when _____

ONCE

we were a

NATION

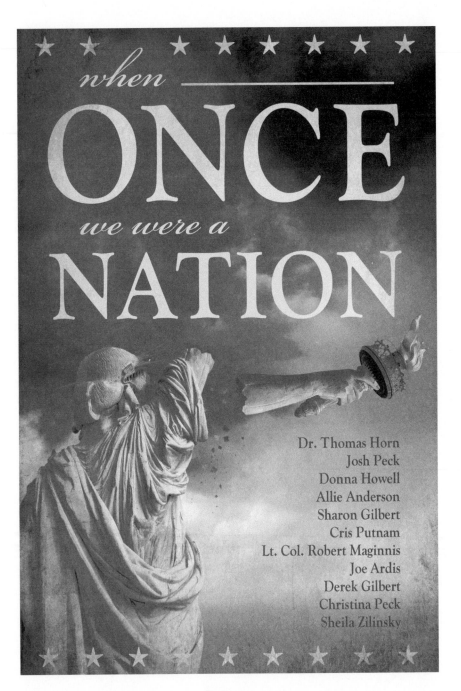

when
ONCE
we were a
NATION

Dr. Thomas Horn
Josh Peck
Donna Howell
Allie Anderson
Sharon Gilbert
Cris Putnam
Lt. Col. Robert Maginnis
Joe Ardis
Derek Gilbert
Christina Peck
Sheila Zilinsky

DEFENDER
CRANE, MO

When Once We Were a Nation

Defender
Crane, MO 65633
©2016 by Thomas Horn

ISBN: 978-0-996-4095-6-8

A CIP catalog record of this book is available from the Library
of Congress.

Cover illustration and design by Jeffrey Mardis.

All Scripture quotations from the King James Version; in cases
of academic comparison, those instances are noted.

Contents

chapter one

—————— WHEN ONCE WE WERE A NATION OF ——————
Rugged Individualism and Pioneering Determination
By Dr. Thomas R. Horn

Recently for my birthday, my daughter Althia surprised me with the most amazing gift—a framed *Phoenix Gazette* feature article dated May 7, 1937, titled "New Generation of American Pioneers Treks Westward, Fleeing 'Dust Bowl' And Seeking New Place to Make Homes." The *Gazette* was one of Arizona's top newspapers in the 1930s, and the story was an interview between a reporter and my grandparents, mother, cousins, and numerous other families who were parked alongside the road seeking shelter for their caravan under the trees, having been forced from their Oklahoma farms to pick fruit for survival. One of the original editions of the newspaper article had been in my grandfather's possession since it was originally published, kept in a small wooden box near his recliner while I was growing up, then inherited by me on his passing. I had cherished that clipping as well as the other items in

1

New Generation Of American Pioneers Treks Westward, Fleeing 'Dust Bowl' And Seeking New Place To Make Homes

Driven from their homes in the "dust bowl" states of Oklahoma, Arkansas, Texas and Kansas, hundreds of small scale farmers are trekking westward, seeking new homes. They are finding the hardships almost as desperate as those of the pioneers. They remained in these states until their resources were exhausted, then loaded their automobiles and started westward, looking for work on new farms. Most of them work in the fields. Right now strawberry picking occupies a large number. Here are pictures taken in the Salt River valley, showing some of the drouth "refugees." At the left are Mr. and Mrs. A. M. McLaughlin, who arrived near Glendale. They both work in the hay fields. Before Oklahoma became part of the "dust bowl" they were making a "good living" on a farm. Now, but hoping for clouds, which they describe vividly, swept the grain fields after a little rain — ruining crops. "We couldn't even raise enough grain for seed toward the end," McLaughlin said. "Finally, we had to leave." The old model say, the tent and a few other necessities are all the...

McLaughlin salvaged when they left. They have two children. Seated from the left is a typical low-rent tourist camp near Phoenix. Many must bowl-ers stop at these camps, halting long enough to earn money, and continue westward. The third picture is a group of "refugee" children playing in a trailer, which their families used to haul belongings. Some of the children, as of the family of Thad Farmer, formerly of Muskogee, Okla. At the extreme right is the 15-year-old junior Kern. He's shown in a camp near Glendale, doing the day's washing. Members of his camp are working in the fields. Junior has rheumatism; he can't work. Junior and his family formerly lived in Benton county, Arkansas. They left in last June. Trouble plagued them, however. Junior's father died only a short time ago when he was struck by an automobile along the highway. This causes the mother and other children to go into the fields to work, for a living.

(Gazette Staff Photos)

'Dust Bowl' Refugees Meet Hardships In Westward Trek

Suffering hardships almost as desperate as those encountered by the pioneers, a new generation of Americans is pushing westward, estimated recently that 100,000 farmers, are moving westward to...

OFFERS TO QUIT RAIL CONTROL

WASHINGTON, May 7 — (AP) — Frank F. Kolbe, New York broker...

PYTHIANS BEGIN NOGALES TREK

NOGALES, May 7 — (AP) — The Pythians to a Jamaican here between ... sections of Arizona to commemorate the 56th anniversary of the founding ... the K. P. convention, said today he expected between ... for the convention ... arrival of Gov. C. ... midnight at which ...

1937 feature article about Tom Horn's grandparents and kinfolk fleeing the "Dust Bowl"

the little chest—war stamps from World War II, a small screwdriver-like tool, old work permits, and so on—until those heirlooms burned in my home in 2011. Thankfully, I had always remembered the date on which the original story had been published, because on the reverse side of the feature about Grandpa and Grandma was the historic report, "Zeppelin Explodes," all about the German passenger airship Hindenburg that had caught fire the day before, May 6, 1937, killing thirty-six people when it blew up while attempting to dock with its mooring mast at Naval Air Station Lakehurst in Manchester Township, New Jersey.

Before news had spread around the world about the Hindenburg, the top story interest the *Gazette* reporter had been assigned involved my family's Great Depression survivors trekking through Arizona on their way to the promised land—sunny California, with its sprawling fruit orchards and miles of row crops where work was waiting for desperate manual laborers.

Depression and "Dust Bowl" This Way Come

There is a reason they call it the "Roaring Twenties." World War I had just ended, wartime economy transitioned to peacetime economy, consumerism surged, industrial production boomed, and the United States had just become the wealthiest country in the world. For the first time, more Americans were living within the new bright lights and big cities than in farmlands. Technology in the cinematic arena whispered of an all-new and unprecedented "speaking film" on the silver screen's horizon, while entertainment via live stage saw raised hemlines sweeping provocative fringe across the bare knees of flapper girls. Slow and conservative dances were largely replaced by the rapid Fox Trot, Charleston, Texas Tommy, and Brazilian Samba. Electronics including radios, refrigerators, and vacuum cleaners were implemented in almost every household. Horses and wagons were abandoned in the interest of the innovative automobile. Everywhere one looked within city borders, glasses were raised to celebrate economic success; laughter echoed through dance halls above the din of merriment; grace notes poured through brass instruments and bounced off the walls in jazz parlors; fast-paced piano pieces tickled the consciousness of patrons, inspiring them to order desserts following their seven-course meals; clouds of "harmless" cigarette smoke hazed around chandeliers in fancy food and drink establishments; and businessmen dangled pretty ladies from their arms as they wrestled their peers for the privilege to pay the evening tabs.

The people had been engaging in a gaudy spree in a country that never sleeps.

Meanwhile, amidst the nationwide festivities, the hype of profit paved the way for regrettable carelessness…

The Beginnings of the Great Depression

There were, of course, contributors to the economic downfall that haunted the U.S. throughout the Great Depression other than the stock market crash on Wall Street, but the crash has largely been attributed by economists as the central, or at least most visible, cause. Prior to the Roaring Twenties, many bankers of Wall Street had reserved their business deals for the elite class, most often other bankers. But as the general public showed a sharp increase in the interest of purchasing personal security through the liberty bonds during the war (promoted by celebrities such as Charlie Chaplin), an investment mind frame took the nation by storm. It was no longer only the elite who partook in such ventures, and banks were profiting from deals with the middle class.

National City Bank President Charles Mitchell saw this opportunity to market corporate bonds and common stocks to everyone within the general population. If the people were so willing to buffer the government's capital funds via liberty bonds, they would be even more

4

excited about the prospects of investing in their own security through prosperous industry that promised to benefit them further with extravagant new technology to match their increasingly extravagant culture. By Mitchell's command, brokerage offices were launched all over the U.S. Before long, stocks and bonds had grown to staggering heights, and many jumped on the bandwagon of gold while the market was thriving. Financial investors had given their every cent to what appeared to be respectable and safe speculations...but their investment focus was on price movements and temporal inflation instead of the wiser fundamental values of long-term security outside stocks. Some saved their money in the bank as it came in spades through the stock market, and others bought businesses as well. However, because of how the inbound crash would affect the banks as well as the consumers, these endeavors were of marginal importance for many.

It seems like nobody saw the risk for what it was. Hordes of stockholders flocked to moneylenders, banks, and brokerage firms; so great was their confidence in the bull market that they borrowed well beyond their means in order to speculate, and the more demand there was for shares as a result of this investing culture, the higher the prices became for shares. Only 10 percent was required to put down for margin on stock, so one thousand dollars cash-in-hand represented ten thousand dollars in stock. How easy it was for a man or woman to turn a couple of dollars into a couple hundred dollars within only a couple of weeks. Industry, factories, manufacturers, technology, and companies that stood as major pioneers of invention all benefitted from the heaps of financial support the infrastructure of the market was building; bankers and individuals all profited from the interest earned on payday. Everybody was winning!

When the money rolled in, it was thrown straight back into stocks and bonds for a speedy turnaround...that is, when it wasn't being spent on seven-course meals, hats, scarves, purses, gold cuff links, automobiles, electronics, and lavish homes with outrageous mortgages. Money was being "made" in record time and for people of all social circles, and they were living large, believing that this new, lucrative way of life would last forever. And nobody could blame them for thinking in such a way when even the pros, such as the illustrious Yale economist Irving Fisher, famously predicted that the stock market had arrived at "a permanently high plateau."[1] The president of the United States, Herbert Hoover, even said, "We in America today are nearer to the final triumph over poverty than ever before in the history of any land."[2] (Hoover's comment was a statement that would haunt him later on and for the rest of his presidency until he was voted out of office by a landslide during the next election after having become the people's scapegoat for the Great Depression.) Yet with all of this "moneymaking," a great number of the American population appeared to owe more than they owned when it came to actual cash.

In addition to the practice of living off of, spending, and reinvesting borrowed monies, behind the scenes, mastermind investors began taking advantage of the unaware public with insider trading. They personally promoted and invested in stocks that they had nonpublic information about, essentially shepherding the people to trail just behind them and put their funds into puffed-up stocks. These inside traders would pull their earnings and get out at the most strategic moment (again, based on nonpublic information), leaving all who had followed them to inherit the losses, and they would prevail with the optimal earnings over and over again…and the debt of the people—as well as the empty promises of a glorious payday—grew even more overwhelming through market manipulation. Some warned that these gratuitous speculations from a naïve people would lead to incredible economic depression, but despite these warnings, ultimately, the nation's unquenchable thirst for riches resulted in more loans for more eventually empty stocks.

On Wednesday, October 23, 1929, after a hasty and overnight loss of confidence in the system (nobody is entirely sure why this happened with such veracity and so abruptly on one single day, and the causes of the swift shift in confidence remains highly debated, but it's likely that it occurred as a result of Americans observing the London Stock Exchange crash just prior), share prices plunged on the New York Stock Exchange when the buyers suddenly became the sellers. The next day, Thursday, October 24, now referred to as "Black Thursday," the trading floors were crawling with people; everyone wanted out of their stocks, but nobody was investing. Documentation of that day reveals that the crowds were so stunned and terrified by the sudden fluctuation that as updates were being read to the thousands and soon tens of thousands making up the masses outside the Exchange building, gasps, cries of anguish, and even fainting erupted. Widespread panic swept the states from border to border all across the country. Notable bankers (including Charles Mitchell) raced to the trading floor and loudly and proudly poured millions of dollars into U.S. steel stocks in front of onlookers in hopes of rejuvenating the faith of the traders. It worked, but only temporarily. Over the weekend, the stock market continued on as usual, but an increasing trepidation and feeling of foreboding left Americans unsettled. By "Black Monday," October 28, those who had been involved in market manipulation (as well as those who saw the proverbial writing on the wall) saw their open door to get out while they could, and they did so, dropping the Dow Jones Industrial Average by 13 percent by the end of business.

On "Black Tuesday," October 29, 1929, the most devastating stock market crash in the history of the country instantly brought a shocking silence upon the Roaring Twenties. In the same national alarm that had marked the previous Thursday, everyone wanted out, and there was nobody left investing. By the end of business, the market had lost $14 billion.

Banks were inundated with multitudes of frightened responders. From everywhere all at once, bank accounts were emptied and cash stored elsewhere while the banks still had anything to give. In no time at all, bank reserves were tapped dry, the crowds were denied their own savings, and banks across the country locked their doors, many of which never reopened. Cries—both angry and forlorn—lifted up from the city streets, an impromptu chorus of chaos and upheaval.

Millions of Americans instantly went from "rich" to destitute as the debt collectors came to take what was owed them. People lost every material possession they owned. Poverty, homelessness, and depression immediately became the financial plague that would wrack the states for years to come. Emigration to other countries soared to record numbers, involving both the return of immigrants back to their home countries, and native U.S. citizens' decision to start fresh on foreign soil in Canada, Australia, or anywhere they could bargain for passage to. Construction was halted midway through the raising of new businesses and homes that had been visualized by dreamers only weeks before.

As weeks drew into months, huts were erected on the side of the roads and near lakes or rivers by those who were losing the roof over their heads. These little shanty houses quickly drew in more and more crowds of homeless men, women, and children, until they had formed their own miniature "villages" or "towns" full of Wall Street stock market crash victims. Because the victims most often attributed the crash to President Hoover, these shanty towns were coined "Hoovervilles."

Hooverville shanties were constructed of cardboard, tar paper, glass, lumber, tin and whatever other materials people could salvage.... Cardboard-box homes did not last long, and most dwellings were in a constant state of being rebuilt. Some homes were not buildings at all, but deep holes dug in the ground with makeshift roofs laid over them to keep out inclement weather. Some of the homeless found shelter inside empty conduits and water mains.[3]

Photos still circulate of these "homes," and in some cases they show destroyed furniture and disassembled large instruments (such as pianos) being used as walls. Although some shacks or tents featured a coal stove that had been stripped from their homes, many were left without heat in the fatal cold. Young children starved as their mothers waited entire days in line at soup kitchens for only a small tear of bread. Often, residents of the Hooverville shanties would hang signs around their doors, and in some cases on their person, advertising their skills and looking for work; the payment they required was frequently only a meal or two they could bring home to their wives and children, although some biographical accounts tell of those who would literally work for anything, such as baby blankets or used shoes. Mothers and fathers slept on the damp ground or molded mattresses while children huddled together on stacks of cardboard.

Relief was needed everywhere, all across the United States, but it was seldom found. Around twenty thousand now-homeless army veterans had been promised a bonus for their service in WWI, but the sum was not due to be paid until the year 1945. (Violent riots between these veterans, referred to as the "Bonus Army," and law enforcement ensued just outside the White House during the summer of 1932, causing President Hoover to barricade himself within.) With nothing solid keeping them in one place, and no possessions to haul, stock market crash victims swiftly became travelers to neighboring cities and states to look for shelter or food.

And just when it seemed it couldn't get any worse, it did.

Crowds gather outside the Bank of the United States after its failure, 1931.
Image: public domain.

Soup kitchen, opened by renowned American gangster Alphonse Gabriel "Al" Capone in Chicago, 1931, as an attempt to clean up his public image. The sign above the door says, "Free soup, coffee, and doughnuts for the unemployed." Men in the line pictured here appear to be fairly well clothed and content, but many of them would leave this line and bring their own small ration to their wives and children waiting for them in the homes they were about to lose or in a Hooverville shack, and then take to the streets to beg for work in the most presentable of the attire they still owned. Image: public domain.

One angle of a Hooverville establishment in Manhattan, 1935. A man sits outside casually reading the paper in a nice hat with his legs crossed; even homeless men could not allow themselves to appear to the public as dirty, starving, or destitute, as only the strongest, most able-bodied, and most trustworthy looking men might be offered work at any given moment. Image: public domain.

Crowds gather outside an employment agency, circa 1935. Image: public domain.

Small children sit outside their Hooverville tent next to signs that read "Hoover's Poor Farm Tobacco Fund" and "Hard Times Are Still 'Hoover'ing Over Us," circa 1935. It was not uncommon for one or both parents to leave their kids behind in a Hooverville town with their own "jobs" to tend to and go in search for money, food, or work. Other similar photos of this time depict small children holding signs that beg passersby to give their father a job. Image: public domain.

The Dust Bowl of the "Dirty Thirties"

Beginning in 1933–1934, and continuing intermittently through 1940, twenty-five thousand square miles of farmland primarily in Texas, Oklahoma, New Mexico, Kansas, and Colorado were swallowed by thick, monstrous clouds of dry dust in one of the longest and most devastating droughts of American history. It became known as the "Dust Bowl." Dry-land farming methods had not been adequately applied, and wind erosion wrought havoc upon agricultural areas like nothing our country had ever seen before, or would ever see again. Layers upon layers of the blackest dust covered what was once the glorious greenery of the great U.S.A. This decade would then be referred to—in an ironic and tragic contrast to its previous—as the "Dirty Thirties."

Farmers wore handkerchiefs over their faces, tried to breathe through the black winds, and spit up mud balls by the end of the work day. Women and children holed up in their homes and nailed the windows shut, but it helped little against the seemingly never-ending layer of black that settled upon their countertops and furniture, in their beds, in the threads of their clothing, all over their bodies, and within their lungs. Later, many went on to document what it felt like to exit their homes and observe giant walls or "black blizzards" of dust, like tornadoes, flying toward their land. With their harvest destroyed as well as their farming equipment and sometimes their homes (after the more aggressive of these storms, many homes had to be torn down), farmers also became travelers, with tens of thousands of families uprooting their lives to look for a fresh start elsewhere, most often to California. (By 1935, over five hundred thousand American farm civilians had become homeless.) Sadly, they discovered that the economic downfall of the nation left little for them to turn to in the cities.

Although *some* depictions of the Dust Bowl migration have been exaggerated for the sake of dramatic, Hollywood, and media storytelling (and there are those historians who even suggest the celebrated *Grapes of Wrath* retelling challenges the truth at times by reporting the worst

Dust storm in Rolla, Kansas, April 1935. Image: public domain.

Dust storm heading straight for Spearman, Texas, April 1935. Image: public domain.

Farmer runs with his two boys through a dust storm in a uniquely visible candid capture, Cimarron County, Oklahoma, April 1936. Image: public domain.

Farming equipment, machinery, automobile, and buildings partially buried under the dust just after a wind storm in Dallas, South Dakota, 1936. Image: public domain.

symptoms of migration and failing to mention families who achieved new beginnings without tragic death, starvation, or loss), many cultural issues arose during this time that completely destroyed the lives and legacies that had been built over generations.

Men, women, and children packed only their most precious sentimental heirlooms and, with little more than the clothing on their back, headed out in "jalopies" (old, worn-out cars), rope wrapped around the exterior from every angle to carry basic survival materials. Most had nowhere to go as they drove aimlessly toward the unknown to look for work; staying with relatives was often out of the question, since entire extended families—and their farmlands—had suffered the same fate. Hardworking farmhands were suddenly aplenty, and surviving farms had more inquiries for work than they could accommodate. Many were sent away from the cities as well, as urban areas were already inundated with the homeless and unemployed, such as those huddled in Hoovervilles.

Some Dust Bowl migrants suffered from dust pneumonia, an inflammation of the lungs' alveoli (Latin *alveolus*, "little cavity": small, tree-like structures with a hollow cavity, central to the body's absorption of oxygen), as a result of one's lungs being filled with dust. Once enough dust has settled within the lungs, the accumulation of foreign substance glues or muddies up the lungs' capability to expel (or clear out) the substance, and the sickness becomes irreversible. In these more extreme cases, death was imminent. Others suffered from malnutrition, as food was a scarce commodity.

And yet, the roads were not traveled upon solely by displaced farming families. Lawyers, professors, small business owners, and lay workers of every variety were all just as willing to put their shoulders to the plow for a hot meal or a nickel, some of whom had dapper clothing still in their suitcases from their romps at the jazz clubs a few years prior, should they meet someone who valued appearance at a hire. The shattering one-two punch upon the economy afflicted both the rural and urban areas. Those who lived in comfy homes and whose businesses were still surviving were met with frequent interruption in their daily duties by men who promised *they* were the best and most honest workers available. Competition was everywhere.

From potatoes to cotton to lemons to oranges to peas to berries and so many others, the automobiles clunked and sputtered from field to field producing people of all ages willing to pick anything, to plow anything, to till anything, to do the dirtiest of jobs for the smallest pay, and when the harvest was complete, the engines crackled to life once more as the entourage moved on to the next agricultural shrine. Between stops, anything found on the side of the road was a treasure worth pulling over to collect. A sunburnt potted plant that had fallen from someone else's wares wagon could be nursed back to health and sold for a penny at the next town, providing the traveler had a green thumb and extra water. A box of plates that had fallen and shattered into thousands of pieces was a beautiful mosaic just waiting to be canvassed. A random sheet of metal was a new roof at the next shack. An old board could hold anything together. There was a use for everything, and nothing went to waste. With enough creativity, a penny or nickel could be earned with every piece of abandoned trash; with enough resourcefulness, any material item could be turned into a mobile home reparation.

At times, familiar faces were spotted as the migrants frequented the fields, and people chose to travel together from harvest to harvest, creating a kind of spontaneous mobile community. After a hard day's work, it wasn't uncommon that the migrants would gather under the shade of someone's makeshift shelter and sing songs, dance, tell stories, and give updates about nearby work opportunities, *despite* the fact that there was an ever-present race to arrive at the next assignment while there were still plants to pick from. The sudden, national eviction of people from all backgrounds did many times cause strife, as men and women were forced to keep peace within social circles they would have never mingled with before. However, the sudden, national eviction of people from all backgrounds was the very thing that gave them *everything* in common

Famous photo from the era titled *Destitute Pea Pickers in California; Mother of Seven Children* by Dorothea Lange (commonly referred to by the title *Migrant Mother*), February/March 1936. Image: public domain.

In a cotton field alongside Arizona Highway 87, three young children are photographed living in an unsanitary and impoverished trailer, circa 1940. Image: public domain.

now, as they were all in this game of survival together. Who they once were and what they once did stopped mattering when one among them started to cough or lose another pound.

Great Values for a Great Generation

Many have stood behind books, movies, and television depictions of this phenomenon, continuing to flatter and perpetuate a notion that the Dust Bowl migration was a time when Americans were falling like flies, starving to death in broken-down automobiles on the side of the road, and falling to their knees in tearful begging for even the smallest crust of bread to bring back to their bus load of barefoot children...and although there is truth to that depiction on a case-by-case basis, it's not fair to consider that a complete representation of all who were affected during this era.

A large number of families did, in fact, survive the Dirty Thirties with hopefulness and faith in the Christian God, relying on prayer, growing close to one another, and eventually crawling out of horrific debt with all their children still alive and fed. And for just as many heartbreaking memories and statistics that can be listed about the Great Depression and the Dust Bowl, a list of incredible developments counteracts. Not only did these difficult times draw people closer to God, family, and others, lifestyle ethics were established for generations to come who did not fear hard and laborious work, did not waste even the smallest of material possessions, did not spend money recklessly, and did not take for granted the wisdom that needed to be applied toward decisions that altered the government and its leaders and laws.

Like many whose parents and grandparents survived the Great Depression and the Dust Bowl, I grew up a living witness to the "hoarding" habits mentioned above, which my elders held for items of possible value. My grandparents, the McLaughlins, built a trailer park that became a lodging area of small cabins and later small houses with the scrap boards and materials they found and "hoarded" together with some purchased products that they then covered with plaster. They owned and operated that property until El Mirage, Arizona (which, ironically, they helped establish in the early 1940s), forced them (using eminent domain) to surrender to the city. It was on that location where I spent countless hours as a young man, and later as a young preacher, sitting with Grandma in their simple home or with Grandpa outside by the wood pile. I was listening and learning, absorbing a deep philosophy of life that had been honed in the fires of the deepest and longest-lasting economic downturn in the history of the Western industrialized world, itself followed by another World War which also refined and defined everything they believed and practiced. Their stories and life-lessons were absorbed into my impressionable young soul regarding endurance, independence, honesty, hard work, faith, thankfulness, and kind-heartedness (I cannot recall the dozens of times my parents and grandparents refused to charge poor people who sought shelter on their property or meals they gave them to make sure they did not go hungry) that became the bedrock of my philosophical worldview. Elsewhere in this book you will read how the Second World War was won by these resilient individuals whom famed television journalist and author Tom Brokaw once called "The Greatest Generation." Not only did they unify the American clarity of purpose during international conflict (World Wars I and II) but reaffirmed for the next generation and the world what famous nineteenth-century French statesman, historian and social philosopher Alexis de Tocqueville concluded—that "America is great because America is good" (albeit, de Tocqueville also warned, "If America ever ceases to be good, America will cease to be great"—a sober warning for us today).

It was there, while Grandpa McLaughlin whittled on a piece of tree limb (what time he wasn't challenging his rooster to a fight!), that I'd ask the deepest questions about life, meaning, God, the world, humanity's place in it, the afterlife, and make other inquiries, including those about survival. He and Grandma, with my mom, uncle, and cousins, had fled the Oklahoma farm after the rains refused to come year after year, leaving their dead crops behind. It was hard for them to do that, to walk away from the homestead that my Great Grandfather Kendall (Grandma's maiden name) had built and then left to them. Grandpa Kendall had been the mayor of Buffalo, Oklahoma (established before statehood), and a successful businessman. He had built a beautiful home on seven hundred acres, which for many years was the gathering place for Northwest Oklahomans to travel to by horse and buggy to cast their votes in state and national elections. Grandma McLaughlin as a child had been pampered by these parents, the Kendalls, and had gone to expensive boarding schools. Grandpa McLaughlin, on the other hand, was a scrappy third-grade dropout, seventeen years her senior (not unusual or "weird" in those days) whom she fell for. Years later, with her high-society clothing and porcelain dolls a distant memory, she, alongside Grandpa and the family, set out to become the rugged individuals and "new pioneers" they would develop into. Short on cash and necessarily high in faith, they became the perfect role models for me and my generation to learn from concerning the things in life that should really matter and be cherished. My grandparents have been gone now for many years, and with them, most of the Greatest Generation. And when by contrast I consider what people value today, I worry. We now live at a time when far too many Americans have no idea where our greatness as a nation came from. People feel "entitled" to what they have not earned and, according to polls, they have an increasing desire for a socialist lifestyle that believes others who *have* worked hard to succeed and do better owe them a way of life, including free higher education, free universal healthcare, housing assistance, and so on. As this book heads to the printer, we are in the most amazing (and scary) political season in which an astonishing number of citizens actually prefer a turn from free market capitalism (which built the most powerful, progressive, and giving society in history) toward the enslavement of pseudo-socialism and "cooperation over the competitiveness of a free market economy" in which "all people in society contribute to the production of goods and services and that those goods should be shared equally."[4] This stands at diametric opposition to the capitalist system our forefathers died to protect in which individual efforts are rewarded and trump the collective (i.e., the New Testament model in which if you won't work, you don't eat) wherein the free market determines the distribution of goods. Derek Gilbert has much to say about this later in this book, but suffice it to say, "things, they are a changing," and not in a good way. The irony is that socialism—while promising a shared level ground—lowers the living standard for all while providing little legal method for prosperity of the individual, while American capitalism historically has resulted in the abundance of capital that has fed the hungry of the world and has built the hospitals and care facilities that to this day assist the needy. This is one reason I believe America needs an awakening—first, a spiritual revival; and second, a cultural awakening defined by the reestablishment of Greatest Generation principles and behaviors that could positively strengthen, recharacterize and rejuvenate our society. Donald Trump, as inarticulate as he is, has captured the essence of this longing with his political jargon: "We can be great again" and "We can win again." Is the Donald right? I'd like to believe on those points he is. I'd like to think that America can once more be a nation of winners, of rugged individualism and pioneering determination. I pray that the book you now hold in your hands is a first small step in this direction and a reminder for many of what once made us the envy of the world. I choose to believe all is not lost, that our nation can once again honor and commit to God, glory, and greatness.

chapter two

────────── WHEN ONCE WE WERE A NATION OF ──────────
Strength
By Robert L. Maginnis

──

T he 1930s and 1940s demonstrated the United States had great
strengths that became evident under the intense pressure of the
Great Depression (1929–39)—the deepest and longest-lasting economic downturn in the history of the Western world—coupled with
a global war that threatened America's very existence. That crucible of
circumstances awakened those strengths and launched America out of
the economic crisis into global leadership via three waves of action: the
period leading up to World War II, the conduct of that war, and American actions once hostilities ended.

World War II was a global catastrophe that involved more than fifty
nations, lasted nearly six years in Europe and longer in Asia, consumed
more than $1 trillion, involved one hundred million men under arms,
and claimed sixty million lives, including six million Jews murdered in
Nazi concentration camps.[5] Although the U.S. came late to the fight, it

made a significant contribution: Four hundred thousand Americans lost their lives, 40 percent of the nation's production went to the war effort, and sixteen million Americans served in the armed forces. Fortunately for the U.S., the war ended well. British Prime Minister Winston Churchill famously said at the end of the war that America stood "at the summit of the world."[6] America's victory earned the unconditional surrender of its adversaries and the admiration of its impoverished war-torn Allies.

The circumstances that led to America being on top of the world could have brought about a very different outcome. After all, no critical national interests were threatened prior to the Japanese December 7, 1941, Pearl Harbor attack, and besides, most Americans enjoyed a false sense of security provided by the giant oceans on either flank. But even those great oceans in the end were insufficient to keep America out of the global war that changed the course of history.

Before examining America's many strengths, we must first appreciate the global war environment that fostered the conflict that eventually brought the unwilling U.S. into World War II.

Many of the causes of the Second World War are directly traceable to the troubled aftermath of the "Great War," World War I (1914–18). The Great War ended with an armistice in November 1918, and two months later, the Allies met with the conquered Germany and Austria-Hungary at Versailles to hammer out a treaty. England and France forced harsh war reparations on their former enemies as well as claimed territories—such as the corridor separating East Prussia from the rest of Germany and the strategic Alsace-Lorrain, with its rich iron fields. Unfortunately, the Versailles and five other treaties that papered the end of hostilities failed to resolve the underlying tensions that led to the Great War—namely, the struggle for economic and military domination and self-determination for political and cultural groups.[7]

The Great War's failure to resolve those underlying issues was further complicated during the post-war era by a rapidly changing environment that led many of those same former belligerents down a new collision path to global war. Some of those interwar changes included rapid industrialization, expanding technologies, empire building (Japan forc-ibly colonizing Asian states), nationalist rivalries, and the emergence of ideologies like Nazism, Marxism and fascism.

Understandably, Europe's quagmire of problems left unresolved by the Great War encouraged America's prevailing isolationist tendencies. U.S. Army General Tasker H. Bliss, the chief of the American military delegation at the Versailles negotiations, said of the situation left at the end of the war: "What a wretched mess it all is. If the rest of the world will let us alone, I think we had better stay on our side of the water and keep alive the spark of civilization."[8]

The world refused to leave America alone, even though Washington pursued an isolationist post-Great War foreign policy. After spurning membership in the League of Nations, an organization first proposed by President Woodrow Wilson as part of his Fourteen Point plan "for an equitable peace in Europe," America quickly rushed into deep isolation by erecting tariffs, limiting immigration, and insisting that Europeans repay their war debts. Congress passed five neutrality acts in the 1930s. But remaining aloof became more difficult as tensions exploded in Europe and Asia.[9]

President Roosevelt anticipated those growing tensions would inevi-tably end America's isolation. In 1940 Roosevelt declared, "As a lone island in a world dominated by the philosophy of force such an island may be the dream of those who still talk and vote as isolationists. Such an island represents to me…the nightmare of a people lodged in prison, handcuffed, hungry, and fed through the bars from day to day by the contemptuous, unpitying masters of other continents."[10]

Roosevelt watched as the storms in Asia and Europe melded into the Axis Powers and anticipated they would soon pull America out of isolationism into the maelstrom. He didn't have to wait too long for the hammer of war to drop on Washington.

In Asia, Japan's rise to hegemonic power started in the nineteenth century as the island kingdom became a modern industrial society that demonstrated its new strength against the Russians in the Russo-Japanese

War of 1904–05. Decades later, Tokyo turned its newfound might against China's Manchuria province in order to seize and then develop that region's industrial and agricultural resources. Japanese colonialization ambitions arguably sparked World War II in Asia first with China, but soon engulfed much of Southeast Asia, the Dutch East Indies, the Philippines and India. Inevitably, the hegemonic Japanese yanked off America's self-imposed veil of isolationism when hundreds of Japanese aircraft attacked the U.S. naval base at Pearl Harbor, Hawaii, which awakened America and prompted Washington's declaration of war on Japan on December 8, 1941.

Half a world away, the situation in Europe evolved precipitously as well. After World War I, the Allies were never able to appease Germany, which explains the rise of Adolf Hitler's National Socialist Germany Workers' Party (Nazi Party). Hitler, a charismatic speaker, leveraged his populist appeal with anti-Semitic rhetoric and tapped into widespread grievances associated with the vindictive outcome of the Treaty of Versailles. Of course, like many people at the time, the Germans were bitter because of the dismal economic conditions associated with the Great Depression. Hitler understood the troubled times and therefore promised to make life better on all fronts, something few Germans came to expect from the failing post-World War I Weimar government.

Hitler's populist message and the dire mood of the German people ushered the Nazi party into power in 1932. The Nazis quickly won the support of the German Communist Party into their political coalition that dominated the Reichstag (parliament), which immediately appointed Hitler chancellor. Once in power, Hitler anointed himself "Führer" ("supreme leader") and then consolidated his powers by dissolving trade unions, muzzling the press, expanding the state police (the Gestapo), and declaring the Nazis the only legal party.

Hitler quickly rearmed Germany and then in 1936 marched thirty-five thousand troops into the Rhineland in violation of Versailles Treaty prohibitions against militarizing that buffer zone between France and Germany. After facing minimal resistance to his breach of the treaty,

Hitler annexed Austria in 1938 and then absorbed part of Czechoslovakia into the Reich (the German realm).

Full-scale war began September 1, 1939, when Hitler launched a *blitzkrieg* ("lightning war") attack into Poland. Almost immediately, Britain and France declared war, but it was too late to help Poland, and early the next year, Hitler continued his *blitzkrieg* by seizing Denmark, Norway, the Netherlands, Luxembourg, Belgium and France. Britain was next in line for Hitler's invasion, which commenced on July 10, 1940, with an aerial campaign ("Blitz") against London and other cities in England, which was intended to precede an amphibious invasion.

Hitler met significant British opposition to his Blitz, which evidently influenced him to turn his sights east to Russia, a decision he would regret and a violation of a pre-war secret agreement with the Soviets. Prior to the war, Hitler agreed with the Soviets that they would not attack each other for ten years. In fact, they agreed to divide Eastern Europe between them—spoils of the planned war.

With this introduction to World War II, we now turn to the three waves—pre-war, war, and occupation—that brought America out of its geopolitical isolation to demonstrate great strengths that led to the U.S. becoming the world's undisputed leader.

Pre-War Strengths

America demonstrated at least three significant strengths before it joined the Second World War.

Strength of Service

Even though America was a reluctant war participant, there was widespread recognition at home in the late 1930s that the rising storms in Europe and Asia would eventually draw the U.S. into the crises. That view prompted America's leaders to preemptively call our nation to arms.

That call to arms created a mammoth job because America in the late 1930s was ill-equipped to face formidable adversaries so far from the homeland. Therefore, it needed to quickly raise, train, and arm a vast military and at the same time aid our Allies hard-pressed by the aggressive and powerful Axis Powers.

Meeting those challenges required massive government spending, the conversion of existing industries to what President Roosevelt called the "Arsenal of Democracy," changes in national consumption, and restrictions on American life.

The most challenging effort that became an obvious strength was enlisting Americans of all ages to the war effort. Fortunately, Americans saw the necessity to unify, not necessarily to defeat the threats posed by the Japanese and Germans but around the "necessity for victory." That strength allowed the nation to quickly man the nation's manpower-hungry armed forces.

Congress' Selective Training and Service Act created the Selective Service System that came into being in September 1940. That effort initially faced strong congressional anti-interventionist sentiments, but opposition quickly collapsed as the Nazis gobbled up most of Western Europe and threatened to invade Britain in July 1940.

Draft registration began in October 1940 with the intention of conscripting nine hundred thousand men between the ages of twenty-one and twenty-seven for one year. Of course, a year later, on the eve of the Pearl Harbor attack and as war raged, conscription was extended but only by a congressional one-vote margin, once again because of the anti-interventionist sentiments. Then the Japanese attacked Pearl Harbor on December 7, which virtually erased any opposition to further conscription.[11]

The Selective Service rapidly expanded our armed forces from 175,000 strong in 1938 to more than twelve million G.I.s (an acronym for "Government Issue" and slang for members of the U.S. armed forces) on active duty at its peak in 1945. All told, some sixteen million

Americans served in the military during World War II and almost fifty million men registered for the draft from a total population of 132 million, while relatively few, perhaps 170,000, tried to avoid conscription.[12]

These "citizen soldiers" were drawn from every state and all economic and social strata. Although we had many volunteers, more than ten million entered the armed forces through the draft.

Just as our armed forces grew in manpower, it also expanded in terms of armaments and war equipment thanks to widespread support on the home front. In 1939, America admittedly was far behind the Axis Powers in war preparations, which had mobilized years earlier. However, once America's industrial might was turned on, it soon became a "mighty superpower." Our industrial base eventually provided almost two-thirds of all Allied equipment during the Second War: 297,000 aircraft, 193,000 artillery pieces, 86,000 tanks, 80,000 landing craft, 5,600 merchant ships, 1,500 navy ships, 20 million small arms, 41 billion rounds of ammunition, 6 million tons of bombs, and 2 million trucks.[13]

The sheer quantity of American war production was impressive, but over, time the quality of our manufacturing efforts gave us a clear fighting edge as well. Initially, American aircraft, tanks, and other war-making equipment were inferior to those produced by the Axis Powers. But soon with new science, technology, and innovative fabrication techniques, America's weapons systems gave the Allied Powers a clear edge.

It is an undisputed fact of history that America went on to win the Second World War in part because we out-produced and out-manned the Axis Powers. Yes, our enemy had great wartime leadership and a massive head start, but we soon overwhelmed them and in the end they could not replace their losses in equipment and manpower at a sufficient level. They could not compete against American production and innovation.

America's pre-war Arsenal of Democracy also rapidly grew its military infrastructure seemingly overnight as well. The Army Corps of Engineers built thousands of barracks, factories, hospitals, and other facilities at new installations across the country that included 345 bases, 116 sub-bases, and 322 auxiliary air fields.[14] Even the 1,520 mile Alaska-Canada Highway was miraculously built in a short six months (March 8 to October 28, 1942) through the wilderness in order to transport military goods to military facilities at Fairbanks, Alaska.[15]

American agriculture exploded its production as well. In the early 1940s, agricultural production increased by 17 percent and the production of livestock grew 28 percent. Even though the war was the priority and in spite of rationing at home, Americans' personal consumption of food and beverages during the war years more than doubled.[16]

America's economic strength was also demonstrated in its gross national product, which doubled during the war years, rising from $91 to $213 billion. At the end of the war, by all accounts, half of the world's manufacturing capability and two-thirds of its gold stocks were in the United States. America had become rich and very strong.[17]

The pre-war period was a time Americans responded to calls for unity within and among its Allies by serving either in the armed forces or in support of the Arsenal of Democracy.

Strength of Unity and Sacrifice

America was sacrificial, a strength critical to the war effort. In 1944, President Roosevelt said, "I need not repeat the figures. The facts speak for themselves.... These men [our armed forces] could not have been armed and equipped as they are had it not been for the miracle of production here at home. The production which has flowed from the country to all the battlefronts of the world has been due to the efforts of American business, American labor, and American farmers, working together as a patriotic team."[18]

During the Second World War, America devoted 40 percent of its gross national product to the effort, which meant significant sacrifice: rationing, experiencing shortages, and paying much higher taxes. These realities put enormous stress on families, especially the one in every five American families who had one or more members serving in the armed forces. Further, many servicemen's wives and other women—nineteen million, or 36 percent of the labor force—stepped into factories to keep our troops supplied, and at nights, many of these same geographical single moms went home to keep their families together through tough times.

Women had an especially significant impact on America's aviation industry. More than 310,000 women—two-thirds of the aviation industry's total workforce at the time—were working in that industry by 1943. which was. The image of "Rosie the Riveter" painted by famed artist Norman Rockwell for the cover of the *Saturday Evening Post* popularized the most iconic image of working women during the war. That image was used in a national campaign that stressed the patriotic need for women, and it worked to recruit women even though they on average were paid about half of the wages the males received.[19]

Americans of all stripes fueled the fiscally hungry federal government through a combination of higher taxes and bond purchases. The war cost the federal government more than $300 billion, an enormous amount given that from 1939 to 1945, the annual federal budget grew from $9 billion to $98 billion.[20]

During the war years, the federal government increased personal taxes across the board. Before the war, fewer than eight million Americans filed individual income tax returns, but by 1945, those numbers rose to fifty million, and the now-familiar payroll deduction became a wartime staple. But federal taxes paid only half of the wartime government costs. The balance of the needed money had to be borrowed, and in most cases, those funds came from small investments in war bonds purchased by Americans.

Americans sacrificed by cutting back on personal consumption and recycling most everything of value. Materials like glycerin in kitchen fats were collected for use in making gunpowder and lipstick tubes were melted into bullet cartridges. Tin cans were melted and used to build aircraft, and the steel from used razor blades was eventually recycled into machine guns. Other household goods such as rags, paper, silk, and string were recycled to advance the war effort as well.[21]

There were special calls for specific materials needed to advance the war effort. In June 1942, President Roosevelt called on the country to find or produce more rubber. He asked Americans to collect "old tires, old rubber raincoats, old garden hoses, and rubber shoes—whatever you have that is made of rubber."[22] Very soon, Americans contributed 450,000 tons of scrap rubber.[23]

The Boy Scouts responded by collecting paper door to door for recycling in response to General Eisenhower's Waste Paper Campaign.

The so-called Victory Garden was a widespread effort to increase food supplies. Americans across the land from urban to rural areas started some twenty million Victory Gardens that produced more than one-third of all vegetables, over one billion tons of food. Americans then canned much of that food at home by consulting "Victory Cookbooks" for recipes.[24]

The pre-war period clearly demonstrated America's unity and strength of sacrifice.

Strength of Innovation

American innovation was a strength that became evident in the pre-war era.

Americans have always been a very creative people, a strength that became especially evident leading up to and during the Second World War. Richard Overy's book, *Why the Allies Won*, attributes much of our war success against the Axis Powers to both our robust productivity and especially our innovation. He wrote that our "effective deployment of modern technology, against an enemy forced to fight with little air cover, few tanks, and dwindling quantities of trucks and guns, made the difference between victory and defeat."[25]

Prior to the war, President Roosevelt harnessed our yet-to-be-tapped proclivity for innovation when he established the Office of Scientific Research and Development (OSRD), which led to critical war-related innovations such as the atomic bomb, radar, the proximity fuse, penicillin, whole-blood substitutes, and new pesticides.[26]

The production and use of the atomic bomb likely saved many tens of thousands of American lives, because our alternative to its use was a bloody ground invasion of the Japanese mainland. The atomic bomb project started with OSRD and then was transferred to the Army Corps of Engineers' Manhattan Engineer District, which built and operated more than three dozen facilities employing 150,000 people to include top-secret cities at Oak Ridge, Tennessee; Hartford, Washington; and Los Alamos, New Mexico.[27]

Lesser-known innovations had a significant impact on the war effort as well. The discovery and mass production of synthetic rubber was especially important. The Japanese occupation of Southeast Asia cut off most of the U.S.' crude rubber supply, leading to a serious shortage of rubber, a critical material for the war effort. Soon American William Jeffers discovered synthetic rubber and the production process, which quickly met our war requirements. This was another problem solved thanks to American innovation.[28]

No doubt American innovation was a strength that significantly contributed to winning the Second World War.

War-Era Strengths

America demonstrated admirable strengths in the war: She fought for a just cause and was a good ally, fought justly, and grew in faith.

Strength of Just Cause

America fought World War II based on a just cause, but not without some reservations. That was strength.

WHEN ONCE WE WERE A NATION

In 1940, America faced a grievous threat from the Axis Powers bent on conquering all of Europe and the Far East. America's role in that war eventually and significantly contributed to the liberation of Europe and Asia and brought about a free and stable Germany and Japan. But were our motives to join that war truly just? The answer isn't as straightforward as one would like to believe based on historical facts.

Earlier in this chapter, I profiled the geopolitical situation leading up to the war and the popular justifications for entering the war, such as the unprovoked Japanese attack on Pearl Harbor. Certainly, even today, Americans asked whether our role in World War II was justified, according to Gallup, answer with an overwhelming (90 percent) "yes," and in fact, most Americans label the Second War as "the last good war."[29]

Concluding that World War II was a just war is based on a well-known concept, the "just war theory" (*jus bellum iustum*), derived from the writings of St. Augustine, a fifth-century Christian theologian who considered the concept in Romans 13:4 that God has given the sword to government, which must act honorably.

Augustine argued that Christians working with their government should not be ashamed to protect peace and punish wickedness; fighting just causes is encouraged. His theory was popularized and expanded on over the centuries, and it came to espouse three central criteria: the good must outweigh the harm, the war must be a last resort to resolve the conflict, and there must be a just or moral cause for undertaking the war.

Initially, America refused to get involved in the wars raging in Asia and Europe. Our strong isolationist proclivity at the time, coupled with our efforts to recover from the Great Depression, contributed to our hesitance to enter the fray. Further, we didn't join the hostilities until our homeland (Pearl Harbor) was attacked (thus we entered only as a last resort). Certainly popular opinion at the time believed war was necessary to keep from being enslaved by cruel and ruthless dictators, which helped our leaders justify our entry (the good outweighed the harm).

President Roosevelt sought to establish the third criteria, the moral argument to undertake war in his so-called Quarantine Speech on October 5, 1937.[30]

Innocent peoples are being cruelly sacrificed to a greed for power and supremacy.... Let no one imagine that America will escape.... There is no escape through mere isolation or neutrality.... War is a contagion, whether it be declared or not. It seems unfortunately true that the epidemic of lawlessness is spreading. When an epidemic of physical disease starts to spread, the community joins in a quarantine of the patients in order to protect the health of the community against the spread of the disease. I call today for a similar quarantine. A quarantine of the lawless, a quarantine of those that threaten world peace.

Ted Grimsrud, author of the *Good War That Wasn't—And Why It Matters*, and a professor of theology and peace studies at Eastern Mennonite University in Harrisonburg, Virginia, challenges the widely held view that America's role in World War II was "just." His voice warrants consideration.[31]

Grimsrud outlines some inconvenient truths about that war.[32]

- During the 1930s Germany bought more arms from American companies than all but two other countries. (Therefore, America was hypocritically taking advantage of the economic benefits of war by associating with a future enemy while at the same time holding to its neutrality in spite of evident atrocities attributed to the Axis Powers. Charles Higham writes in Trading with the Enemy: An Expose of the Nazi-American Money-Plot 1933–1949 that numerous American companies traded with the Nazi regime before and during the war. Specifically, Standard Oil shipped enemy fuel through Switzerland for the Nazis in France; Ford trucks were used to transport German troops; I.T.T. supplied bombs the Germans used against London.)[33]

- Poland, the first nation Germany invaded, was also ruled by a military dictator. Further, America's ally in China was not democratic either.
- The Russians would have defeated Germany without our involvement.
- America did not join the war "to save the Jews."
- Japan's hegemonic actions in Asia conflicted with America's own imperialistic interests in the region.

Grimsrud rightly points out America's most flagrant example of geopolitical hypocrisy regarding our entrance into the conflict: "When the U.S. aligned itself with the Soviet Union and Nationalist China, American leaders made it clear that their war effort simply was not animated by principled opposition to tyranny—no matter what the purpose statements declared."[34] Remember, the Soviets brutally annihilated millions of fellow Russians and the Nationalist Chinese were brutal as well.

Even the outcome of the war resulted in something worse and unexpected for the U.S., according to Grimsrud, a self-identified pacifist. The war transformed America "from a relatively demilitarized, relatively democratic society into the world's next great empire." Grimsrud explained that the post-war America applied its new power by rapidly expanding its military and then it overthrew governments such as Iran, fought undeclared wars (Korea and Vietnam), and failed to turn away from militarism even after the end of the Cold War.[35]

Professor Grimsrud's arguments are very compelling and demonstrate the hypocrisy of our leaders' judgment. Besides, leading up to the war, Americans were deeply divided about intervention. At the time President Roosevelt supported intervention on the side of Great Britain, the only anti-Nazi democracy remaining in Europe after the fall of France in June 1940. However, Roosevelt's war desire was checked by a majority of

Americans influenced by Charles Lindbergh, the world-famous aviator, who was a staunch anti-interventionist and the unofficial leader of the movement to keep America out of the war.

Roosevelt thought he knew better than Lindbergh and his followers when, using his executive power, he launched America's so-called Lend-Lease program with congressional support to aid the Allies. That move was not a neutral action; rather, it was understood by Germany as an act of war. Further, Roosevelt ordered other actions, which clearly exposed his pro-war agenda: He ordered the seizure of Axis shipping, froze Axis funds, transferred tankers to Britain, and aided the Russians by providing them with offensive arms.

British historian J. F. C. Fuller wrote that President Roosevelt wanted war. He "left no stone unturned to provoke Hitler to declare war on the very people to whom he so ardently promised peace. He provided Great Britain with American destroyers, he landed American troops in Iceland, and he set out to patrol the Atlantic seaways in order to safeguard British convoys; all of which were acts of war…in spite of his manifold enunciations to keep the United States out of the war, he was bent on provoking some incident which would bring them into it."[36]

Roosevelt's motivations for joining the war were likely based on mounting threats to our national interests and an honorable outcome to the conflict. After all, in 1941, he and British Prime Minister Winston Churchill issued a formal declaration of Allied war aims, the "Atlantic Charter." That document expressed the collective goal of seeking "no territorial changes that do not accord with the freely expressed wishes of the peoples concerned," that they would "respect the right of all peoples to choose the form of governments under which they will live," and that they would strive "to see sovereign rights and self-government restored to those who have been forcibly deprived of them."[37]

We are left with the question: Does the end state of World War II justify the means? Historians will continue to argue these issues, but on balance, many wrongs were righted and peoples were freed to better lives, and the atrocity-plagued Axis regimes in Berlin and Tokyo were toppled. Thereafter, America emerged from the war to a very different future than the one espoused by her isolationist majority.

Roosevelt's hypocrisy aside, it does appear that America joined the war for a just cause, perhaps in spite of itself, which is yet another American strength. This is a view shared by Churchill, who said, "You can always count on Americans to do the right thing—after they've tried everything else."[38]

Finally, we should not ignore the hand of God in the decision-making process. Hitler and his senior officials were deeply involved in the occult. Japan was a nation worshipping emperors and other gods. By no stretch of the imagination, America and her Allies, while certainly not perfect, were fighting the forces of evil. God had a purpose and His plan was carried out.

Strength of Being a Good Ally

America was a strong ally prior to and during World War II. In March 1941, the Lend-Lease Act became the principal means for the U.S. to aid foreign partners during the war. That act authorized the president to transfer arms or other defense articles to "the government of any country whose defense the president deems vital to the defense of the United States."[39] Those articles were transferred without compensation to Britain, China, the Soviet Union, and other countries, accomplishing at least two ends: helping our partners in the fight against the Axis Powers and not overextending America in the battle.

Once America entered the war, the Axis Powers were largely doomed—primarily because of the Arsenal of Democracy, which turned out a B-24 heavy bomber every hour, and a single shipyard could produce an ocean-going Liberty merchant ship from scratch in a week. The Axis couldn't keep up with American aid to its partners. In total, America produced thirty-four thousand excellent B-17s, B-24s and B-29s and simultaneously put a six-thousand-ship navy afloat—the largest in history.[40]

America joined the fight as a giant partner. It eventually sent millions of troops throughout the Pacific islands, North Africa, and Italy, then finally to Western Europe. Further, America staged two simultaneous bombing campaigns with its Allies against Germany and Japan while conducting global surface and subsurface campaign against Axis navies.

As America shipped war goods to its Allies, those weapons systems, over time, vastly improved in effect, which before long gave the Allies a combat edge over the Axis Powers. Our M1 rifle, B-29 bomber, P-51 Mustang fighter, Gato-class submarine, Essex-class aircraft carriers, and Iowa-class battleships soon ruled the war's battles.[41]

Allied cooperation was a major strength. On January 1, 1942, the U.S. officially united with twenty-five other nations as Allies and formed the basis for the United Nations to oppose the Axis Powers. At the time, the informal, "Big 3" alliance of the United Kingdom, the Soviet Union and the United States emerged as the key decision-makers for all future Allied strategic decisions.

The level of Allied cooperation went beyond Lend-Lease to forming the twenty-six-member United Nations. Early in the war, President Roosevelt and Prime Minister Churchill sparked a level of bilateral cooperation never seen in the history of warfare. Soon, Anglo-American cooperation became embodied in the combined chiefs of staff, which was far more than a means of consultation. That relationship made the position of Supreme Commander Allied Expeditionary Force possible, which was filled by U.S. Army General Dwight Eisenhower, a man with a proven ability to work amicably with Allies in Europe. Eisenhower enjoyed authority over all the armed forces branches of all Allied countries whose militaries participated in D-Day, Operation Overlord (June 6, 1944).[42]

The level of Allied integration reached deep into each partner nation's armed forces, with units from one nation falling under the command authority of a commander from an Allied unit. This trend continues today with the North Atlantic Treaty Organization, which seeks to standardize weapons and procedures across the twenty-eight-member militaries. The best outcome of the cooperation among the Allies in World War II is a program established after the war by General Eisenhower and British Field Marshall Montgomery in 1947.

The American, British, Canadian, Australian Armies Program, which now includes the small nation of New Zealand as well, continues today to reach levels of materiel and doctrinal interoperability never seen across so many nations in the past. This strength across Allies is thanks to America's initiative first seen at the beginning of the Second War, which continues to fortify America's fighting forces even today.

Strength of Fighting Justly

Americans, with few exceptions, fought justly in World War II.

Earlier, we established that the just war principles were satisfied by America's entry into the war, and now we examine the manner by which Americans fought that war. Was it conducted in a just manner (*jus in bello*)?

The rules governing conduct within war are based on the principle of discrimination. First, armed enemy soldiers are legitimate targets and may be killed, but unarmed civilians are immune, and deliberate attacks on them are prohibited. Second, disarmed enemy soldiers are also immune, and acquire rights as prisoners of war. Finally, there is a principle of proportionality that requires the ends sought in a particular action to be proportionate to the harm done. Clearly, an unintended but permissible result of targeting an enemy may be the death of some civilians—that is, as long as the civilians were not the intended target.

Combat veterans understand that war is a nasty business where "kill or be killed" is the intended outcome, but modern war, which includes World War II, has made the classic just-war principles a high and tough standard to achieve. Specifically, World War II added a new twist to fighting a just war, because technological change afforded both sides the means to render massive death and destruction. After all, in hindsight, history provides ample evidence that the Axis Powers conducted an unjust war—atrocities, treatment of noncombatants, proportionality—and both their people and leaders paid a high price. The question before us here is whether America and her Allies conducted the World War II in a just manner that could then be identified as a strength.

We will explore this question by examining perhaps two of the most difficult allegations about America's conduct in World War II: Some in our ranks committed atrocities, and our strategic bombing campaigns killed many civilians.

In 1947, Edgar Jones wrote for *The Atlantic* a sobering and very critical account of American warriors in World War II. His allegations warrant consideration and a response before anyone declares that our conduct of that war was just and therefore a strength.[43]

Jones acknowledged, "I do not pretend to speak for all veterans," and then he outlined his career that spanned "40 months of war duty and five major battles [which included Iwo Jima and Okinawa] ...I was only an ambulance driver, a merchant seaman, an army historian, and a war correspondent, never a downright GI."[44]

Jones doubts our men were satisfied with "their hollow victory." He argued the GI had "bitter contempt for the home front's abysmal lack of understanding, its pleasures and comforts, and its nauseating capacity to talk in patriotic platitudes."[45]

He labeled the GI as "not a deep-thinking man" who left "the peace talk to the civilians." The GI was placed, explained Jones, in a "position where he had to kill or be killed, he did not trouble himself with pretenses that he was a crusader. He fought because his people at home expected him to fight, and he let them seek the necessary justification for his own ruthlessness."[46]

"Nine out of ten servicemen wanted nothing more to do with wars after their first week of basic training," Jones observed. "Whether stationed in Washington or on a scrap of coral sand, the average GI considered himself to be the purposeless victim of malignant justice." Then Jones restated a phrase he often heard from GIs at the time: "From where I stand, this whole thing stinks."[47]

He rhetorically asked, "What kind of war do civilians suppose we fought, anyway?" Jones dismissed the notion that Americans are more noble and decent than other people, and in two sentences outlined atrocities he alleged were committed by far less than 1 percent of our troops. "We shot prisoners in cold blood, wiped out hospitals, strafed lifeboats, killed or mistreated enemy civilians, finished off the enemy wounded, tossed the dying into a hole with the dead, and in the Pacific boiled the flesh off enemy skulls to make table ornaments for sweethearts, or carved their bones into letter openers."[48]

Jones went on to explain: "If we [America] were on trial for breaking international laws, we should be found guilty on a dozen counts. We fought a dishonorable war, because morality had a low priority in battle." He admits that very few GIs committed unwarranted atrocities, but also volunteered that "the same might be said for the Germans and Japanese." He blames the exigencies of war for many war crimes and the rest on the mental distortion that war produced. He went on to explain, "But we publicized every inhuman act of our opponents and censored any recognition of our own moral frailty in moments of desperation."[49]

"It is not my intention either to excuse our late opponents or to discredit our own fighting men. I do however, believe that all of us, not just the battle enlightened GIs, should fully understand the horror and degradation of war…. War does horrible things to men…. It demands the worst of a person and pays off in brutality and maladjustment. It has become so mechanical, inhuman, and crassly destructive that men lose all sense of personal responsibility for their actions. They fight without compassion, because that is the only way to fight a total war."[50]

Yes, there is evidence that some Americans committed atrocities, as Jones states, and many were rightly convicted while others inevitably escaped the arm of justice but not their eventual accountability to their

Maker. The broader question is whether the manner by which the vast majority of the GIs fought was just and therefore an American strength.

The simple answer is a resounding "yes." American GIs fought for the most part justly in spite of their often dire circumstances, a conclusion based on two compelling reasons. Sixteen million Americans served in our armed forces during a time of great national crisis, and the overwhelming majority fought hard and long and many died while others came home with physical and psychological wounds. These men were called upon to do something unnatural—kill—and they did what they were called to do, victorious over an unconscionable enemy that threatened America's very existence. Further, although the crass realities of killing led a few troopers to commit atrocities, many of those violators were convicted—a sign of the attempt to fight justly by their superiors.

The second difficult allegation questions whether America fought in a just manner when it conducted strategic bombing campaigns.

The American air forces conducted strategic bombing campaigns that destroyed German and Japanese cities, culminating in the nuclear devastation of Hiroshima and Nagasaki. Those attacks killed many thousands of civilians and left many cities crumbled wastelands.

Massive bombing attacks were launched by both sides prior to America joining the war, and the U.S. joined the Allied campaigns once in the fight. It is important to understand that prior to entering the war, many American leaders unequivocally condemned the bombing of civilians. In 1938, the U.S. Senate expressed a common sentiment by issuing an "unqualified condemnation of the inhuman bombing of civilian populations" conducted by the Japanese and Fascists bombing in Spain. President Roosevelt appealed to all sides following Germany's 1939 invasion of Poland that armed forces "shall in no event, and under no circumstances, undertake the bombardment from the air of civilian populations or of unfortified cities."[51] Unfortunately, our soon-to-be ally, Great Britain, violated Roosevelt's admonition months before we joined the war.

The English decided to bomb civilians soon after the fall of France in June 1940, and shortly after, German aircraft started to rain bombs on British cities in preparation for an expected Nazi amphibious invasion of the island nation. The British desperately responded to the German Blitz by bombing German cities in an attempt to forestall the anticipated Nazi invasion by using a strategy Churchill coined as the "dehousing" campaign. Churchill's intent was to bomb the German people in cities to deny them homes hoping to seed a revolt against the Nazis, something that never happened.

Churchill's "dehousing" campaign became somewhat of a standard for American bombers, even though in time, maturing technology gave us improved bombing accuracy. However, during the war, American leaders remained self-righteous by constantly condemning the Axis powers for targeting civilians even though Allied aircraft continued to bomb civilian areas such as in Dresden and Hamburg. At that time, February 1945, Secretary of War Henry Stimson addressed the issue: "We will continue to bomb military targets and...there has been no change in the policy against conducting 'terror bombings' against civilian populations."[52]

The same viewpoint was evident when it came to using a nuclear bomb on Japanese cities. Specifically, in the wake of the nuclear attack on Hiroshima, President Harry Truman's press release insisted it was against "a Japanese army base" and "we wished in this first attack to avoid, insofar as possible, the killing of civilians."[53]

Admittedly, President Truman faced an incredibly difficult decision. The president had two choices: Use the untested nuclear bomb to compel the Japanese to surrender without further fighting, or send hundreds of thousands of Americans to invade the Japanese homeland and accept the high probability that Tokyo would mobilize the entire nation as kamikazes and result in a bloodbath for invaders and defenders alike. Truman is quoted as saying at the time that the joint chiefs "were grim in their estimates of the cost in casualties we would have to pay to invade the Japanese mainland" and that "all of us realized that the fighting would be fierce and the losses heavy."[54]

At the time, the American public was either gullible or numb to the bombing of civilians because there was virtually no public protest. Perhaps their lack of protest is attributable to the absence of information about the attacks and the devastating results for civilians. Another explanation often heard, especially from veterans, was that the air attacks were justified as retribution for the Axis' aggression and atrocities, and bombing civilians to quicken the war's end was less of an evil than had the Allies suffered defeat; besides, invasion would take an unacceptable toll in American blood.

After the war, the Nuremberg tribunals in Germany and the war crime trials of Japan's leaders focused as much on the harm inflicted on civilians as any other atrocity. Certainly an unbiased observer would have seen the hypocrisy in the Allied prosecution of Axis leaders for their own promiscuous bombing of civilians. Even our erstwhile ally, the Soviet Union, condemned America for barbarous methods of bombing civilians.

Senior officers in America's armed forces were concerned about the precedent set in the Second War regarding bombing civilians. In 1949, a number of U.S. Navy admirals criticized U.S. Air Force colleagues for their war-time bombing practices. The media called the public dissent the "Revolt of the Admirals" who in congressional hearings argued against targeting civilians in the future. Rear Admiral Ralph Ofstie contended that "strategic air warfare, as practiced in the past [read WWII] and as proposed for the future, is militarily unsound and of limited effect, is morally wrong, and is decidedly harmful to the stability of a postwar world."[55]

The secretary of the Air Force, W. Stuart Symington, objected and bluntly dismissed the criticism. "It has been stated that the Air Force favors mass bombing of civilians," he said. "That is not true. It is inevitable that attacks on industrial targets will kill civilians. That is not an exclusive characteristic of the atomic bomb, but is an unavoidable result of modern total warfare." [56]

World War II was ugly, vicious, and bloody. Our troops fought hard and mostly honorably. They were horribly bloodied, but victorious, and for that we owe them a debt of gratitude. The same can be said of their leaders and especially the top men who faced a massive responsibility to oppose evil and save our country from defeat. Any questionable decision that appears to have sanctioned unjust bombing must be credited to the men who made those very tough decisions—Roosevelt, Churchill, Eisenhower, Marshall, and McArthur. However, for those who would judge these men for their heart-wrenching decisions, then let them cast the first stone. Most of us, who will never face such wrenching decisions, are thankful for such men tough-minded strong leaders who we credit with saving our country.

Strength of Faith

Americans grew closer to God thanks to the war and especially thanks to the fear associated with combat. The combat-related conversions of many troops explains in part America's resurgence of faith after the war.

American religiosity today isn't that much different than it was in the pre-World War II and the war years except for evidence of wide-spread faith found on the battlefields. In fact, coming out of World War II, America was not very religious, but that trend quickly reversed as combat-hardened and prayer-dependent troops returned home.

The phenomenon of growing religiosity after the war is attributed to combat veterans returning home with a deep faith formed under the constant threat of death. Evidently, according to a study of those veterans, many troops found great solace in their faith, which increased the heavier combat became.

A study published in the *Journal of Religion and Health* found that when service members were fearful in combat, they reported that prayer was a big motivator. "The most important thing is that the more veterans disliked the war, the more religious they were 50 years later," said Craig Wansink, one of the study's authors and a professor of religious studies at Virginia Wesleyan College.[57]

That study, "Are There Atheists in Foxholes? Combat Intensity and Religious Behavior," found that as combat became more intense, more soldiers reported praying, rising from 42 to 72 percent. Further, soldiers who faced heavy combat attended church 21 percent more often and soldiers who described their war experience as positive attended 26 percent less often.[58]

Michael Snape, the British author of *God and Uncle Sam*, provides great insight into our understanding of World War II "foxhole religion," and he alludes to the phenomenon that helped America grow closer to God after the Second War.

Snape reviewed thousands of personal accounts from war-time chaplains and service members alike to conclude, as do the authors of the study above, that the intensity of religion seemed contingent on the proximity to combat-related danger.

It's noteworthy that the expression "There are no atheists in foxholes" is ascribed to William Cummings, an American Catholic priest and army chaplain who took part in the defense of Bataan and "died of exposure and starvation" on board a Japanese prison ship in 1945.[59] The importance of religion was widely echoed by American service members across the war years.

- Sergeant Alvin McAnney wrote his wife from Luxembourg in 1944: "They can laugh about foxhole religion but every front line soldier embraces a little religion and are [sic] not ashamed to pray. When you face death hourly and daily you can't help but believe in Divine Guidance. My faith in God has increased a thousand fold. He pulled me thru when nothing else could."[60]
- A vignette published in the *Invasion Diary* by Richard Tregaskis recounted a "supposedly authentic" story about a foul-mouthed GI who had loudly called upon God to save his life during an

artillery barrage, which prompted a response from an unidentified GI in a nearby foxhole. "Hey, Joe, why don't you knock off that cryin' for help, and talk to somebody you know?"[61]

- Glenn Frazier, a soldier who survived the Bataan Death March, paraphrased the Twenty-Third Psalm to fit the context of his situation and identify the source of his hope:

Yea though I walked 106 miles through the valley and in the shadow of death.... I knew the Lord was my shepherd. They forbid me to lay down in green pastures for six days and seven nights. I was marched by running water but was forbidden a drink. The Japanese prepared their tables before me but I was forbidden food. They maketh me march without mercy. But only God could restoreth my soul.

It is also noteworthy that throughout the war, the intensity of battle dictated the level of attendance at religious services.

- The *Christian Science Monitor* reported in 1943: "A fair estimate of the men attending services…was now 75 or 80 percent compared to the old peacetime figure in the services of about 25 percent."[62]
- Army chaplain Percy Hickcox wrote from the Pacific theater: "At the beginning of my fifth year of service as a chaplain in this present conflict, I am ready to admit that the religion of our soldier is one which is largely determined by crisis. It is the elementary urge of men to turn to God in time of danger just as they turn to their chaplains in time of trouble."[63]
- A chaplain assistant wrote from Belgium in January 1945: "About 95 out of every 100 men in our outfit have either been to some service or in to see the chaplain since we left the States. Worship and communion really means something here, where

48

the sound of rifle fire means death instead of range practice. Every battle boosts attendance for men want the assurance and hope of their Christian faith when they face death."[64]

- Chaplain Harry Abbott with the 1st Armored Division in the North African Campaign wrote that he was surprised by the large attendance at services. One sergeant spoke up to explain: "Chaplain, those German 88's are making believers out of us."[65]

- A chaplain with an American airborne unit said, "I know that the majority of men who jump do ask for God to help them. Why, you can't help but ask as you throw yourself from an airplane and realize that if the chute does not open you will die suddenly and violently."[66]

- Sergeant George Tullidge III with the 507th Parachute Infantry Regiment wrote advice to his younger brother to develop a steady habit of "Bible-reading, the keeping of good company, and filial obedience to their mother and father."[67]

- Leo Claude Martin of the 501st Parachute Infantry Regiment said his "company commander led his men in prayer before [the] Normandy jump" and that religious convictions clearly "helped" performance.

- Another important indicator of battlefield-related religious fervor among our men was the frequency they prayed to God.

- Chaplain Francis Sampson wrote about surviving a night of intense German fire: "How we survived that night I shall never know, except that the calm, fervent prayers of those wounded didn't leave God any choice in the matter but to answer them."[68]

- George Farmer, a Disciples of Christ chaplain with the 95th Infantry Division outside of Metz in the fall of 1944, visited soldiers in an underground bunker. Before leaving each bunker, the chaplain asked if the troops would join him in prayer. Every man reportedly answered, "Yes, sir." "The men as a unit...got on their knees and I felt a great responsibility upon me.... It was a great challenge to me to try to turn their extremity into God's opportunity."[69]

- The April 1944 edition of *What the Soldier Thinks* states: "The judgment that 'there are no atheists in foxholes' is close to the truth, if one is to examine the statements of officers and men on the power of prayer to help fear.... Prayer is more likely to be a help to enlisted men than to officers, but even among officers, a majority from [Europe and the Pacific] say that it helped them a lot when the going was tough. Almost two out of three enlisted men say the same and less than one man in five says the thought of prayer never occurred to him. Among officers, one in four says he never thought of it."[70]

- General George Patton promoted prayer among his Third Army troops. Third Army's Chaplain James O'Neill wrote: "As chaplains it is our business to pray. We preach its importance. We urge its practice... Urge all of your men to pray, not alone in church, but everywhere. Pray when driving. Pray when fighting. Pray alone. Pray with others. Pray by night and pray by day. Pray for the cessation of immoderate rains, for good weather for Battle. Pray for the defeat of our wicked enemy.... Pray for victory. Pray for our Army, and pray for peace."[71]

- *The American Soldier*, a post-war study by the Social Science Research Council, surveyed soldiers to conclude that "the fact that such an overwhelming majority of combat men said that prayer helped them a lot certainly means that they almost universally had recourse to prayer and probably found relief, distraction, or consolation in the process."[72]

- The quick end of the war in Europe and the unexpected abrupt end of the war in the Pacific was a relief to our war-weary troops and an answer to their collective prayers. Many of those sixteen million men and women who returned home from war felt humbled, thankful because four hundred thousand of their fellow service members didn't survive, and if not for God's grace, they would have been among those who never returned.

• Louis Zamperini was one of those who came back from war a broken man, but then he quickly turned to Christ for hope. He competed in the 1936 Berlin Olympics and was set to compete again in the 1940 games in Tokyo, which were canceled due to World War II. Zamperini served in the Army Air Corps aboard a B-24 Liberator before his aircraft experienced mechanical problems and then crashed into the Pacific Ocean. He and two surviving crewmates spent the next forty-seven days stranded on a raft, surviving on collected rainwater and killed birds that landed on their raft. Their raft drifted into Japanese territory and soon they were taken prisoner of war and held captive for two years, a time of both physical and psychological torture. After release, Zamperini turned to Christ at a Billy Graham crusade, founded a camp for troubled youth, forgave his Japanese tormenters, and became an inspirational speaker. His life inspired a biography by Laura Hillbrand, *Unbroken: A World War II Story of Survival, Resilience, and Redemption,* and a 2014 film directed and produced by actress Angelina Jolie.[73]

• Men like Zamperini who suffered so much during the war were ripe for the transforming love of Christ while others, who came home already transformed, became the seed of a spiritual renewal across America that contributed to a post-war surge in faith and church attendance.

Post-War Strengths

Winston Churchill said World War II left Europe "a rubble-heap, a charnel house, a breeding ground of pestilence and hate."[74] Into that chaotic situation America and her Allies poured compassion, hard work, and lots of aid over many years to transform Germany and Japan into major Allies and incredibly successful economic states. That's a testimony to American strength.

Strength of Leadership in Post-War Occupation

After Germany's defeat, the four primary Allies in Europe—the United States, Great Britain, the Soviet Union and France—occupied the German state for almost eleven years with one exception: The Russians occupied East Germany until the end of the Cold War. U.S. leadership was an obvious strength during the occupation, especially when contrasted with the Soviet Union's usury-like stewardship of East Germany.

The Allies met several times before the end of the war in Europe to decide how to deal with Germany after the conflict. In 1943 at the Tehran Conference, President Roosevelt and Soviet leader Joseph Stalin agreed to divide Germany and occupy it jointly. Two years later at Yalta, these men further refined the Tehran agreement by shifting the eastern border of Germany to the west, a generous albeit naive gesture to the Soviets. Further, these leaders discussed but never agreed on Soviet demands that Germany pay reparations, much like the French and British demands at Versailles at the end of World War I. The final East-West meeting between Stalin and by then new President Truman was held at Potsdam, where they confirmed the earlier agreements.

Fast forward to Victory in Europe (V-E) day (May 8, 1945). At that point, General Eisenhower had 1,622,000 men in Germany out of a total force in Europe numbering 3,077,000.[75] Once the shooting stopped, the occupation immediately began and GIs transitioned from warriors to a stabilization force. Their duties ranged from controlling the population and stifling the remaining Nazi resistance to manning borders, enforcing curfews, repairing telephone lines, starting up factories and re-energizing the German economy.

Just as the troops settled into their occupation jobs, nearly a million and a half prepared for redeployment to the Pacific theater to fight the

Japanese, while nearly six hundred thousand others who had the longest war service were headed home for discharge. Meanwhile, wartime East-West cooperation soured after the Axis Powers surrendered. Soon the Allies minus the Soviets agreed to a joint occupation, with each country taking charge of a zone as well as a sector of Germany's capital, Berlin, while the uncooperative Russians occupied East Germany and East Berlin.

The Soviets quickly stripped East Germany of all manufacturing equipment, which scuttled any hope of a quick post-war recovery. Meanwhile, the U.S. wanted to avoid making Germany economically dependent on outside aid, so we poured aid into German industries beginning with what became known as the Marshall Plan.

In 1947, Secretary of State George C. Marshall spoke at the Harvard commencement, where he issued a desperate call for a program to rebuild Europe. "Our policy is directed not against any country or doctrine but against hunger, poverty, desperation and chaos. Its purpose should be the revival of a working economy in the world so as to permit the emergence of political and social conditions in which free institutions can exist."[76]

Soon the U.S. Congress embraced Marshall's proposal, and by March 1948, the Economic Cooperation Act (or the Marshall Plan) passed. That act eventually led to the U.S. investing over $22 billion (more than $182 billion in real twenty-first-century dollars adjusted for inflation) in economic foreign assistance across sixteen European nations.[77]

The Marshall Plan saved many Europeans from mass starvation, gave Europe the stimulus necessary to rapidly regrow its industries, facilitated the spread of democratic and free market ideals, spurred outside investment, and cemented the region against the dangerous influence of Russia's East European communist satellite states. Further, it created markets for American goods while doing nothing for Soviet-occupied Eastern Europe except to make them envious and dissatisfied with their Soviet occupiers.

Even though America offered to include the Soviet-occupied areas in the Marshall Plan, Stalin rejected that offer, believing America intended to interfere in Russia's internal affairs and, after all, he thought the West's offer was really intended to wean the East away from Moscow's new sphere of influence. That's likely correct analysis on Stalin's part.

Although the Allies repeatedly encouraged the Soviets to join in reunifying the two halves of Germany, as they had agreed to do during war-time conferences, the Russians refused reunification, believing the Germans were still a security threat. However, it soon became obvious that Moscow was really more concerned about its own hegemonic ambitions, not German remilitarization.

Moscow's real ambitions soon became very apparent with a series of disputes with the Western Allies over Berlin. The first sparks flew with the Berlin blockade, which was later followed by the Berlin Quadripartite Agreement (an arrangement whereby the Soviets undertook not to impede transit traffic between West Berlin and the Federal Republic) and then the construction of the Berlin Wall, "officially" starting the Cold War that lasted until the collapse of the Soviet Union in 1991.

In June 1948, the Soviets took steps to permanently divide Berlin by blocking all road access between West Germany and West Berlin to protest Western efforts to integrate their zones of occupation in Western Germany. In fact, the Soviets evidently expected the West to abandon Berlin to Moscow rather than resist the blockade. However, the U.S. with its Allies launched a massive airlift to deliver supplies to the people of Berlin, an effort that was immensely popular among the Allied nations. Once the blockade was lifted eleven months later (May 1949), the geopolitical landscape was radically different. During those interim months, the Allies established the Federal Republic of Germany and the North Atlantic Treaty Organization, thus a bright line between the East and West was firmly in place.

Meanwhile, on the other side of the world in Northeast Asia, the occupation of post-war Japan was less complicated than Europe, which favored America's interests. Between 1945 and 1952, General Douglas MacArthur was in command of the Supreme Command of Allied Powers (SCAP) that used its occupation of Japan to enact widespread military, political, economic, and social reforms.[78]

Although winning Japan's surrender required the use of two atomic bombs that claimed many thousands of lives, ultimately Tokyo's capitulation to Allied demands for surrender came from Emperor Hirohito, who announced that decision in a radio broadcast to the Japanese people on August 14, 1945. The Emperor said in that announcement: "After pondering deeply the general trends of the world and the actual conditions obtaining in our empire today, we have decided to effect a settlement of the present situation by resorting to an extraordinary measure.[79]

"We have ordered our Government to communicate to the Governments of the United States, Great Britain, China and the Soviet Union that our empire accepts the provisions of their joint declaration [unconditional surrender]."[80]

The groundwork for the post-war occupation of Japan was made during a series of war-time conferences that included America's Allies. Those representatives agreed to focus occupation efforts primarily on stabilizing the Japanese economy and preventing Japan's remilitarization.

Although each of the Allies participated in an "Allied Council" that oversaw the occupation, General MacArthur had the final authority. He assembled a team of American officers and other experts to closely supervise the occupation. It is noteworthy that some of those experts were liberal Democrats who subscribed to President Roosevelt's New Deal policies such as the recognition of labor unions, an idea that became part of Japan's new economy.

Once on the job in September 1945, MacArthur approved a three-phase occupation plan: punish and reform; revive the economy; and formalize peace with the formation of an alliance. The first phase lasted through 1947 and involved significant changes, such as punishing Japan's past militarism, the conduct of war crime trials, and banning former military officers from political leadership.

SCAP made quick and significant economic change to include land reform designed to benefit the tenant farmer at the expense of rich landowners. Then MacArthur replaced Japanese business conglomerates, family-owned firms known as *zaibatsu*, with a free-market capitalist system. Meanwhile, to sustain the country during those dire economic times, the U.S. government provided food aid, which the Japanese government sold to raise funds for its operation.

Political reforms were significant as well. MacArthur realized fundamental reform required inside help, and there was no one better to recruit to that task than Emperor Hirohito. The general curried Hirohito's favor by preserving the institution of the royalty in society, albeit as a figurehead like the British royal family and by treating the emperor with respect—especially in public ceremonies.

MacArthur's cultural brilliance earned the emperor's favor that made dramatic political change much easier. Specifically, SCAP dictated a new constitution to the Japanese that established a parliamentary system, emphasized civil rights (especially for women), and included a clause that renounced military action. Then, with the emperor's full support, MacArthur's draft constitution won widespread public support even over the objections of the Japanese ruling party.

By 1948, SCAP realized that Japan's economy needed significant rehabilitation, in part because widespread discontent made the island nation ripe for the spread of communism that had already found a foothold in the region thanks to the communist victory in China's civil war. Therefore, economic rehabilitation of Japan became the SCAP's top priority, which included tax reform and heavy investment. In fact, one of the greatest economic helps was the outbreak of the Korean War in 1950 that made Japan the principal supply depot for war-bound United Nations forces.

The third and final stage of MacArthur's occupation plan was a transition to a formal peace treaty and an alliance. Those agreements left American bases in Japan, an outcome that cemented Japan's bilateral security relationship with America.

America was the critical leader behind the rebuilding of Japan and Germany that transformed those nations into major U.S. Allies and indispensable trading partners. That outcome was only possible because of America's post-war strengths: compassion, generosity, leadership, and democratic vision. Compare these two economic giants with the areas formally under Soviet control after the war that are far better off now, yet still lag in development.

Strength of Justice

After World War II, America and her Allies held officials and regime partisans from Japan and Germany accountable for their war crimes and other war-time atrocities. Special tribunals were created in both countries to prosecute and punish the major war criminals, as well as smaller, less well-known tribunals The manner and fairness of the tribunals was evidence of an American strength in justice.

In Europe, the four major Allied powers—France, the Soviet Union, the United Kingdom, and the U.S.—established the International Military Tribunal (IMT) in Nuremberg, Germany, to prosecute and punish war criminals including senior Nazi political and military leaders as well as Nazi organizations.[81]

The charter of the IMT (or Nuremberg Charter) outlined the tribunal's constitution, functions, and jurisdiction. There was one judge from each of the Allied powers on the tribunal, and each country also provided a prosecution team. The charter gave the IMT the authority to try to punish persons who "committed any of the following crimes": crimes against peace, war crimes, and crimes against humanity.

The IMT prosecutors indicted twenty-four Germans, including Nazi officials like Hermann Göring and Rudolph Hess, as well as German industrialists, lawyers, doctors, and high-ranking military officers. Of course, the Nazi leader Adolf Hitler had committed suicide just before Germany's surrender. Six Nazi organizations like the secret police, the "Gestapo," were indicted as "criminal organizations." The thirteen trials of those major war criminals/organizations were carried out at the Palace of Justice in Nuremberg and took place November 20, 1945, to October 1, 1946.

The IMT found all but three guilty, of which twelve were sentenced to death—one in absentia, and one, Hermann Göring, who committed suicide the night before his execution with a cyanide capsule. That left ten condemned who were executed by Master Sergeant John Woods, who told *Time* magazine he was proud of his work: "The way I look at this hanging job, somebody has to do it...ten men in 103 minutes. That's fast work," explained the sergeant.[82]

The Nuremberg trials were not the only war crime trials in Germany. The U.S. Army hosted a series of trials over four years in the small Rhineland city of Duren. One such trial convicted a German officer, Captain Curt Bruns, for the murder of two American prisoners of war during the Battle of the Bulge. Another case involved an American pilot who had bailed out over the village of Preist in the Rhineland. Peter Back, a local Nazi *Blockleiter* (community warden who spread ideology), twice shot the unarmed pilot in front of local policemen who did not attempt to prevent the murder. At trial, Back was sentenced to death and the policemen to life imprisonment.[83]

Other tribunals considered those who ran the Nazi camps. General Eisenhower asked for and received approval to prosecute concentration camp commandants and guards as war criminals as well. Eisenhower explained that those accused of "abominable deeds" both during the war and the occupation must be held accountable, and he believed punishing the guilty would have "a salutory effect on public opinion both in Germany and in Allied countries."[84]

Tribunals were established in Japan to try war criminals as well. General MacArthur established a similar tribunal structure to that in Nuremberg for Japanese war criminals. The International Military Tribunal for the Far East (IMTFE) presided over trials of senior Japanese political and military leaders for war crimes.[85]

The 1945 Potsdam declaration demanded Japan's "unconditional surrender" and that "stern justice shall be meted out to all war criminals." MacArthur granted the IMTFE broad authority to determine the composition, jurisdiction, and functions of the tribunal. Like the Nuremberg tribunals, the IMTFE included judges from each Allied country as well as a prosecution team.

The IMTFE tried individuals for crimes against peace, war crimes, and crimes against humanity, just as the Nuremberg tribunal. The only significant difference was that the IMTFE covered a much longer period, from the 1931 Japanese invasion of China to its 1945 surrender.

The tribunals took place in Tokyo from May 1946 to November 1948. Nine senior Japanese political leaders and eighteen military leaders were prosecuted, finding twenty-five defendants guilty and sentencing seven to death, including General Hideki Tojo, who served as Japanese premier during the war. Sixteen others were sentenced to life imprisonment or lesser terms. Tojo and six others were executed December 23, 1948, in Tokyo.

There were other trials for war crimes in addition to the central Tokyo IMTFE high-profile tribunals. Courts outside Japan tried about five thousand Japanese accused of war crimes, of whom more than nine hundred were executed for their crimes.

America and her Allies demonstrated great strength by establishing well-run and just tribunals that carefully collected, studied and presented evidence that led to convictions and sentences against the Axis leadership and their representatives.

Strength of Charting a Bright Future

America ended the occupation of Germany on May 5, 1955, after the Allies established the Federal Republic of Germany and accepted West Germany into the North Atlantic Treaty Organization. Under the terms of the end of the military occupation, West Germany was allowed to establish a military and resume the manufacture of arms except for chemical and atomic weapons.

MacArthur started to draw down the occupation of Japan in 1949 with sweeping changes to SCAP's power structure. Then on September 8, 1951, the San Francisco Peace Treaty was signed appointing April 28, 1952, as the official end of the Allied occupation. However, thirty-one thousand U.S. military personnel remain in Japan today under the terms of the Treaty of Mutual Cooperation and Security between the U.S. and Japan.

Today, almost seventy years after the end of the Second World War, both Germany and Japan remain strong democratic and economically prosperous. Why? They are great nations today because a strong America defeated the Axis powers and then sacrificially rebuilt those nations. Their success is a tribute to American strength. And then, with their mission in Japan and Europe successfully accomplished, the young, battle-hardened Americans went home where they applied that same winning strength to expand the American economy and make America into a great nation.

Conclusion

As mentioned earlier, famed author Tom Brokaw labeled World War II veterans and their supporters at home "The Greatest Generation." Yes, they were heroes in the truest sense because they evidenced, in spite of very tough challenges, the ten strengths outlined in this chapter. But they were great for very simple reasons as well.

Our World War II-era forefathers had clarity of purpose. They understood that either they must quickly unify in the face of great crises, or risk defeat—and the America they had grown to love would cease to exist.

The Greatest Generation did unify around clarity of purpose, and they also easily identified their enemies, then poured every ounce of their effort and willpower into defeating that "evil." They didn't trifle with political correctness about labeling the regimes in Berlin and Tokyo as "evil"; no, they knew those "evil" enemies had to be totally destroyed before they wreaked untold and irreparable damage. Too much was at stake to do otherwise.

Finally, those American heroes, much like their Revolutionary War forefathers, risked everything to muster their collective strengths. With total dependence on God, they went forth under the cover of constant prayer to prepare for the serious business of war, then fought justly. After victory, they compassionately redeemed their former enemies.

That, my friends, is evidence that once America was a nation of great strength!

chapter three

WHEN ONCE WE WERE A NATION OF
Capitalists
By Derek Gilbert

W e Americans have always taken pride in our nation as a land of opportunity, a place where a good idea, a little entrepreneurial spirit, and some hard work can pay off in financial independence. And for much of our history, this has been true. Today, 240 years after declaring independence, we like to believe the "American dream" is alive and well thanks to free-market capitalism, where government stays out of the way of business and lets markets naturally determine winners and losers.

This belief has been shaken over the last eight years. Americans have watched in frustration and disbelief as our federal government, over the objections of two-thirds of us, bailed out Wall Street and General Motors, funneled billions of dollars into financially shaky renewable energy companies, and then compelled us to buy health insurance, whether we wanted it or not, thereby taking direct control of 17 percent of the U.S. economy.[86]

It is disturbing. A belief in free-market capitalism is practically coded into our DNA. The tale has been repeated often enough that it is taken as a documented fact: The first settlers of the Massachusetts Bay colony tried socialism and nearly starved to death. Only after giving the colonists permission to keep the food they grew above and beyond what was needed to keep the community alive did the struggling colony begin to prosper.

While it's a great story, it isn't entirely accurate. Yes, the colony did take a communal approach to building, planting, and harvesting in its early years, but that was out of necessity. Desperation, really—there weren't enough bodies for every family to fend for itself. Still, it is true that the Pilgrims saw their fortunes turn for the better when they adopted an approach that incentivized self-interest.

That is the basis of capitalism. Simply put, capitalism is an economic system based on private ownership of the means of production and the operation of those means for profit. Economic activity is driven by the desire for workers to reap the benefits of their labor, and market forces self-correct based on the natural tendency of people to invest time and treasure into activities that are most likely to yield a profit.

Terms like "free market" have been thrown around very loosely in recent years. The North American Free Trade Agreement (NAFTA) and the Trans-Pacific Partnership (TPP) have been presented to the American public as incentives to trade, which presumably means more jobs for American workers. The devil is in the details, of course, and the details—which, in the case of the TPP, have been hidden not just from the public, but from Congress—suggest that the real winners are globalists, bankers, big pharmaceutical companies, and, of course, attorneys.

Changes in trade policy over the last half-century have mainly benefitted corporate owners and CEOs. The average wage for American workers only increased from $19.18 an hour to $20.67 (in adjusted dollars) between 1964 and 2014.[87] Over that same period, the ratio of corporate CEO compensation to that of average workers jumped from 20:1 to nearly 300:1.[88] It isn't hard to understand why populist rhetoric finds a receptive audience among young voters. The generation entering the workforce today is likely to be the first since the founding of the American republic that will be worse off financially than those that came before.

The United States—actually, most of the world—has been mired in an economic downturn since 2007. The Great Recession, which officially lasted from December 2007 to June 2009, was linked to the collapse of the housing bubble in mid-2007 (the subprime mortgage crisis) and the subsequent worldwide financial meltdown of 2007–09. However, in spite of the figures released by the United States government, the economy never really recovered for the vast majority of Americans. Except for a few pockets, such as the shale oil and natural gas industry (which has since collapsed due to cheap Middle Eastern oil), real unemployment has been much higher than the government's official figures[89] and household incomes have steadily declined.

The 2016 presidential campaign has put basic economic terms like "capitalism" back into the limelight. As of this writing, one of the five remaining major party candidates for president, Democrat Bernie Sanders, is a socialist. Socialism, in contrast to capitalism, is a range of economic systems that are generally based on social ownership and control of the means of production.

While his critics recoil at promises of "free" college education (a concept that only makes sense to the economically illiterate), guaranteed health care, and a $15 hourly minimum wage, Senator Sanders has publicly disavowed a key tenet of socialism, saying, "I don't believe the government should own the means of production."

Sanders supporters point to the excesses of big investment banks, which received billions of dollars in taxpayer funds (actually trillions— see below) because they were deemed "too big to fail," the spiraling cost of health care, and other perceived inequalities as justification for scrapping capitalism and using the power of government to level the playing field for the middle class.

So what has gone wrong? Is capitalism broken? Were Karl Marx and Friedrich Engels, authors of *The Communist Manifesto*, right after all? Does private ownership of the means of production inevitably lead to oppression of the working classes?

To diagnose the economic malaise plaguing the United States, one must analyze the state of the American middle class. The so-called backbone of the country has been described by politicians of both major parties as the engine that drives the economy, so it follows—assuming that premise is correct—that the factors squeezing the middle class are responsible for the country's economic stagnation of the last decade.

By analyzing this issue, we can perhaps shed light on a broader question, one that is especially relevant in this election cycle: Is the American economy struggling to get back to consistent economic growth because of flaws inherent in capitalism, or because the American economy is no longer truly capitalist?

To those of us born after World War II, it comes as a surprise that the American middle class of the second half of the twentieth century is an anomaly in human history. Yes, there were always opportunities in America for those with ideas for a better mousetrap. But even as late as the 1940s, in spite of heavy manufacturing capacity in the North, the United States was still mainly a rural society. At the outset of WWII, half the country lived outside urban areas and roughly one in five families was engaged in farming. Except for a brief period during the 1920s, a white-collar consumerist middle class did not really exist.

That changed during World War II. The sudden, urgent need for mass-produced implements of war turned America into a manufacturing powerhouse. It also is no coincidence that the United States was the only industrialized nation on the planet that escaped the war with its infrastructure intact just before three decades of unparalleled economic growth and the emergence of the world's first society dominated by a prosperous middle class.

Between the end of the Second World War and 1979, wages and overall compensation for production and non-supervisory workers roughly kept pace with increases in worker productivity. Using 1947 as a baseline, productivity increased 119 percent by 1979 while average hourly compensation rose 100 percent.

Between 1980 and 2009, however, productivity increased another 80 percent while average earnings rose by only 8 percent.[90]

Since 2010, productivity has leveled off. Productivity growth, which drives standards of living higher, averaged 2.6 percent annually between 1995 and 2010, but only 0.4 percent per year since.[91] Declining productivity means the "pie" of real wealth is no longer expanding.

And the slice of that pie for American workers has been shrinking for decades. Since 1970, earned income as a share of Gross Domestic Product (GDP) has declined from 51.5 percent to 42.5 percent.[92] Real median household income in the U.S. peaked at $57,843 in 1999 and dropped to $53,675 by 2014, a loss of 7 percent in fifteen years.[93]

Again we must ask, why? Is capitalism inherently unfair? Or does this massive transfer of wealth to the uber-rich reflect a transformation into a post-capitalist society?

Some history: The early years of the American colonies were a new experiment in wealth creation. In contrast to the situation in seventeenth-century Europe, natural resources—timber, furs, farmland—were in abundant supply while the population, and thus the available labor force, was small. England happily took the output of the colonies—mainly raw and processed grains (wheat, corn, rice, flour, bread), dried and salted fish, naval stores (tar, pitch, turpentine), and tobacco. In exchange, Britain supplied finished goods to the colonies.

Colonists who arrived after the difficult early years, when survival depended on irregular deliveries of food, tools, and other supplies from England, generally prospered. The abundance of food and firewood led to higher birth rates and better health in general than in Europe. The population of European settlers in the colonies increased from about 2,300 in 1620 to over 250,000 by 1700, and nearly 2.8 million by the time of the American Revolution.[94]

That unique set of circumstances is not likely to be repeated. As European settlers arrived in eastern cities, population pressures encouraged the more adventurous to move inland. While most of the colonists, especially those on the frontier, engaged in subsistence farming and handicraft production for home use, the demand in Europe for tobacco, grains, and other raw materials spawned a thriving shipbuilding industry in the colonies. Britain in return supplied finished goods, and the British government guaranteed markets for its manufacturers by restricting what could be produced in the colonies.

Over time, the patterns of exchange grew into what became known as the Triangular Trade. This refers to trade routes between the North American colonies, England, and west Africa, described in unflinching terms in the song "Molasses to Rum" in the musical *1776*.

Molasses to rum to slaves, oh what a beautiful waltz
You dance with us, we dance with you
Molasses and rum and slaves
Who sails the ships out of Boston
Ladened with bibles and rum?
Who drinks a toast to the Ivory Coast?
Hail Africa, the slavers have come
New England with bibles and rum.[95]

In simple terms, raw goods were sent to England; finished goods, including textiles, guns and ammunition, were sent from England to Africa; slaves and spices were transported back to the colonies.

The economic development of the United States cannot be fully understood without acknowledging the impact of slavery. The first Africans to set foot in the English colonies as slaves arrived in Virginia in 1619, and the practice of slavery was legal in parts of the nation until the War Between the States nearly 250 years later.

During the colonial period, the majority of African slaves worked the tobacco plantations of the upper South, Maryland and Virginia. After the American Revolution deprived the colonies of their European tobacco markets, slavery shifted to the lower South, especially after the invention of the cotton gin. By the eve of the Civil War, the American South may have produced as much as 80 percent of the world's cotton, which provided more than half the export earnings of the United States.[96] In 1850, more than three-quarters of the 2.5 million enslaved Africans employed in agriculture in the United States were working on cotton plantations.[97]

There is no question that slavery in the mid-nineteenth century was an essential part of the American economy. The value of the American slave population in 1860 was three times the amount of capital invested in railroads or in manufacturing, about seven times the value of all currency in circulation, and forty-eight times the total expenditures of the federal government that year.[98]

Given those figures, it is difficult to characterize the American economy on the eve of the Civil war as a "free market."

Still, economists to this day debate the net effect of slave labor on the American economy. While it seems obvious that farms and plantations should benefit from artificially cheap labor, it wasn't quite as simple as that. Some economists and historians point out that reluctant workers were likely to deplete soils more quickly. They were likewise unwilling to learn new skills, as there was no real incentive for their effort, making scientific agriculture impossible. Southern farms thus became less competitive than their Northern counterparts. The focus on King Cotton on Southern plantations may actually have contributed to the growth of Northern agriculture as farms in the Midwest were planted to meet the demand for food not produced in the South.[99]

After the American Civil War, the United States was gradually transformed from an agricultural to an industrial society. The easy availability of raw materials, such as timber, iron ore, oil, coal, water, and other resources; the development of new technologies; and a large labor force created by the abolition of slavery and large-scale immigration provided clever (and often unscrupulous) business leaders the opportunity to establish the United States as the world's largest economy by about 1880.

This was assisted, perhaps unintentionally, by the United Kingdom's adoption of a policy of free trade in the nineteenth century. This allowed the United States the opportunity to expand its industrial capacity at the expense of what had formerly been the world's leading economic power.[100] Until about 1800, Britain, like much of Europe, pursued a policy of mercantilism, an economic theory that emphasizes a positive trade balance, especially in finished goods, to augment state power at the expense of rivals. This was especially successful in the seventeenth and eighteenth centuries, when England could exploit its colonies for economic gain. Restricting what could be produced in North America kept the growing colonies a captive market while limiting competition to Britain's expanding manufacturing base.

But by the second half of the nineteenth century, England's elites began turning their attention from wealth creation to wealth manipulation. This opened the door to manufactured goods from competitors like the U.S. and Germany, who maintained tariffs on imported goods to protect their growing industries.

Another phenomenon that grew out of the rapid industrialization and modernization of the second half of the nineteenth century was the emergence of "trusts," trade organizations that collaborated to standardize costs and pricing—and prevent the emergence of rivals. While some good came from the order imposed on chaotic industries in their infancy, such as standardizing track gauges for the nascent railroad industry, "corporate trusts" soon faced accusations of abusing market share to engage in anti-competitive practices. Prominent trusts of the era included Standard Oil, the American Tobacco Company, and U.S. Steel.

Throughout our nation's history, Americans have generally had a strong bias toward fair play. Public opinion against the anti-competitive practices of the trusts was so strong that both major parties in Congress worked to pass the Sherman Antitrust Act in 1890, and both William McKinley and Theodore Roosevelt based much of their presidencies on "trust-busting."

The demands of the Civil War followed by the rapid rise of industry in the United States were accompanied by the growth of investment banks to facilitate the demand for capital. Unlike commercial banks, investment bankers were not allowed to accept deposits or issue notes. Instead, they served as intermediaries, bringing together investors with those who needed capital. As with the industrial trade organizations, the banking industry eventually stratified, until by 1890 a few powerful firms—J. P. Morgan & Co.; Kuhn, Loeb, & Co.; Brown Brothers; and Kidder, Peabody, & Co.—dominated investment banking in the U.S. A House committee in 1913 found that the officers of J. P. Morgan sat on the boards of directors of 112 corporations with a market capitalization of $22.5 billion. The total capitalization of the New York Stock Exchange at the time was estimated at $26.5 billion.[101]

A pattern of booms and busts persisted in the years between the Civil War and the Great Depression. The bank panic of 1907, which might have been worse except for the personal intervention of J. P. Morgan and other wealthy financiers to inject liquidity into the banking system, directly led to the creation of the Federal Reserve Bank of the United States in 1913. The Fed was conceived as a lender of last resort to member banks to stave off the collapse of financial institutions during bank runs. A "run" is when a large number of a bank's depositors withdraw their money at the same time. Because banks are usually required to hold only a fraction of their deposit liabilities as cash-on-hand,[102] a run can force a bank to collapse.

Lax regulation in the United States, which continued until the passage of the Glass-Steagall Act at the height of the Great Depression in 1933, allowed banking firms to operate commercial and investment divisions with no internal firewall. Thus deposits from the commercial banking side of a business provided a ready in-house supply of capital for the investment banking side. Glass-Steagall, passed after the collapse of a large portion of the commercial banking system, required separation of bank types according to their business. So, for example, J. P. Morgan & Co. continued as a commercial bank while Morgan Stanley was formed as an investment bank.

The cause of the Great Depression is debated by economists to this day. The opinion of this author, which is admittedly not the majority view, is that rapid expansion of credit through speculative investing in the 1920s created a wealth "bubble" that burst when the unsustainable credit cycle inevitably collapsed.

Over the last century, it seems that American financial elites have decided to follow in the footsteps of their British forebears. The trend in the U.S. has been away from an emphasis on wealth creation and toward wealth manipulation. A parallel trend has been toward the deregulation of the banking industry. It is well beyond the scope of this chapter to discuss the many factors that led to the savings and loan crisis of the 1980s and '90s, which cost American taxpayers over $150 billion,[103] or the subprime mortgage crisis of 2007 and the global economic malaise that followed (from which we have not yet emerged). Suffice it to say that economists generally agree that deregulation of the savings and loan and investment banking industries encouraged the risky investments that brought down those houses of cards.

Unfortunately, it doesn't appear that we've learned from 1907, 1929, 1933, 1985, or 2007. Commercial and investment banks today, rather than bringing together investors and entrepreneurs to finance economic growth, focus on trading exotic financial instruments such as collateralized debt obligations (CDOs), credit default swaps, tri-party repos, and others.

Defining those terms in detail would add a long chapter to this book (maybe titled "When Once We Were a Nation Where Banks Actually Did Banking"). Instead, we will offer a general description: CDOs, which were at the heart of the 2007 subprime mortgage meltdown, are securities backed by a variety of income-generating assets such as corporate bonds, government bonds issued by less developed countries, or, of course, mortgage loans, which encouraged lenders to approve as many as possible during the real estate boom. (Remember the television ads for 120 percent loan-to-value mortgages?)

In one amusing example, German investors accused Deutsche Bank of fraud for selling more than $750 million worth of shares in funds based on American life insurance policies. Apparently the anonymous Americans who'd taken out the policies didn't have the courtesy to die quickly enough for the investors to turn a profit.[104]

Frankly, some of these financial instruments have so little to do with economic output that investment bankers might as well be trading baseball cards.

Traditional banking—holding deposits and making loans—is simply not where the largest banks put their efforts anymore. Loans to businesses are just 11.5 percent of the balance sheets of Wall Street's Big Six (Bank of America, JPMorgan Chase, Wells Fargo, Citi, Morgan Stanley, and Goldman Sachs), and the federal government, through Fannie Mae and Freddie Mac, now own or guarantee 90 percent of new home mortgages.[105] The local branch of BoA, Citi, JPMC, or Citi is there mainly to get the corporate office access to FDIC deposit insurance and the Federal Reserve Bank's "discount window," its program of low-interest loans to commercial banks.[106]

Speculation is the name of the game. That's where real money is made. The value of the global market for financial derivatives is estimated at $553 trillion,[107] and the five biggest Wall Street banks—those listed above, minus Wells Fargo—hold more than 90 percent of all derivatives contracts.[108]

To give you an idea of how much money that is, the annual Gross Domestic Product of the United States is about $17 trillion. Global GDP in 2014 was estimated at $77 trillion.

Let that sink in. The biggest banks in America, which created an economic disaster that the American government has so far committed $16.8 trillion to delay,[109] are holding contracts on speculative investments *worth six and one-half times more than the annual economic output of the entire planet.*

This type of high-risk/high-reward speculation was fueled by a cheap money policy adopted by the Federal Reserve Bank during the tenure of former Alan Greenspan, chairman from 1987 to 2006. A graph plotting the performance of the S&P 500 against the percentage of American adults employed shows that the lines diverged in 1990, with stock prices continuing to climb while employment peaking in 2000 and declining steadily since.[110] Life is far better on Wall Street than on Main Street.

Ironically, investment bankers, who are in theory the very heart of America's free-market system, instantly turned into simpering socialists when a government bailout was all that stood between them and the unemployment line.[111]

The two big financial crises of the last hundred years—the Great Depression of the 1930s and the ongoing Great Recession—led to unprecedented levels of federal intervention in the economy. The administration of Franklin Roosevelt launched the New Deal, a package of programs intended to stimulate the economy and provide a social safety net for people. Social Security, which was criticized by conservatives during the Depression as an attempt to "Sovietize the country," is now taken for granted so completely that any politician who talks of changing, much less eliminating, Social Security is guaranteeing a limit on his or her term in office.

As successful as bankers have been at bending the American concept of free markets to their will, the health care industry has been even more ingenious, transforming the federal government into a collection agency for health care insurers. In 2008, Barack Obama was elected president, partly on a promise to overhaul America's bloated health care system. Costs for health care were spiraling and reform was definitely needed.

However, the boondoggle produced by the Democrat-controlled

Congress, the Affordable Care Act ("Obamacare"), has done the opposite of what was promised. Costs have soared, enrollments were lower than projected, and the system is so badly devised that even the insurance companies that more or less wrote the legislation are losing money.[112] And because of this mandatory tax (even if it is considered a tax only for Supreme Court purposes), health care will actually surpass housing as the largest expenditure by Americans sometime in 2017.[113]

In a nutshell, the federal government now controls what will soon be the largest segment of consumer spending by Americans.

So, how to draw some meaningful conclusions about the worth of capitalism from this thumbnail sketch of American economic history? Admittedly, we've skipped over many factors that have played a role in shaping our economy, in particular the trend toward globalism in the guise of free trade.[114] Briefly, though, we can identify a few key factors that were foundational to the United States as we know it:

- Vast amounts of untapped natural resources, including land, water, timber, coal, oil, and ore
- Technology far superior to that to the indigenous population, making land acquisition artificially cheap[115]
- Geographic location—separated from East and West by oceans—protected it from foreign intervention
- Escaped both twentieth-century world wars with industrial base unscathed, while competitor nations, such as England, Germany, Japan, and Russia, suffered heavy losses in population and infrastructure

Obviously, these conditions were unique in history. Never before had a people on the verge of rapid technological development stumbled onto such an immense supply of natural resources, nor has any nation in history enjoyed the natural strategic barriers to invasion that have protected the United States.

It is also clear that America's "free market" has never been really free. During the colonial period, the economy was heavily regulated by England. From the late eighteenth century through the Civil War, slavery distorted the true cost of agriculture, which was the bulk of American economic output. In the second half of the nineteenth century, the emergence of powerful oligopolies warped our economic system in favor of the wealthy. And from the second half of the twentieth century through the present day, the influence of Wall Street has shifted the basis of the American economy from creating wealth through manufacturing to consuming goods produced elsewhere (mainly China) and paying for those goods by taking on unsustainable levels of debt.

All the while, the influence of the federal government on economic activity, through regulation and taxation, has created an economy that is more controlled than the framers of the Constitution would have dreamed in their most fevered nightmares.

But the key point is this: *The problems identified by critics such as Karl Marx and Bernie Sanders are not inherent to capitalism.* The root cause of the distortions in the American economy that favor the rich is one that Jesus Himself identified: "You always have the poor with you."[116]

This was not a pessimistic prediction; it was a condemnation of the human heart—of sin. He knew better than anyone that there would always be those who enrich themselves at the expense of others. (And, as Paul acknowledged, there are always others who just won't work.)[117]

Karl Marx and Friedrich Engels correctly identified many problems with capitalism. Capital does tend to concentrate in the hands of the wealthy, especially when the wealthy engage in anti-competitive behavior. But that behavior is endemic in *humans*, not capitalists. Transforming a capitalist society into a socialist one doesn't cure the root problem. It only puts the power of government behind it.

While capitalism doesn't guarantee a level playing field or a fair shake, it comes closer than any other economic system to providing an incentive for hard work—a reward that correlates to effort. Under any type of socialist system, which places the distribution of wealth in the hands of government, there is far less incentive for workers to be productive. The fruits of labor are taken away and redistributed, ostensibly for the good of the many. Under such a system, human nature, which is fundamentally selfish, is to be only as productive as absolutely necessary. Additional work only benefits others, which isn't a satisfactory answer to the first question that comes to all of us when we're asked to work: "What's in it for me?"

Only those who are truly selfless—a character trait that's rare enough even among Christians who try to follow Jesus' example of the suffering servant—can find the motivation to give their all when they know the profits of their work will be given to others. How many of us volunteer to work overtime or on a holiday without extra pay to make it worthwhile?

As we Americans look back over our proud history and lament the transformation of "the land of the free and the home of the brave" into a nation dependent on government handouts, we should be honest enough to admit that we have been blessed by circumstances that tilted the game in our favor.

We should also recognize that our system of economics has never been as capitalist as we would like to believe. In spite of that, the limited government envisioned by the framers of the United States Constitution allowed people enough freedom to invent, invest, and prosper that America has been a land of hope and change for millions of people of all races and creeds for four hundred years.

Whether this nation can continue to prosper and live peacefully with one another is an open question. It is a different world from the one that saw the foundation of the first English colonies in North America. Some would say we have progressed; and in our technology and our attitudes toward those of different color and culture, that is true.

In other ways, however, we have stepped backward even farther than our science has advanced. Progressives imagine themselves forward-thinking because they celebrate lifestyles that were common in the ancient Near East 3,500 years ago. The self-reliance that defined America during its first 350 years is being replaced by a growing belief that the state, which already requires our participation in a barely solvent retirement plan, should provide cradle-to-grave health care, free education, and presumably a guaranteed monthly income, too—ignorant of Rome's history and the transformation of its free citizens into a permanent underclass pacified with bread and circuses.

But that empire also facilitated the global distribution of the greatest gift in human history, the gospel of Jesus Christ. Perhaps, in the years ahead, the loss of liberty and economic freedom in America will be offset by a similar explosion of evangelism and passion to make disciples of all nations. May it be so.

chapter four

—————— WHEN ONCE WE WERE A NATION OF ——————
Faith

By Christina Peck

T here have been arguments throughout the years on whether or not this nation was founded on Christian faith. Why did people sail here and set up colonies in the first place? Why did they rebel against their mother country? Were we ever a nation of Christian faith? What proof do we have that our country was founded on faith?

All types of people—not just Christians—came over and settled here. Christians—along with atheists, agnostics, and masonic followers—made their way to America. Some may even go as far as to argue that the Christian God is not in the Declaration of Independence, historical documents, or presidential addresses. Regardless of the types of people elected into our public offices, I can say confidently that America was founded on Christian faith.

Let's start with the first question: Why did many people leave their country and sail to America? The British as well as many others had made the trip to America for years before the colonies were established. In the early 1500s, the Pilgrims came over in search of a better life. They wanted to worship God freely and not be held under the rule of a monarchy.

The Pilgrims set up colleges under the Christian faith, Harvard University being a popular one. When that institution was founded in 1636, its student handbook included the following rule:

Let every student be plainly instructed and earnestly pressed to consider well, the main end of his life and studies is to know God and Jesus Christ, which is eternal life, John 17:3; and therefore to lay Jesus Christ as the only foundation for our children to follow the moral principles of the Ten Commandments.[118]

The original thirteen colonies began in 1607 under King James VI. The colonists abided by the taxes and laws of England for more than a hundred years before gaining their independence. Their original goal of sailing to America was jobs. The settlers came to plant tobacco, grow fruits and vegetables, raise animals, and make clothes to sell and trade. It wasn't until the late 1700s, under the rule of King George III, that the colonies strove to become free. Though the Declaration of Independence was signed in 1776, America was not recognized as a free nation until 1783, when the Treaty of Paris was signed, officially ending the Revolutionary War.

The time between 1773 and 1783 was the most volatile. This was when our Founding Fathers started a revolution to be free from Britain's rule. The Boston Tea Party was just the beginning. The colonies felt that they were being taxed unfairly due to the war between Britain and France that had been going on for seven years. As a result, Britain had accumulated a large debt. Next, the 1767 Townshend Revenue Act and the 1773 Tea Act were introduced. After those acts were put into place, the colonists realized they were being taxed in order for Britain to get out of debt.

During our nation's inception, the Founding Fathers wrote the Constitution, the Declaration of Independence, and the Bill of Rights, among other important documents. One by one we will go through these documents, quotes from American leaders, and presidential addresses to find the proof of our nation's founding faith as well as the faith of the first presidents.

Certain articles on the Internet claim that the Constitution omits any mention of religion. That is simply untrue. For example, it plainly states:

> If any bill shall not be returned by the President within ten days (except Sundays) after it shall be presented to him, the same shall be a law.[119]

Sundays were included here an exception because they are considered to be the Sabbath, a day of rest. Also, consider the Declaration of Independence, which clearly reads:

> We hold these Truths to be self-evident, that all Men are created equal, that they are endowed by their Creator with certain unalienable Rights that among these are Life, Liberty and the Pursuit of Happiness.

Why mention a Creator if we are not a nation built on faith? From there, the Declaration of Independence lists many reasons the colonists wanted to break away from a monarchy. To sum it up: If they didn't follow the rules or if they believed differently than the king, they would be persecuted, tried for treason, and—most times—they would be hung or beheaded. The punishment was so harsh because this type of rebellion was considered a heresy to the throne.

The Bill of Rights was given to the state legislators on September 25, 1789, and it became effective as of December 15, 1791. The third article of the document states:

Congress shall make no law respecting an establishment of religion, or prohibiting the free exercise thereof; or abridging the freedom of speech, or press or the right of the peaceably to assemble, and to the Government for redress of grievances.[120]

This means we have our right to fellowship, worship, and speak freely peacefully. This doesn't mean starting fights and verbally abusing anyone for his or her worship of God.

One phrase that is often misinterpreted is "separation of church and state." This does not mean church should be kept out of the government, as popular belief dictates. Rather, it means keeping the laws of government out of the church,[121] assuring our right to worship God freely while preventing the government from making laws against it. This was a direct response to the political environment in England that the settlers had left behind. The churches of England belonged to the state; monarchy and parliament owned the church. This is why Thomas Jefferson said we should keep the two entities separate, ensuring our religious freedom.

Next, let's like to look at our presidents, the letters they wrote, the addresses they made, the lives they led, and the values they possessed as followers of the Christian faith. We will also look at a few of our Founding Fathers to examine what they stood for and what was expected of them as leaders of our country.

First, consider these quotes from John Adams, our second president. In his diary entry on July 26, 1796, he wrote:

The Christian Religion is above all the Religions that ever prevailed or existed in ancient or modern times, the religion of

Wisdom, Virtue, Equity and Humanity. Let the Blackguard Paine say what he will; it is Resignation to God, it is Goodness itself to man.

Further, on December 25, 1813, in a letter to Thomas Jefferson, Adams wrote:

I have examined all religions, as well as my narrow sphere, my straightened means, and my busy life would allow; and the result is that the Bible is the best Book in the world. It contains more philosophy than all the libraries I've seen.

Then, on November 4, 1816, in another letter to Jefferson, Adams wrote:

The Ten Commandments and the Sermon on the Mount contain my religion.

Because anyone can say anything, let's look at some of Adams' actions that proved his faith. Adams was a Puritan who later became a Unitarian like most of the other Founding Fathers. He and his wife, Abigail, attended First Parish Church in Britaintree (later renamed Quincy), Massachusetts, where they were active members throughout their lives.[122] John Adams also believed in the separation of church and state because he believed that governments corrupt religion.[123] This just further shows that the principle is to keep government laws out of churches.

One especially exciting president was Abraham Lincoln, our sixteenth president. The information available on President Lincoln alone could fill an entire volume of books on his life and faith. As we may remember from earlier days in history class, he was born in Kentucky in 1809 and grew up in a Baptist church. With a passion for reading, he later moved to Illinois to study law. As an adult, he never joined a specific congregation, yet still kept the faith. On July 31, 1846, he is recorded as saying:

> That I am not a member of any Christian church is true; but I have never denied the truth of the Scriptures; and I have never spoken with intentional disrespect of religion in general, or of any denomination of Christians in particular.... I do not think I could myself be brought to support a man for office whom I knew to be an open enemy of, or scoffer at, religion.[124]

After the death of his eleven-year-old son in 1862, Lincoln held true to that statement. He instead became close to a Presbyterian minister named Phineas Densmore Gurley.[125] In spite of Lincoln's tremendous loss, he turned to God and never lost sight of the faith his country was founded on. According to his wife, his faith only increased during his presidency. To illustrate this, consider this proclamation he made for a national day of prayer and fasting on March 30, 1863:

> It is the duty of nations as well as of men to own their dependence upon the overruling power of God, and to confess their sins and transgressions in humble sorrow, yet with assured hope that genuine repentance will lead to mercy and pardon, and to recognize the sublime truth, announced in Holy Scripture, and proven by all history, that those nations only are blessed whose God is the Lord. And, insomuch (sic) as we know that by His divine law nations, like individuals, are subjected to punishments and chastisement in this world, may we not justly fear that the awful calamity of civil war which now desolates the land may be but a punishment inflicted upon us for our presumptuous sins, to the needful end of our national reformation as a whole people? We have been the recipients of the choicest bounties of Heaven; we have been preserved these many years in peace

and prosperity; we have grown in numbers, wealth and power as no other nation has ever grown. But we have forgotten God. We have forgotten the gracious hand which has preserved us in peace and multiplied and enriched and strengthened us, and we have vainly imagined, in the deceitfulness of our hearts, that all these blessings were produced by some superior wisdom and virtue of our own. Intoxicated with unbroken success, we have become too self-sufficient to feel the necessity of redeeming and preserving grace, too proud to pray to the God that made us. It behooves us, then, to humble ourselves before the offended power, to confess our national sins and to pray for clemency and forgiveness.[126]

Lastly, we can look to the Gettysburg address. With his journey of loss and growing faith, Abraham Lincoln left everyone speechless on November 19 1863 with his words about what the United States had been founded on. He opened his statement with how this country was founded and even included a quote from the Declaration of Independence:

Four score and seven years ago our fathers brought forth, upon this continent, a new nation, conceived in liberty, and dedicated to the proposition that all men are created equal.

Out of all the presidents, I personally feel that Lincoln was the truest to his faith and remained humble through adversity. He could have forsaken God in times of trial and suffering, but instead ran to Him. He truly believed that "all men were created equal" and demonstrated that by putting an end to slavery and helping unite the country.

Through the years, our religious freedoms have been slowly diminishing. By and large, those who consider themselves Christian are considered by many to be intolerable and judgmental. Other religions speak out against us and tell us to be silent, misusing the "separation of church and state."

Speaking of prayer and Christian teachings in our schools, we may find ourselves wondering what happened. Why can't we speak freely about our faith in public schools? There is no law stating we can't pray in school. Remember the rule in the Harvard student handbook quoted at the beginning of this chapter? What happened to the idea that every student should be taught about Jesus Christ and the Ten Commandments? Also, consider this quote by George Washington:

It is the duty of all Nations to acknowledge the providence of Almighty God, to obey his will, to be grateful for his benefits, and humbly to implore his protection and favors.[127]

Contrary to popular belief, it is perfectly legal to hold Bible studies and prayer meetings before and after school hours. But why has it turned into a taboo subject? We have been made to believe that we cannot freely speak about our faith in schools; yet, if anyone else has a different belief, we cannot speak out about it.

Before 1969, when the Supreme Court ruled that it was no longer acceptable for teachers to open with prayer in public schools, it was completely acceptable to pray in classrooms and at lunch, and to read our Bibles without being told that we were breaking a law. It was recently reported that a young child singing "Jesus Loves Me" on the school playground was told by an adult to change the words from "Jesus loves me" to "my mom loves me."[128] In another instance, a young girl was told not to carry her Bible in the hallway of her school.[129] Even more shocking, a Florida high school teacher was suspended for three days because he posted his disapproval of same-sex marriages on Facebook. He used his own computer in the privacy of his own home, on his own time—yet was disciplined for it. He was given back his job when the school board realized he had broken no laws.

Is there a law we missed somewhere saying we can't practice our religion? The truth is, no, there isn't. We have just been told this by others who are intolerable of Christianity. Consider these rules pertaining to Christianity in public schools:[130]

Student Prayers

Students have the right to pray individually or in groups or to discuss their religious views with their peers so long as they are not disruptive. Because the Establishment Clause does not apply to purely private speech, students enjoy the right to read their Bibles or other scriptures, say grace before meals, pray before tests, and discuss religion with other willing student listeners. In the classroom students have the right to pray quietly except when required to be actively engaged in school activities (e.g., students may not decide to pray just as a teacher calls on them). In informal settings, such as the cafeteria or in the halls, students may pray either audibly or silently, subject to the same rules of order as apply to other speech in these locations. However, the right to engage in voluntary prayer does not include, for example, the right to have a captive audience listen or to compel other students to participate.

I believe these laws are ridiculous and we should get back to our fundamentals as a nation. I'm going to point out, though, that nowhere does it say it is acceptable to treat Christian students like they are breaking a law for praying aloud or privately.

"See You at the Pole"

Student participation in before- or after-school events, such as "See You at the Pole," is permissible. School officials, acting in an official capacity, may neither discourage nor encourage participation in such an event.

As stated, no one has the right to discourage any student from participating in religious prayer sessions. Here is one more rule stating that discussing religious topics with peers is allowed:

Religious Persuasion versus Religious Harassment

Students have the right to speak to, and attempt to persuade, their peers about religious topics just as they do with regard to political topics. But school officials should intercede to stop student religious speech if it turns into religious harassment aimed at a student or a small group of students. While it is constitutionally permissible for a student to approach another and issue an invitation to attend church, repeated invitations in the face of a request to stop constitute harassment. Where this line is to be drawn in particular cases will depend on the age of the students and other circumstances.

What is happening to our rights? We are letting others decide what we can and cannot say as Christians. Sadly, I feel we are falling back into what we left in the first place. It's considered intolerable if a Christian pastor refuses to marry a homosexual couple, or if a Christian company refuses to make a cake for a homosexual couple. What happened to the idea that the government is supposed to stay out of our religious organizations or that it is not supposed to tell us what we can or cannot refuse to do for our beliefs?

According to the secular world, we are intolerant and persecute the sinners. We are at the point now when we are calling evil good and good evil. Isaiah 5:20 states:

Woe unto them that call evil good, and good evil; that put darkness for light, and light for darkness; that put bitter for sweet, and sweet for bitter!

John Adams was right when he said, "Government corrupts religion." In a way, I believe George Washington saw what would come in our nation. Going all the way back to the beginning of it all in our last point of this chapter, we are going to discuss George Washington, his faith, and—most importantly—his prophetic vision.

We should all remember the story of the cherry tree that young Washington cut down. When his father asked what had happened, the boy admitted, "I cannot tell a lie," and confessed. He continued throughout his life as a man of faith, though he was private about his beliefs.[131] He was never shy about mentioning God when he was speaking of government leadership. For example:

It is impossible to rightly govern the world without God and Bible.

If only our leaders would still lead by this quote! Instead the Bible and God have been almost completely omitted from our decisions in politics and education. This is leaving our children and future generations clueless about what freedom means and about the faith we once had as a nation. What does this mean for America? Without God, how can we continue?

Washington, in a vision about this very thing, saw three great perils come upon the Republic (our nation). The most frightening peril was the third. However, according to his vision, the nation would rise against it and overcome it. It is comforting to know that, regardless of how things are in our present day, we as a nation will rise up again and get right with God. Before that happens, we are in for a rude awakening. To close this chapter, consider this final quote from Washington's vision:

"Let every child of the Republic learn to live for his God, his land and the Union." With these words the vision vanished, and I started from my seat and felt that I had seen a vision wherein had been shown to me the birth, progress, and destiny of the United States.[132]

Even if this vision doesn't come to pass in this way, we can take great comfort in knowing that, in the end, every nation will return to God. We can look to our Bible for this proof. Philippians 2:11 reads:

And that every tongue should confess that Jesus Christ is Lord, to the glory of God the Father.

chapter five

──────── WHEN ONCE WE WERE A NATION OF ────────
Mentors
By Althia Anderson

1956 Sunset

Myrtle sat in her rocking chair staring intently as the point of her needle repeatedly penetrated the woolen gray cloth in her hands. The skirt that she was almost done hemming would be worn to church the following Sunday by her daughter, Laura. She glanced to her right at Laura, who sat on the porch swing that held a captivating view of the town nestled in the valley below, one that had recently flourished, thanks to the economic stir of post-WWII America.

To her left, in a second rocking chair, sat her father, Abel, and in the field beyond him she could see her husband in the distance wrapping up his evening chores.

Laura's face was buried in her latest book, a member of the newest literature genre that the young people were calling "science fiction," when all of a sudden, she slammed the book shut and stared expectantly at Myrtle as if she had some burning secret she was just dying to tell but was awaiting an invitation to spill the beans.

At Myrtle's prompting, Laura began to speak of how, that week at school, the teachers had been "simply beside themselves" with the disciplinary problems of the students as of late. Apparently, according to authority figures in school, the "teenagers" (a recently coined phrase describing people between the ages of thirteen and nineteen) of this generation were nothing like the young adults of previous generations.

Previous generations had been more focused, making concrete plans for their future and following them ambitiously, stopping only long enough to consult God and country about their plans, which usually involved family or military pursuits. But this newest generation seemed given to earthly pleasures like leisure time, soda parlors, and even games such as ping pong.

With animated expressions, Laura related stories of teens passing notes and chewing bubble gum in class, listening to that new, rebellious "rock-and-roll" music, and staying out late into the night, sometimes past 10:00 p.m.! Of course, the students were then so sleepy the next day that they were hardly alert in class, thus they were easily distracted and their studies suffered. All of this had become such a problem that the principal of the school had to get involved, calling an assembly to address the issue. He announced that films on social issues and behavior would be brought in to the school and viewed during the day to help teach and reinforce good manners and behavior with the students.

Myrtle glanced over at Abel, who returned her concerned and knowing gaze. They were thinking the same thing: As surely as the evening breeze wafted through Laura's neatly bobby-pinned curls, the winds of change were upon this generation. She regarded Laura as the young girl returned to her reading, and silently thanked God that her daughter had the good sense to avoid the destructive and troublesome antics of her peers.

That Was Then, This Is...Wow...

Fast forward to present day: Jeremy tossed the note that his mother had left on the counter aside. He almost didn't need to read it, the message was so predictable. She would be working a second shift to pick up extra hours, so she would be home late. She had lovingly made sure the freezer was stocked with dinner supplies and reminded him that his homework needed to be done before he played any video games. He rolled his eyes, reflecting that school was stupid and that one day's homework wasn't going to bring his failing grades up anyway.

Not even noticing the usual city sounds of sirens and shouting coming through the window from the street below, he worked his way to the freezer and dug around, perusing his options. He decided on a Pepperoni Pocket, which he tossed in the microwave. While waiting for his dinner to cook, he fumbled through the email on his smartphone, quickly scrolling past one subject line after another until a particular one caught his eye: "Hot 18-Year-Olds Want to Say Hi."

Intrigued, Jeremy clicked on the email, opening it. A head shot of an attractive girl, barely older than his own fourteen years, stared up from the phone, her sultry eyes promising that the next screen would reveal more than just a pretty face. Jeremy's finger hovered over the link. The microwave beeped, announcing suppertime.

Momentarily distracted, he grabbed his dinner and made his way to the TV. He turned on his video game, shooting both the good guys and the bad guys in a mess of blood and guts...until a knock came at the door.

Approaching but not opening the door, Jeremy cautiously asked who was there. The familiar voice of his friend Rick called out playful obscenities at him, coaxing him to open the door. Jeremy obeyed, and Rick came charging into the room, grinning. Rick was older by a few years, and his gang-affiliated tattoos and rough demeanor always offered a sense of adventure and belonging that Jeremy felt drawn to.

Announcing that he knew of a place where they could get hooked up with "anything" they wanted, and promising Jeremy the "night of his life," he led Jeremy out of the apartment building and down the street.

Is This the End of Innocence?

The two above scenarios seem so brazenly opposite that it makes one wonder what has happened to our society. How have we fallen so far in such a short time? When a person really examines that question, a number of outstanding issues can come to light. But what is the crux of the problem, and where did we get off track? Well, the obvious answer is that this country needs God, and that only a true revival can really turn our situation around. But let's take a closer look at the hub of a huge contributing factor that we face today: the lack of parenting and mentorship for our vulnerable and unguided youth.

What Happened to Home?

In the year 1953, the divorce rate was 25 percent, which had skyrocketed since the meager 3 percent divorce rate reported in 1867. By the year 1985, 50 percent of marriages were ending in divorce.[133] This means that in barely over thirty years, the rate had doubled. A society that boasted the illusion of the happy family on popular television shows such as *Leave it to Beaver* and *The Brady Bunch* seemingly had a storm brewing below the surface.

Judging by the above statistic, it is reasonable to assume that by the year 1985, about half of the marriages producing children were actually creating single-parent homes. Between the years 1970 and 2012, the number of children living with two parents in the home decreased to 64 percent.[134]

Studies have shown that children of divorced parents are increasingly victims of abuse and neglect; they exhibit more health, behavioral, and emotional problems; they are more often involved in crime and drug or alcohol use; and they are even more likely to attempt and commit suicide. They lose their virginity at younger ages and are more likely to become teen parents. They have higher percentages of educational problems and disabilities, and even a higher school drop-out rate. And, to top it off, a lower percentage of these children claim a religious faith.[135]

Studies have shown that over 30 percent of children from divorced families are likely to show emotional problems, and that more than 43 percent demonstrate behavioral disorders.[136] The situation becomes further problematic when the home goes from one parent back to two parents because of a remarriage, and then stepchildren/siblings are introduced. According to recent studies, the first three years of a child's life are the most "critical in shaping the child's brain architecture,"[137] so this is an even more increased complication if the child is very young.

Each year, more than one million children are subjected to their parents divorcing, adding to these already climbing numbers. This doesn't even begin to count all the children born to single, never-married parents.

So why state all these numbers? What is my point?

Remember the above statistic about 50 percent of marriages in 1985 ending in divorce? Figuring based on only the marriages that ended in the '70s and '80s, it is estimated that the average child from these failed marriages would probably be somewhere within their thirties or forties now.

These are the parents of our upcoming generation.

Are You My Mother? The Disappearance of the Female Role-Model

During early America and through about the '50s, women were the primary caretakers of the family. Men were at work, and women were keeping house. With women as the primary shoppers, and even product marketing was geared toward appealing to the female gender. This was the person who took care of the kids when they were sick, and who planned, cooked, served, and cleaned up after meals. She did the laundry and knew how to properly set a table. She could mend torn clothes or make new ones, and she was the one who made sure that cultural refinements such as etiquette courses or music lessons were completed.

Biblically speaking, a woman is to set a good example for her family, as well as nurture and care for them, be a role model, and teach her children the ways of God (see Titus 2:3–5). The key ingredient to being able to do all of this is for the mother to be *available*. This was largely possible in the '50s, so women could be in tune with the needs of their family and could be accessible to help meet those needs. Children were not left to raise themselves or heat up their own dinner in a microwave. More importantly, when they needed guidance, prayer, or encouragement, their mother was never far away.

Is this how the role of mother played out in every household back in the good old days? No, of course not. I'm spelling out an ideal scenario here. Did the female gender commit some sort of crime by beginning to go after careers and other ambitions? Again, not at all. But in our current society, we have lost a sense of balance that has almost completely removed the female role model from our homes, leaving a generation of girls who have unanswered questions about everything, from how to cook a great lasagna to whether to use birth control. Further, children raised without mothers tend to show that "later in life, they have trouble making normal relationships, and they struggle with abandonment and security issues" according to BabyMed.[138]

Desperately Seeking Daddy

The role of the father has undergone significant metamorphosis over the generations as well. For most of history, the marked observation would note the father as the breadwinner of the family. But the depth of his role should not be overlooked. The father was the constant of the family. He was the one whose arrival home was always anticipated as a highlight moment of the evening by the family each night. He was the solid rock the family could count on. He was the one whom mom turned to when she didn't have the answer. He was the one who, in a crisis, could come up with a plan. He was the heavy who would go to bat for you when you found yourself in an unfair situation with a teacher at school. After all, father knows best, right?

Biblically speaking, he's the head of the household, the one who gives good teaching, and the one who is to be the authority figure within the home (see Ephesians 5:23, Proverbs 4:1, Proverbs 1:8).

According to a recent article in the *Huffington Post*, the role of a father is central to the emotional well-being of his children, and an affectionate father can contribute "cognitive, language, and social development, as well as academic achievement, a strong inner core resource, sense of well-being, good self-esteem, and authenticity."[139] This is because the early interactions with a father create the very parameters within which a child builds future relationships. And, here is the frightening part: According to the same article, a child adopts this criteria so deeply into his or her subconscious that it lays its foundation "not only (into) your child's intrinsic idea of who he/she is as he/she relates to others, but also, the range of what your child *considers acceptable and loving*."[140]

The nutshell: Boys grow up emulating Dad, and girls grow up to look for a man like Dad. When Dad is removed from the picture, a huge, foundational puzzle piece is lost, leaving the children involved without all the necessary tools for maturing, identifying with self, and even forming and carrying out loving relationships.

According to the National Center for Fathering, children in fatherless homes are more likely to experience poverty, drug and alcohol abuse, and health and emotional problems. They also tend to drop out of school. Boys are more apt to become more involved in crime, and girls are more likely to become pregnant as teens. These children are more than twice as likely to attempt or commit suicide.[141]

The Aftermath of the Single Parenting Society

The biblical roles of men and women are created to work together to form a perfect matrimonial team, both for living out life together and for raising healthy, well-rounded children. The man is to be the head of the wife, to be an authority and a solid, secure role model for his family. The wife's role is to nurture and direct her children toward God, while helping to provide their physical needs and working in tandem with her husband, their father. Both roles are needed. This was the way God intended for this to operate.

As stated before, around half of children are living with only one parent. This means the remaining parent must then take on the roles of both parents. One person is left to try to bring home an income, meet physical needs, deal with social and educational issues, and somehow still have enough energy to remain in a nurturing state of mind at the end of the day.

Let's also keep in mind that previous generations were often located closer to each other geographically. Many families have even shared land. If a parent left or passed away, grandparents, aunts and uncles, or other relatives were in a position to step in and help. If a father figure might be missing, a young man could look to his grandfather for mentorship. The same might be true for the young girl, who could look beyond an absent mother to a grandmother or aunt. It was less frequent that a single parent was truly operating alone. But in recent years, as unemployment becomes more rampant, higher percentages of single parents are relocating to urban settings to improve their opportunities. This geographic isolation of the single parent is becoming more common, leaving the child's support system more fragmented than that of previous generations.

Many children in homes with one parent find themselves alone and unsupervised for a great part of the day. This is often due to the remaining parent's employment, school, or other attempt to better the situation.

Children left to their own devices often fall prey to countless problems that can arise within their world and become an issue while the "already-stretched," remaining parent is out trying to create a better life for their child. This is a good scenario, with a parent who is honestly trying to give his or her best to the child. Imagine how much worse it could be if the parent doesn't try at all!

The world is filled with traps and pitfalls that await the unsupervised child, especially teenagers. Combine these opportunities for trouble with the emotional baggage of having an element as crucial as a parent absent from their lives, and it could be a recipe for disaster for a young individual.

Multiply that by approximately 50 percent of our young population, and you have present-day America.

The Digital Daycare

Every day, background checks are run to verify the credibility of daycare workers, school employees, nannies, and even summer camp counselors. And rightly so. Our children are our most precious and vulnerable commodity, and they need us to take every precaution to make sure they are safe.

The irony is that at the end of the day when they are at home, many of us go about our evening, catching up on laundry, writing out bills, or watching TV while they go to their rooms and play on a smart phone, tablet, personal computer, or other device. They are, this entire time, being entertained, and they seem quiet enough, so many of us don't think to object. After all, better that they are in the safety of our home than out roaming the streets unsupervised, right? Maybe…

Little do we realize that by allowing online interaction, many times we invite complete strangers into our homes, those who are entertaining our children right under our noses. Who are these people? What are

WHEN ONCE WE WERE A NATION

their real intentions? What moral—or immoral—principles are these people teaching our children? What visual pictures are being embedded into our kids' minds? Are our children growing to trust these people--maybe even to the point that they think they are friends? Would our children consider meeting these individuals in person?

Many people think they can answer these questions casually, certain that they know everything their children are up to and that they can predict what their children will and won't do when an Internet stranger is concerned. But keep in mind that one of the largest growing underground criminal industries is human trafficking, and that a large portion of the recruiting is carried out online. Many girls who fall victim to human trafficking actually believe when they set the meeting that they are going to meet a benevolent friend or even a romantic prospect.

This is an extreme example, but even simpler instances of Internet activity can expose a young person to all sorts of destructive influences. Graphic images, once in a young man's mind, can wreak havoc on his life and lead to bigger problems. Cyber-bullying can cause kids to become depressed, withdrawn, or even suicidal. We need to step in and filter what our children are putting into their minds, and monitor *who* is putting it there.

Rent-a-Family

Some youths raised in single-parent families are easy targets for those recruiting into gang activity. According to Mike Carlie, PhD, techniques used by gangs to recruit new members include promises of money, sex, and power. The physical symbols of the gangs promise recruits that they will belong to something bigger than they are. They are even made to believe that they will now be a special part of a "club" and be loved.[142]

This is only the beginning for the young people who allow themselves to become involved in this activity. Soon to follow will be drugs, sex, crime, and violence—leading to patterns of destructive behavior and dangerous circumstances that many teens may never be able to find their way out of. And all of this happens because they are looking for that sense of family they long for.

But at what cost?

Babies Having Babies

The statistics for teen pregnancy among girls raised without a father are overwhelming. The UCSB (University of California) study of children from fatherless homes determined that teen girls from such homes were more than *twice* as likely to become pregnant than other teen girls.[143]

Remember that "strong inner core resource, sense of well-being, good self-esteem" that the *Huffington Post* credited to loving fathers earlier in this chapter? Girls who don't have these qualities are looking for them. It is human nature to need and want love, to long to be accepted, and to yearn for validation. Remember how we said earlier in this chapter that the foundations of all relationships are ideally created by the interactions with the father?

If the father is missing, so is that foundation.

And a lost little girl is wandering around, looking for that puzzle piece. This is a problem that perpetuates itself, because a pregnant teen who gives birth usually does so as a single mom, creating another generation that will grow up without a father.

Media Madness

It really isn't necessary to spend a lot of time diving into all of the countless ways that the media messes with our children's minds every day. It promises everything from glamour, respect, reverence, and so much more to the young man who can involve himself in sex, drugs, or crime. It pledges success and self-esteem to the young woman developing an eating disorder who hopes that being one size smaller will finally buy her that sought-after love she so earnestly chases.

Whatever the needs of a young person may be, media is there promising the *wrong* answer is precisely the *right* answer. Teens who are vulnerable, lonely, and in need of direction are sitting ducks for these lies.

Garbage In, Garbage Out

When we fail to regulate what our children are putting into their minds, how they are spending their time, and who it is spent with, we leave their future to their own discretion. Even the most level-headed and well-rounded teen is still that: a *teen.* A young person, who needs guidance, mentorship, tutelage, constructive criticism, and *most of all,* love.

If we do not make a difference now in the lives of our youth, soon they will be raising up a new generation more confused than the current one. If we do not step in and standardize what our children are exposed to now, we are basically leaving tomorrow with no standards at all.

Remember, these are the *future parents* of the next generation.

John Wesley said, "What one generation tolerates, the next generation will embrace."[144] If we don't take a stand and redirect our children now, everything we turn a blind eye to will be embraced in the following generation.

Do you like what you see when you look around?

Kids These Days

In my years of working in the education system and in other settings with children and teens, it has always baffled me to watch interactions between some adults and certain troubled teens. Many of the youth whose "reputations precede them" are actually not what you would expect. Many of come from challenged homes and respond positively to a kind word. Sure, they are teens, and fully capable of selfish, mean, and even bullying acts—but isn't anyone who has never been shown love? I have found that by being kind and speaking to them with respect, over time, most of them reciprocate. They often become polite and are entirely different with me than they with many other adults within the setting.

School System Soap-Box

Many people like to blame the current education system for our problems when the truth is that the problem is at home. Is our school system flawed? Of course. There are some things in it that need to be over-hauled. But visiting a local school, you will more likely than not find a lot of overworked, underappreciated staff members who do what they do because they want to make a difference. And where we have failed at home, many of them are *trying* to pick up the slack. If you want to see a change in your local school, become a volunteer and make a difference.

Become part of the solution you want to see take place.

The Gender-Gist: Fact or Fluid?

One problem teens today are facing is that of gender orientation and all of the confusion that has ensued on this topic as of late. It is much too lengthy and convoluted to address with any substance here, but I will offer one point for the reader's consideration: there was a time when gender roles were clearly defined and a child had role models living out examples of each.

During that time, there were women who taught little girls to sew, bake, cook, and keep house. Femininity was embraced, and a little girl learned that being female was special for all the things it was ordained by God to be.

There were men who taught young buys to hunt, fish, and fix a car. They were taught to be strong, authoritative, and innovative. Masculinity was a source of pride for a man, and an appealing characteristic to his peers. He was taught to take charge and be a godly leader to those in his care.

This is not to say that these functions are the sole value of the individual, nor that a person should be *limited* to these activities. Modern society has demanded that men and women both step outside of traditional roles and fill the needs for their families as they arise. But in a generation in which all lines seem gray and children have no definition within these parameters, it is no wonder that confusion on this matter runs rampant and unchecked.

A Call to Action

There was a time when adults saw the need for mentorship with our youth and stepped up to the plate. In filling these roles, many good organizations were formed. Boy Scouts, Girl Scouts, Big Brothers & Big Sisters of America, Boys & Girls Clubs, even local and national church programs like Royal Rangers, Missionettes, and Awanas are products of these efforts made by caring individuals who knew that our children needed mentorship and direction.

Many of these programs are still thriving. Some people would argue that their current effectiveness has been hampered by recent political changes, but that is neither here nor there. The point is, many adults today owe a great deal of who they are as a person to volunteers within these programs who cared enough to invest in young peoples' lives when a role model (like a parent) may have been absent.

This is where the rubber meets the road. Everything covered in this chapter can either be material to complain about, or a motivation to make a difference. If you are a single parent, don't be discouraged by everything that has been said. You have a very difficult and often thankless job, and I applaud you for doing all that you do.

If you are not a single parent and you can get involved, do so today! Even a little bit of time each week or month can make a difference. Think you don't have time? Try cutting one TV show per week out of your schedule and start there!

Find a local church, club, or community center where you can volunteer. Is there a single parent living up the street from you? Can you reach out to that family? Speak kindly to those you interact with and let God's love flow through you to heal lives. Don't be judgmental; there is enough pain in the world already. As stated before, a simple kind word spoken to a troubled teen can mean that he or she will open up to God's direction for his or her life through that interaction with you.

You can be the difference.

You can help re-direct the lives of a future generation.

You can help this country reach the turning point it so desperately needs, one life at a time.

chapter six

─────── WHEN ONCE WE WERE A NATION OF ───────
Etiquette and Polite Norms
Dr. Thomas R. Horn

E arly in American history, the "art of debate" was routinely taught and practiced from high schools through universities, court-rooms, and many pulpits. The eloquence of argument against perceived logical fallacies was not just for politicians, but a necessary and learned exercise involving well-crafted protocols, procedures, and rules, through which one could persuade others through reason, logic, diplomacy, facts, insights, values, wit, and rhetoric to embrace a particular idea as more or less plausible to reaching a conclusion. Besides winning in debates, proper discourse and etiquette provided a "code of behavior" for "polite" society expected by "gentlemen" and "ladies" in respect to people and cultural norms. Young women learned early on how to behave in society—including how to speak, dress, hold their posture, etc.—and boys were taught to treat girls and their male counterparts with courtesy and respect; to say "yes ma'am" or "thank you, sir." Stratified society expected citizens to carry themselves in these appropriate ways and to interact with one another in a dignified manner (not that everybody obeyed these rules, of course, but most were made to understand that what was expected could improve their opportunity for acceptance and advancement in the world). Such polite conduct as an art form was not confined to the social elite, either. "Good manners for ordinary people in everyday situations were set forth in the United States by two prominent and influential arbiters of taste, Emily Post and Amy Vanderbilt. Drawing on her own wide experience in social, political, and diplomatic situations, no less a personage than Eleanor Roosevelt published her own typically practical *Book of Common Sense Etiquette* (1962)."[145]

Fast forward to today and we find an entirely different reality. Etiquette, courtesy, and civil discourse have largely given way to increasingly rude, crude, and verbally abusive individuals in a culture where even "Christians" treat each other with a passing contempt that would have horrified previous generations.

Charisma News recently illustrated this phenomenon with a clip from the *Jim Bakker Show* in which Lori Bakker, Jim's wife, was reading this selection from Galatians 5, verses 22–26:

> But the fruit of the Spirit is love, joy, peace, longsuffering, gentleness, goodness, faith, meekness, temperance: against such there is no law. And they that are Christ's have crucified the flesh with the affections and lusts. If we live in the Spirit, let us also walk in the Spirit. Let us not be desirous of vain glory, provoking one another, envying one another.

The important point the Bakkers made from this text involved how much vitriol they and other ministries face today from "Christians," and that God hates it when such discord is sewn among the brethren. The timely comments by the Bakkers reminded me of something I had intended to address for a while involving so-called Internet trolls—narcissistic, Machiavellian, psychopathic, and sadistic individuals who actually enjoy sewing discord and polarizing people, especially among believers.

And when I say *enjoy*, I mean that in the coarsest way possible: Modern society is plagued by sick-minded individuals who actually get "turned on" in demonic and twisted ways while trolling.

But don't take my word for it.

Not long ago, *Psychology Today* highlighted a study that actually confirmed what many of us have sensed for a while: Internet trolls are a symptom of a deeper cultural malaise and are not just horrible misanthropes; they're actually part of deranged society in profound ways.

"Let's start by getting our definitions straight," professor Jennifer Golbeck wrote. "An Internet troll is someone who comes into a discussion and posts comments designed to upset or disrupt the conversation. Often, in fact, it seems like there is no real purpose behind their comments except to upset everyone else involved. Trolls will lie, exaggerate, and offend to get a response."[146]

The research Golbeck quotes from was conducted by Erin Buckels of the University of Manitoba and his colleagues. Titled "Personality and Individual Differences—The Dark Triad of Personality," it was published in the journal *ScienceDirect.*[147] The material investigates whether there is a direct link between so-called "trolling" and growing personality disorders defined by a Dark Tetrad: Machiavellianism (willingness to employ cunning and duplicity to manipulate and deceive others), narcissism (egotism and excessive or erotic interest in oneself over others), psychopathy (enduring antisocial behavior, diminished empathy and remorse, and disinhibited behavior), and sadism (the tendency to derive pleasure, especially sexual gratification, from inflicting pain, suffering, or humiliation on others).

Of the wickedest findings made by the researchers is how **sadism** turns out to be the strongest admitted characteristic of trolls, *and* *that such persons do indeed find regular sexual fulfillment in tormenting others.*

Keep that in mind the next time you sacrifice your online energy trying to pacify a troll. *It's very possible you'll be having unintended, one-way sex chat with a creep!*

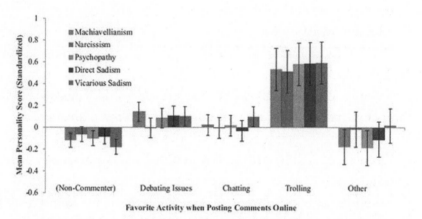

Fig. 1. Dark Tetrad scores as a function of favorite online activity in Study 1. Error bars represent standard errors.

Of course, it's not just laypeople whose social media is increasingly infested with rampant incivility and ad hominem attacks by trolls. Businesses and ministries have likewise wasted enormous time and resources in recent years swatting at Baalzebub's flies as they hatch their vitriolic eggs. To deal with the growing problem, the *Chicago Sun-Times, The Daily Beast, Popular Science,* Vice Media's *Motherboard, The Verge,* and others have gone so far recently as to shut off their online comment sections altogether.

Good for them.

In fact, it may be time for all of us in media to return to the old fashioned "letters to the editor" method for interacting with public commentary. This is where staff members screen submissions, keep and publish the good, and "round file" (verb: "to throw in the garbage") time-wasting materials before anybody of importance ever has a chance to see them.

For the last few years, that's exactly what we've done at Defender Publishing and SkyWatch TV. Ask anybody who works in this ministry and they'll tell you how my method for dealing with trolls is lovingly referred to as "BLOCK, FILTER, DELETE!" This system accomplishes the following:

First, we block the individuals from making additional comments in the future.

Second, we place the email (if that is how the message was sent) in the spam filter so that we will never know if the trolls continue sending comments.

Third, we delete whatever drool the trolls have attempted to leave on our message boards and social media sites. If they're on our email list, we delete them from that as well.

We *never* read or respond to anything once it's obvious we are dealing with a troll.

I've recommended the same process to other large ministries that followed suit and later thanked me. Basically, my advice to all who will listen is simple: **DON'T FEED THE TROLLS!** Never reply to or try to explain yourself to a troll. Never give them an ounce of your energy. They're not interested in truth, fellowship, or council. They feed off anguish, and hope to gain access to your audience (most trolls only have tiny followings—if any at all—on their own webpages and social sites) in order to legitimize or make a name for themselves while increasing overall misery. They don't just *love* doing this; we now know such parasites actually have a *lust* for it. But is this sickness more than just a sign that Americans and much of the world have lost our capacity for civil discourse? Is literal evil supernaturalism behind the loss of diplomacy?

Evil Spirits Set Minds and Tongues Afire

During our formative years in ministry, few people more profoundly influenced our theology and practical Christianity than pastor and theologian Dr. Robert Cornwall. Bob—or simply "Cornwall," as his friends knew him—had a photographic memory, and in order to pay his way through Bible college as a young man, he had gotten a job proofreading books for a publisher of scholarly works. As a result of maintaining this job for years and having an uncanny propensity for recalling facts, Cornwall retained the majority of material he read and became one of the most well informed and brilliant thinkers we ever had the privilege of knowing or being mentored under. Cornwall was also a great storyteller and could thrill audiences at churches and in conferences by weaving details of true-life events with deep theological propositions. A particular story that raised profound spiritual-warfare implications (and eyebrows at the time) revolved around one of the first churches he pastored as a young minister in a sleepy little town near the Oregon coast. As described by Cornwall himself at Redwood Family Camp meeting in the 1970s, he had barely settled into leadership at the church when strange things began to happen for which he had no explanation. Objects in the building seemed to move around on their own, especially overnight when the building was supposed to be unoccupied. He would hear the piano playing and go into the sanctuary to find nobody there. Doors would slam, pews would be discovered positioned backward against the wall, and his notes would disappear—then reappear. Members of the church reported similar phenomena, and Cornwall eventually learned that the activity had been going on for years.

One night, hours after he had gone home to bed, Cornwall's telephone rang and the police chief was on the other end of the line. He wanted to know what kind of party Cornwall was sponsoring at the church.

"What do you mean, a party?" Cornwall asked.

"Neighbors are calling. They say it's so loud they can't sleep. We thought maybe the youth group was having an overnight event that was getting out of hand."

Assuring the officer that nobody was supposed to be in the building, Cornwall agreed to meet him at the church. On arrival, they noticed the lights inside the auditorium were going off and on, the piano was banging loudly, and what sounded like shouting of some kind could be heard throughout the edifice. The officer drew his sidearm while Cornwall unlocked the front door. As they pushed the entrance open, all activity inside the facility abruptly ceased. The lights were still on, but the noises had suddenly gone silent. Cornwall moved through the building with the officer and found every entryway locked, with no signs of break in. This experience was documented in the police report—which, at the time, Cornwall was happy to let us confirm with the chief along with other unexplained events.

Together with his board members and ministry leaders, Cornwall began a series of special prayers over the building in what today some might call a "cleansing" ceremony to purge the house of worship of malevolent spirits mimicking trickster ghosts or poltergeists (German *poltern*, "to rumble or make a noise," and *geist*, meaning "spirit"— invisible entities that manifest by creating noises or by moving objects around). But the results of these prayers were mixed, and Cornwall could not understand why. Whenever members of the church were inside the building and prayed, the phenomenon stopped. As soon as they would leave the facility, it would start up again. This went on sporadically for some time, until one day the chief—now a member of the church— called Cornwall and asked if he could meet him downtown at the police department, saying he had found something important and wanted the pastor to see it. Arriving on schedule, Cornwall was handed an envelope that contained a copy of the original deed to the church property and other interesting documents. One of these records was very enlightening. It revealed that the structure—which was nearly one hundred years old and had been boarded up for over a decade before the organization Cornwall was a member of purchased it and turned it into a church— had originally been constructed by an occult group as a meeting place for their "order." It had been dedicated as a residence "for spirits of Lucifer as they move to and fro upon the earth."

Cornwall was shocked. Legalese existing within the building's first title and deed provided lodging for satanic spirits. Equally disturbing, the experiences at the church suggested demons were operating under some legal claim to be there.

As soon as possible, a new church was erected across the street from the old one, and subsequently the original building was torn down and an asphalt parking lot was poured over the plot of land on which it had sat for nearly a century. From that day forward, all paranormal activity on the property ceased, and a powerful and important theological proposition was born in Cornwall's mind—that under certain conditions, Satan and his spirits have legal rights to property and people.

While some may step back at this point and ask what comparable authority over earth Satan continues to hold following the redemptive work of Christ, most scholars agree that until the Second Coming of Jesus and the final judgment of men and angels, this planet remains under limited jurisdiction of Satan as "the god of this world" (2 Corinthians 4:4) and under the influence of "the rulers of the darkness of this world" (Ephesians 6:12). During this time, contracts and covenants with such spirits allowing access or entry into one's property or life do not have to be officially recorded as in the story of Cornwall's church above. They can be oral or assumed agreements, not to mention "adverse possession," or what laymen call "squatter's rights." In the physical world, this is when a person openly uses somebody else's property without contractual permission over such a long period that eventually the "squatter" gains legal claim to the land, due to the original owner not taking legal action against him or her. These are ancient statutory principles that pertain equally to material and spiritual dynamics. They imply that wherever activity favorable to malevolent spirits occurs by consent, is tolerated, or action is not taken to force the "squatter" to cease and desist, footholds and even personal rights can be surrendered to hostile forces over people and locations. This is similar to the contract some make with dark forces as a result of incivility to others.

But what does this have to do with the state of our union?

In my 1998 book, *Spiritual Warfare: The Invisible Invasion*, I documented how, throughout history, entire geographies became strongholds of demonic activity as a result of what governments and citizens were willing to tolerate in foreign, domestic, public, cultural and social policies. Specifically, I cited biblical examples like the city of Pergamum, which Scripture identified as having become a seat of satanic influence (Revelation 2:12–13). More recent examples would include the history of Nazi Germany and similar cases. This phenomenon—territorial demonization—also occurs on a small scale, wherever space or property (real property including home office space, land, personal property as in possessions, commercial property, public property, and even intellectual property) is provided for purposes hostile to moral or biblical law.

As an example, many years ago as young Christians, my wife Nita and I walked through a local mall during the Christmas season and came upon a New Age bookstore conducting a grand opening. In a derisive tone, I said to Nita, "Can you believe the lack of intelligence of some people?" I strolled casually into the store, snatched a book from the shelf, and began offering sarcastic commentary as I read from its pages. I could tell she was uncomfortable with what I was doing, so I placed the book back on the shelf and proceeded out of the store. Suddenly, a dull sensation hit the pit of my stomach and shot upward through my chest into my cranium. My head started spinning, powerful nausea took hold, my hands began to shake, and I could tell I was about to collapse. It was literally as if something invisible had jumped on me and was injecting rapidly spreading poison throughout my body. Feigning interest in sales items, I moved away from the shoppers and began praying under my breath, asking for forgiveness for my smart attitude, for my lack of caution, and for my lack of concern for the lost. I prayed for deliverance from evil and for healing of my body and mind. After more than an hour of such intercession, I was finally restored. As a young preacher, I discovered a valuable lesson that day: The princes of this world are powerful and territorial, and we should enter spaces that have been dedicated to them only with the proper attitude and when guided by the Lord.

Even then, experiences with exorcism many years later taught me that Satan's jurisdiction and legal rights to property and people are extrapolated to an entirely different level when the phenomenology involves inner space as opposed to external, physical territory. This is because "habitable space" and spatial occupancy—the amount of substance (or demons, in this case) that can fit into a specific area—are different between material and spiritual dimensions. A unique argument, one that has existed since the Middle Ages and highlights this concept, involves the question of how many angels can fit on the head of a pin, illustrating that even the ancients pondered advanced physics, space-time, quantum gravity densities, relativity theory, and hyperdimensional materiality (though the ancients knew nothing of these terms), allowing for different maximal density of "beings" within what otherwise appears in the physical world to be the same "space." Dr. Anders Sandberg, in the research paper, "Quantum Gravity Treatment of the Angel Density Problem" for the Royal Institute of Technology in Stockholm, Sweden, actually derived a number for the density of angels at critical mass that could fit on the head of a pin. He arrived at $8.6766*10exp49$ angels ($3.8807*10exp-34$ kg), thus theoretically fixing through physics how an entire legion of demons (forty-two hundred to fifty-two hundred spirits, plus auxiliaries) in the fifth chapter of the New Testament book of Mark could possess the inner space of a single man.[148]

An important question related to this mysterious relationship between people surrendering inner and external territory to evil spirits—and the boundaries of that association—involves the difference between those who are deceived into unwittingly giving place to the devil and thus become "demonized," and those who knowingly form alliances with evil supernaturalism. The contrast between these types of persons may be defined in the most frequent New Testament expressions used to refer to demonic possession: 1) *daimonizomai*, meaning "to be demonized"; and 2) *echon daimonion*, which means "having a demon," and can actually denote a person who possesses the demon, not the other way around. In the Bible, this might describe persons like Saul, who sought out a woman possessed by a "familiar spirit" to summon the deceased Samuel, even though he knew God's commandment not to allow such practices in Israel (1 Samuel 28), and possibly Judas Iscariot, into whom "Satan entered" (Luke 22:3) as a result of his decision to do what his heart may have told him was betrayal of God. In *echon daimonion*, it is therefore one of the premises that territory can be surrendered to evil spirits by persons actually reaching out to and "taking hold of the demon" through willingly choosing to do what they otherwise know is satanic (such as Internet "trolling" or sewing discord among friends). That some people are not only aware of this marriage with evil, but energetically nurture it, is difficult for most of us to understand—yet the reality exists and is growing. An example of one such person was brought to us for treatment decades ago while we were still involved with exorcism. It involved a young woman who was released from a mental institution to spend a week under the care of her family, and her family, who sought help from the church because they believed her condition was the result of diabolical possession. Having been approached by a relative of the girl, we were told how, over time, she had become withdrawn and eventually delusional. She began hearing voices and held lengthy conversations with what appeared to be empty rooms. Finally, her condition became so detached from physical reality that she had to be placed in a psychiatric facility. As time went on and her condition worsened, prayer for her by her family was met with hostility and then outright violence, and her parents were desperate for help. After consulting with our group, an agreement was reached to have the young woman brought in for evaluation. We requested privacy and asked that a limited number of family members be present.

Her caregiver agreed, and the story of the girl and what happened that week remains private. What we can say is that hers was the only case ever examined by our group in which the rare determination was made that while this person was truly possessed, exorcism was not an option. The simple reason was (the reader would understand if the unthinkable facts could be published) that she actually wanted the demons. They had a right to be there.

Interestingly, some years later, Nita and I were back in the same city and noticed that our host pastor looked tired. We asked him if it had been a busy week, and he proceeded to tell us about an exorcism he had participated in a few days earlier. As he recounted the story of a certain possessed woman and how the church had fasted and prayed for a week, followed by seventeen hours during which a select group of ministers in a private room drove multiple demons from her, we realized he was talking about the girl from the institution. We remained quiet as he repeated the exhausting story, telling of the many personalities and voices they encountered during the drawn-out ritual. He claimed that when the last spirit finally came out of her, she sat up and for the first time appeared lucid. When they asked her if she wanted to accept Jesus as Savior, she began cursing and crying, complaining that he and the others had made her friends go away. Through chest-heaving sobs, she began calling out to unknown persons by name. As she did, the pastor said he felt something move across the room into her. Her eyes rolled back, and once again she lost control of her faculties. The exorcism ended.

While the experience above is a glaring illustration of one aspect of *echon daimonion*, in which a person seeks out and "possesses the demon," over the years when on those few occasions we witnessed what was considered authentic possession (as opposed to most cases evaluated as psychological or biological issues), it was typically *daimonizomai*, wherein the individual did not want to be under the spirit's influence.

The Work of Lying "Religious Spirits"

While the pages of nearly all books on spiritual warfare abound with examples of people becoming possessed or demonized by entities as a result of deviant perversion, drug use, violence, occultism, or other depravations of immoral behavior, including infidelity and witchcraft, the most powerful instruments of satanic bondage by far witnessed during my decades of executive ministry were connected to something much more dangerous than personal failings. The superior enemies to which I refer are demons of religion that infest institutional Christianity.

This is not a daring statement.

Just as a lying spirit filled the mouths of the prophets in 2 Chronicles 18, and just as Jesus confronted unclean spirits inside the synagogue (Mark 1:23) and connected some of the priestly leaders of the Temple to the strongest power of Satan on earth (John 8:44; Matthew 13:38, and 23:15), robust *echon daimonion* exists today from the lowest to the highest levels of denominational establishment among institutional members who are possessed (whether they perceive it as such or not) by luciferian ambition. This will come as no surprise to truly born-again and seasoned spiritual warriors, as it is the result of a common military strategy. The church represents the single establishment on earth capable of undoing Satan's plans, and is therefore the natural enemy of the kingdom of darkness and the epicenter against which all spiritual wickedness must ultimately be focused. The church, through its hierarchies and institutional constructs, is therefore the primary target for infiltration by agents of darkness wherever human weakness allows for penetration by daimonions. Among others, the apostle Paul recognized this specific danger, warning the church in Corinth that "false apostles" were masquerading among them as ministers of Christ. "And no marvel," he revealed, "for Satan himself is transformed into an angel of light. Therefore it is no great thing if his ministers also be transformed as the ministers of righteousness" (2 Corinthians 11:13–15).

Consistent with this phenomenon, Father Gabriele Amorth, a renowned exorcist in Rome whose book, *Memoirs of an Exorcist: My Life Fighting against Satan*, was released in 2010, admits to the existence of "satanic sects in the Vatican where participation reaches all the way to the College of Cardinals." When asked if the pope was aware of this situation, he replied, "Of course."[149] Similarly, before he was tragically killed in an automobile accident in 2011, Rev. David Wilkerson reported *daimonion* activity within evangelical institutions as well when he said:

A number of [former] witches are warning that Satanists are infiltrating the church—especially charismatic churches. Some of these [are] telling of a diabolical plot by evil witches to enter congregations posing as super-spiritual Christians. Many of these evil witches, they say, are already firmly established in numerous churches, controlling both the pastor and congregation and causing great confusion, wickedness, divorce—even death. We have received many letters in our office from people who say they believe their pastor must be under some kind of demonic influence—and I believe many of these letters are very legitimate.[150]

Wilkerson, who at one time was a member of the same organization we served, was correct in asserting that some of those who pose as super-spiritual Christians, department leaders, pastors, and even state office holders and denominational headquarters executives are in fact instruments of evil. Thankfully, there are other church members, pastors, and leaders who, as sincere believers, have become increasingly aware of this sinister invasion into organizations by daimonions and in recent years have made special efforts to teach their congregations how to identify the differences between "religious spirits" and true Christianity.

Sometimes "identifying" the misdeeds of "religious spirits" is not really that hard to do.

For example, just about every solid Bible expositor I know has been tirelessly harassed online the last few years by fake defenders of the faith. Yet, not once have these self-proclaimed "guardians of the truth" (including one TV preacher who dedicated an entire edition of his "Ministry" magazine last year to slanderously vilifying all of today's most popular prophecy preachers as apostates [all but himself, of course!]) actually followed the Bible's mandates themselves, directives that very specifically outline how believers are to deal with error in the church. The New Testament books of Matthew, Galatians, Thessalonians, Romans, and others provide guidelines for dealing with differences between true believers. These verses were well known "When Once We Were a Nation of Etiquette and Polite Norms" and teach that if we perceive a brother or sister as falling into error, we are to:

Go to him or her PRIVATELY in a spirit of humility and redemption.

If those we approach will not receive our advice, we go to the elders of the church PRIVATELY and share our concern.

If the elders believe the issue is legitimate, they go to the person PRIVATELY in hopes of restoring him or her.

If the person still refuses council, the church is to have nothing more to do with him or her.

With that in mind, the next time you are online reading some troll's diatribe about Chuck Missler, Gary Stearman, Steve Quayle, L. A. Marzulli, Cris Putnam, Derek and Sharon Gilbert, Jonathan Cahn, Josh Peck, Gonz Shimura, Joel Richardson, yours truly, or any of the other current favorite targets, ask yourself if the hatchet people attacking them ever bothered to obey Scripture and go to the person PRIVATELY with their concerns in a loving spirit of restoration (they haven't), and then "be careful little eyes what you read," because these Scripture-guideline-stomping destructive forces seek to contaminate your mind and spirit (see Proverbs 4:23–27) in order to draw YOU TOO over to the dark side.

Be absolutely clear about this, as well: NOTHING in Scripture allows for setting up websites, blogs, or other mediums to PUBLI-CALLY and routinely lambast believers with accusations—that is the job of Satan and his followers! He is the father of lies and the "accuser of our brethren…which accused them before our God day and night" (John 8:44; Revelation 12:10).

For all the value the Internet has given believers, it also has "unlocked something dark in humanity," says acclaimed author Anthony Horowitz in a newspaper interview.[151] Horowitz, a best-selling children's fiction writer in the United Kingdom, was speaking at the Oxford Literary Festival when he described how Internet trolls are "foul, disgusting and cruel" and that "evil is getting the upper hand."[152] His passionate comments came on the heels of relentless and vicious online feedback he received following a television appearance. Sadly, this too reflects the loss of etiquette and polite norms in modern America and Mr. Horowitz is certainly not alone in this experience, as any notable writer can attest—especially Christians who pen edgy, newsworthy, or prophetic material.

And yes, that includes me and people like me. In fact, every leader with whom I am associated in news, print, television, and social media has been under growing attack the last few years, and not from those you would expect. Religious "Christians," not atheists or unbelievers per se, form the largest part of the swelling ranks of warfare aimed at criticizing true Bible-based works. Because such discontents cannot stop people from hearing God's prophets, they (and the spirit they allow to channel through them) at a minimum seek to divide and confuse ungrounded babes in Christ who, while seeking a deeper relationship with Jesus, end up online. Those who would destabilize these believers have always existed, of course. I witnessed ingrates in every town where I pastored throughout the 1970s–1990s. But today the Internet has given malcontents a place to hive and to hide behind screens while using spiritual-sounding titles and websites to voice their ungraciousness. And while their audiences are very tiny at this time, their contaminated spirits threaten to take root and could explode under the coming legions that

OF ETIQUETTE AND POLITE NORMS

will fuel the empire of the Son of Perdition. Simply put, the words of Jesus that "ye shall know them by their fruits" (Matthew 7:15–16) have never been more important. These instructions of Christ should serve as a warning to all believers to monitor their motives, to examine their hearts, if truly they are altruistic or if in fact they are energized by self-ish ambition, because the latter is the Lucifer-effect that Antichrist will use to energize the coming war between Christian vs. Christian, a time when it will be eternally important to know you are on the right side.

Evil Men and Seducers Will Wax Worse and Worse (2 Timothy 3:13)

During the decades my wife and I served the institutionalized church as pastors and later as executives, we (like most ministry leaders obviously would be) were certainly aware of such "trolls" even before the modern usage of that term was defined. We witnessed the two types of "believers" the Bible calls the "wheat and the tares," and have strong memories of the spiritual differences between the two. Before our house burned down in 2011, while searching for a particular document we had placed in an old photo album some time ago for safekeeping, we took an unexpected stroll down memory lane in this regard. We had gone through at least a dozen books of images and old newspaper clippings, seeing members of churches we had pastored and records of events frozen in time from nearly thirty years inside the organization. Finally, between dusty storage bins and spider webs, we found what we were looking for. We placed the coveted item among the research notes for a future book, then returned everything else to the closets.

That should have been that, but for the next week, the old memories in those boxes kept calling to us about things and friends from the past—people who represented the true mission of the church and were wonderful examples of what it really means to be a Christian. Their names would not be recognized by most today—dedicated believers like O. R. Cross, Henrietta Stewart, Lorraine Morgan, Wyoming Rosebud Dollar, C. K. Barnes, Eugene and Evelyn Fuller, Annie Walton, Eugene Stockhoff, and numerous others of the New Testament clan.

And then there was another group hiding in plain sight among the believers, sometimes even leading them—the ones the Bible calls "clouds without water, carried about of winds; trees whose fruit withereth, without fruit, twice dead, plucked up by the roots" (Jude 1:12).

Among this second class were—and still are—some fantastic heresies. Take "Kingdom Age" theology for instance (also known as Reconstructionism, Kingdom Now Theology, Theonomy, Dominion Theology, and most recently, Dominionism), which singularly has wrought some of the most far-reaching destruction within the body of Christ this century. Dominionism is a type of hyper-Calvinism (though supported by both reconstructionists and nonreconstructionists), which ultimately seeks to establish the Kingdom of God on earth through the union of politics and religion. Though we as American believers have opportunity (and one could even argue, responsibility) to vote for and support moral leadership, we need to balance that temporal concern with the more important eternal knowledge that our true "kingdom" is not of this world, and that combining religious faith with politics as a legislative system of governance such as Dominionism would do hearkens the formula upon which Antichrist will come to power! Note how in the book of Revelation, chapter 13, the political figure of Antichrist derives ultranational dominance from the world's religious faithful through the influence of an ecclesiastical leader known as the False Prophet. Similar political enthusiasm exists among revived Dominionists as this book heads to the printer during a heated political climate, despite the fact that neither Jesus nor His disciples (who turned the world upside down through preaching the gospel of Christ, the true "power of God," according to Paul) ever imagined the goal of changing the world through supplanting secular government with an authoritarian theocracy. In fact, Jesus made it clear that His followers would not fight earthly authorities purely because His kingdom was "not of this world" (John 18:36). So while every modern citizen—religious and nonreligious—has responsibility to lobby for moral good, that should NOT be the MAJOR focus of believers. I would go even further and suggest that combining the mission of the church with political aspirations is not only unprecedented in New Testament theology—including the life of Christ and the pattern of the New Testament church in the book of Acts—but is often a tragic scheme concocted by sinister forces that seek to defer the church from its true power while enriching insincere bureaucrats.

But while great heresies like Dominionism and Inclusion are, or should be, self-evident, other contenders for the most spectacular doctrines of devils in the church today would have to include Ecumenical Environmentalism and Dual Covenant (wherein Jews do not need to accept Jesus as Messiah), which has been aggressively espoused by the Vatican under Pope Francis and Emeritus Pope Benedict as well as allegedly some surprisingly well-known modern evangelical preachers. Yet those aged voices that called out to us recently from our fading boxes of memories also reminded that while it's easy today to get an "amen" while condemning the big lies of Dominionism, Ecumenical Environmentalism, and Dual Covenant, the most insidious doctrines are those "smaller lucifers" that are often harder to perceive. For instance, how easy it is (and was) to see through the glaring examples of self-serving and lavish lifestyles that some of our old televangelist friends sought support for, while overlooking or even excusing Luciferianism (selfishness) that is measured in the tiniest of portions, minute amounts so cleverly concealed within subtle and popular doctrines today that they are nearly impossible to detect.

Ask any evangelist who has tried to take the gospel outside the four doors of the local assembly what I mean by this and hear them repeat stories of how quickly certain church members arose to resist the plan and grumble over the resources that could otherwise be used to benefit *them*. This is the cancer that decades of Prosperity Preaching, inward focusing, and entitlement "me-ism" have produced. Of course, most of these anti-evangelists wrap their Luciferianism in nifty religious phrases—like Judas Iscariot did when he pretended to care for the poor but secretly wanted to steal the value of the oil that was used to anoint the feet of Jesus (John 12:1–6). These types resemble Judas in another way as well: They don't even know how they are thus being used as fleshy gloves, the earthen hands of that invisible spirit, the master of waterless clouds operating within or behind them that hates true fishers of men. But for those with eyes to see, the father of lies (and his trolls) always gives himself away through his envy of others, seeking what he can gain from—not what he can give to—believers and religion, then pretending something is wrong with those he cannot control, those who get things done like Jesus did, disparaging them while he himself accomplishes nothing but division, diversion, and destruction.

Perhaps you have seen this spirit in the actions or heard it in the mouths of people you thought were your partners. When once you (or somebody you knew) had nothing more to give them, they turned away from you—or worse, against you—and revealed the awful truth: Their religious spirit had only ever come for what it could get, gain, and absorb, and when there was nothing left to take, it turned to do what it had always planned, "to kill and to destroy" (John 10:10a). This is because, as Jesus Himself put it, such are the children of murder: "[They] are of [their] father the devil, and the lusts of [their] father [they] will do. He was a murderer from the beginning, and abode not in the truth, because there is no truth in him. When he speaketh a lie, he speaketh of his own: for he is a liar, and the father of it" (John 8:44).

Loss of Etiquette, Demonization, and Christians

Given what we've said in this chapter so far and the inevitability during the study of spiritual warfare that the thorny (if not polarizing) question will arise concerning whether true Christians can become demon possessed, I'd like to state my personal opinion unequivocally that, although *daimonizomai* ("to be demonized") and *echon daimonion* ("having a demon") are manifested within institutionalized Christianity, those who are truly born again can never actually be possessed—as in inhabited—by demons. There are numerous reasons for this conclusion, not the least of which is that there are no instances of "possession" of believers anywhere in the Bible. Not a single verse in the Scripture even warns of the possibility, and there are zero examples in the life of Jesus Christ and the early church of demons being cast out of Christians.

What we do find in Scripture regarding the inner space of believers is that our body "is the temple of the Holy Ghost, which is in you, which ye have of God, and ye are not your own" (1 Corinthians 6:19). In fact, John writes that "he that is begotten of God, keepeth himself, and that wicked one toucheth him not" (1 John 5:18). Therefore, "What communion hath light with darkness? And what concord hath Christ with Belial. And what agreement hath the temple of God with idols? for ye are the temple of the living God; as God hath said, 'I will dwell in them; and I will be their God, and they shall be my people'" (2 Corinthians 6:14b–16). These and similar Scriptures verify for those who have the Holy Spirit residing within them that they are positively redeemed and sealed from the torment of diabolical possession. As John also certified, "If the Son therefore shall make you free, ye shall be free indeed" (John 8:36).

Though in recent years "Christian deliverance ministries" have suggested otherwise, claiming that *daimonizomai* and *echon daimonion* infer the Lord's body can actually be inhabited by demons, it is usually a matter of semantics. Confusion over the meaning of the terms "possession" and "demonization" is somewhat understandable from an exegetical standpoint, especially given how *daimonizomai* is used in Scripture to refer to a variety of problems and demonic manifestations. But because it is dangerous to promote precise definitions where none exist in Scripture, it should be noted that the actual phrase "demon possession" does not even appear in the Bible (Josephus coined this phrase near the end of the first century), and what some teachers classify as "possession" is actually demonization—a spirit from an external posture gains control or influence over a person. As such, literal possession is different than demonization, and ample evidence exists in the New Testament to conclude that whereas believers may never be "possessed," they most certainly can be tempted, influenced, oppressed, and even demonized by evil supernaturalism. To this end, the apostle Paul warned the Christians at Ephesus (Ephesians 4:25–31) not to give "place" (Greek: *topos*) to the devil, meaning a foothold, opportunity, power, occasion for acting, or doorway into one's personal space through which demonic strongholds can be established. Paul even listed particular behaviors that could lead to this fiendish union—lying, anger, wrath, stealing, bitterness, clamor, evil speaking (Greek *blasph mia*: "to blaspheme, gossip, slander others"), and malice, which goes without saying constitutes most Internet trolling. Elsewhere in the Bible, we learn that doorways for agents of Satan to enter a believer's life can also include encumbrances like fear, such as the fear that led Peter to deny Christ in Luke chapter 22 and that Jesus made clear was an effort by Satan to cause Peter to stumble (v. 31), and greed—as illustrated in the story of Ananias and Sapphira in Acts chapter 5, where "Satan" (v. 3) filled the couple's hearts to lie and to hold back a portion of money. Demonization of a Christian through these and similar weaknesses is usually gradual, where small decisions are made over an extended period of time during which the individual gives in to temptation, followed by ongoing and progressive surrender of territory within the mind and finally the flesh. Such steps to demonization may be summarized accordingly:

Temptation: The enemy discovers a weakness and appeals to it.

Influence: The individual entertains the idea and finally gives in to temptation. A foothold is established in the person's life, making it harder to resist the same or related activity in the future.

Obsession: The activity eventually becomes an unhealthy preoccupation and irresistible impulse leading to critical degrees of control over the individual. The power to resist is practically gone.

Demonization: Control over the individual by external power becomes substantial. What at one time was considered sinful and to be avoided is now an addiction. The person may no longer even recognize the tendency as immoral, and little or no fortitude to cease participating in the activity remains.

Possession: This can occur if the individual turns his or her back on God so as to fully embrace carnality, surrendering the body and mind to Satan's control. The desire to resist invasion by discarnate supernaturalism is vacated.

What immediately stands out in these steps and doorways to demonization is how central the mind of man is to the functioning battleground where spiritual warfare takes place. Whether it is lying, anger, wrath, stealing, bitterness, clamor, evil speaking, malice, fear, greed, or another human frailty, the battle begins in our thought life where we are tempted to give in to sin. "That's where Satan can manipulate people toward his ends discreetly and invisibly," writes Chip Ingram in *The Invisible War.* "If he can distort our thoughts, our emotions, and our knowledge, then our behaviors and relationships will fall the way he wants them to. And even if he doesn't manage to turn us to overt evil, a little bit of distorted thinking can neutralize us and render us practically ineffective."[153] In other words, if Satan cannot possess or demonize an individual, he will settle for what he can get, influencing the mind and spirit to whatever extent he can, keeping people ineffective or causing them to become a problem for their families, their communities, or their churches.

Unfortunately, in Christendom, it is within this same mind-domain battleground where vulnerable people can be controlled by satanic forces to cripple the effectiveness of the ministry. God only knows how many resources of time, energy, and money have been exhausted over the centuries as a result of "Christians" like those Jesus warned of when He said, "Many will say to me in that day, 'Lord, Lord, have we not prophesied in thy name? and in thy name have cast out devils? and in thy name done many wonderful works?' And then will I profess unto them, I never knew you: depart from me, ye that work iniquity" (Matthew 7:22–23). In the parable of the tares and wheat, Jesus compared these types to weeds that germinate among devout believers (the wheat), choking their outgrowth until the day that He returns to judge them, while in the metaphor of the sheep and the goats, He described how, during this judgment, these "cursed" ones will be separated from the true believers and "shall go away into everlasting punishment." Matthew records this future event, saying:

> When the Son of man shall come in His glory, and all the holy angels with Him, then shall He sit upon the throne of His glory: And before Him shall be gathered all nations: and He shall separate them one from another, as a shepherd divideth his sheep from the goats: And He shall set the sheep on His right hand, but the goats on the left. Then shall the King say unto them on His right hand, "Come, ye blessed of my Father, inherit the kingdom prepared for you from the foundation of the world:" For I was an hungred, and ye gave me meat: I was thirsty, and ye gave me drink: I was a stranger, and ye took me in: Naked, and ye clothed me: I was sick, and ye visited me: I was in prison, and ye came unto me. Then shall the righteous answer him, saying, "Lord, when saw we thee an hungred, and fed thee? or thirsty, and gave thee drink? When saw we thee a stranger, and took thee in? or naked, and clothed thee? Or when saw we thee sick, or in prison, and came unto thee?" And the King shall answer and say unto them, "Verily I say unto you, Inasmuch as ye have done it unto one of the least of these my brethren, ye have done it unto me." Then shall He say also unto them on the left hand, "Depart from me, ye cursed, into everlasting fire, prepared for the devil and his angels: For I was an hungred, and ye gave me

no meat: I was thirsty, and ye gave me no drink: I was a stranger, and ye took me not in: naked, and ye clothed me not: sick, and in prison, and ye visited me not." Then shall they also answer him, saying, "Lord, when saw we thee an hungred, or athirst, or a stranger, or naked, or sick, or in prison, and did not minister unto thee?" Then shall He answer them, saying, "Verily I say unto you, 'Inasmuch as ye did it not to one of the least of these, ye did it not to me.' And these shall go away into everlasting punishment: but the righteous into life eternal." (Matthew 25:31–46)

When considering theses verses, it should be frighteningly clear that those who lack discipline in their thought life and whose lips are "a world of iniquity… set on fire of hell" (James 3:6) are literally playing dice with eternity. We cannot help but shudder at some of the congregants we have known through the years who similarly surrendered their minds to malevolent religious spirits and afterward left a trail of questions, division, and destruction in their wake. As the reader, perhaps you too at one time observed damage done to a person(s) either online or at a local fellowship before the offending party(s) moved down the road to repeat their mayhem elsewhere, and were confused by what you could or should do about it, if anything. That's partly why I wrote this chapter on the loss of etiquette and polite norms among troublesome individuals because real Christians are often unsure over what role, if any, spiritual warfare should play with respect to them—especially given that Ephesians 6:12 says "we wrestle not against flesh and blood." Yet hermeneutically speaking, it is often impossible to discern exactly how "principalities and powers" engage the church in warfare without taking the human element into account—that sometimes people, because of the choices they make, are the problem, or least a part of it. Second Timothy 4:14–15 illustrates that this is not a contradiction of Ephesians 6:12, as the writer of Ephesians himself refers to a man named Alexander the coppersmith, saying that he "did me much evil: the Lord reward him according to his works: Of whom be thou ware also; for he hath greatly withstood our words [the Gospel]." The great commentator Matthew Henry says this text illustrates that "there is as much danger from false brethren, as from open enemies." Though Paul wrote the book on spiritual warfare, including the phrase, "we wrestle not against flesh and blood," he did not blame immaterial spirits that may have been operating behind Alexander the coppersmith. He named the man himself as the culprit and warned Timothy to beware the damage he could do to the work of the ministry. The point to be made from this is not one of personal revenge toward a wrongdoer, but that wisdom is needed during spiritual warfare because prayer is most profitable when it is directed with specificity—in this case, recognizing the source of the problem, the conduit, even when it is made of flesh.

Jesus likewise verbalized the difference between people who attend religious services (whether brick-and-mortar facilities or today's virtual church world) and become tools for evil as opposed to good, and we note with particular interest His genius in using the small yet powerful word "of" to contrast the two for His followers. In John 8:44, He said of the Pharisees, "Ye are *of* your father the devil, and the lusts of your father ye will do" (emphasis added), while in Luke 9:51–56, when James and John wanted to call fire down from heaven upon Samaritan villagers, He rebuked them and said, "Ye know not what manner of spirit ye are *of.* For the Son of man is not come to destroy men's lives; but to save them" (emphasis added).

This amazing yet insightful little term "of" probes beyond temporal human activity to identify whose dominion one belongs to and what spirit holds one's allegiance and offers one motivation. The Pharisees were "of" their father the devil, while the disciples James and John were still learning the nature of the spirit they were "of." The Word of God was therefore used by the Pharisees as a tool for destruction, illustrating what spirit they were "of," while Jesus and His followers used the same tool to give life to others.

Some years ago, my wife Nita worked in a state department beneath a woman who was driven by similar thirst for Pharisee-like church authority and who not only made a habit of demeaning those under her but actually seemed to delight in being as hurtful as possible to people she viewed as not having the same level of political influence she did (though later she was disciplined for conspiring against state leaders). Her spirit seemed to especially enjoy using the Bible as a weapon to denigrate and control others. Nita did her best to simply stay out of the woman's way, but wasn't always successful. One day, with the woman's department informational packet scheduled to be mailed and a distressed-looking secretary whose job it was to get them collated looking for assistance, Nita jumped in to help. A few moments later, the woman who could wield the Word like an unholy sword (Proverbs 12:18) came in and began reciting a finely tuned sermon from memory. She was good with words and practiced at sermonizing, and this three-pointer was especially designed to illustrate this fact and to demean anybody not as eloquently instructed as she. When finished, she looked at Nita and said, "So, Nita, where are you in God's Word, hmm?" The sermon had its intended effect, and for a few moments Nita felt as unworthy to be in that office as the supervisor had probably hoped she would. *Who am I, really, to serve in this capacity as state director for a girl's ministry?* she thought to herself. *I don't preach, don't prophesy, and don't do miracles. I didn't even have time for devotions this morning.*

As the two-edged swordswoman cocked her head, somehow knowing she had found important organs, Nita answered, "Well, I usually have devotions each day. Right now, I'm using *My Utmost for His Highest* as an outline with my Bible reading." Then, for some reason, she added, "But, I didn't have devotions this morning. Time got away from me, and I had to hurry and hit the road to get here on time." It was a two-hour drive to the office one way.

"Well, Nita," swordswoman replied caustically, turning aristocratically to walk away, "We must make sure that we are in God's Word so that we can be good examples to those under our leadership."

After helping the secretary finish her work, Nita returned to her office and placed her head in her hands. "Lord, why did you bring me here?" she prayed. "There are so many other women who are much more qualified than I am to lead this department. Women who somehow manage to read the Bible every day, quote Scriptures at the drop of a hat, and rattle off a perfect homiletic." Nita brooded and cried over the slight for nearly two weeks. Just to think that she had displeased her supervisor, set a poor example for the secretary, such shame. Then, a few days later, still feeling the pain, still asking God if she should resign so that a more worthy person like the supervisor could fill her spot, a profound but still quiet voice whispered to her, "Nita, your qualification to do what I have called you to do is not measured by where you are in my Word. The question is not 'Where are you in my Word, but where is my Word in you?' Satan knows my Word and can quote it ad nauseam, but it is not within him to do my will." In that moment, Nita bowed her head and asked forgiveness for doubting her placement in the state office.

Nita learned a valuable lesson that day. One I hope you will keep in mind whenever you or somebody you know is under attack in our increasing caustic world. Knowing what spirit one is of and embracing the Word of God accordingly is vitally important, "For the word of God is quick, and powerful, and sharper than any [troll's] twoedged sword, piercing even to the dividing asunder of soul and spirit, and of the joints and marrow, and is a discerner of the thoughts and intents of the heart.... Seeing then that we have a great high priest, that is passed into the heavens, Jesus the Son of God, let us hold fast our profession. For we have not an high priest which cannot be touched with the feeling of our infirmities; but was in all points tempted like as we are, yet without sin. Let us therefore come boldly unto the throne of grace, that we may obtain mercy, and find grace to help in time of need" (Hebrews 4:12–16).

While it was prophesied that "evil men and seducers shall wax worse and worse, deceiving, and being deceived" (2 Timothy 3:13), it is our sincere prayer that a spiritual awakening might burst forth from that throne of Grace mentioned above and bring healing to our land, giving rise once again to a great nation where believers express their love one for another (see John 13:35) through "Etiquette and Polite Norms."

chapter seven

——————— WHEN ONCE WE WERE A NATION OF ———————
Visionaries
By Donna Howell

I n 1999, the world of motion pictures gave birth to one of the most profound plots in all of cinematic history. *The Matrix* depicts a futuristic world wherein humans only physically exist in liquid, egg-like containers while their bioelectrical energy is harvested by intelligent machines like an enormous, collective, human-race battery. "The Matrix" is a simulated reality fed to their consciousness through a cable plugged into the back of their heads. While they truly "sleep" in the terrible, dark, real world of fluid-filled, human-housing-pods around them, they believe themselves to be living normal lives and carrying on daily tasks, completely unaware of the fact that the world they know is merely a computer-generated replica that they have been programmed to comprehend. Early on in the film, after finding cryptic allusions to this "Matrix," Neo (played by actor Keanu Reeves) is contacted by

Trinity, a member of a small group who has discovered the true nature of life on earth, and given the opportunity to meet with Morpheus, the group's leader. Intrigued, Neo agrees to the meeting and, after a brief deterrent by the group called the Agents, is brought before Morpheus and presented with an ultimatum:

MORPHEUS: Do you believe in fate, Neo?

NEO: No.

MORPHEUS: Why not?

NEO: Because I don't like the idea that I'm not in control of my life.

MORPHEUS: I know *exactly* what you mean. Let me tell you why you're here. You're here because you know something. *What* you know, you can't explain, but you *feel* it. You've felt it your entire life...that there's something wrong with the world. You don't know what it is, but it's there, like a splinter in your mind, driving you mad. It is this feeling that has brought you to me. Do you know what I'm talking about?

NEO: The Matrix?

MORPHEUS: Do you want to know...what it is? [Neo nods.] The Matrix is everywhere. It is all around us, even now, in this very room. You can see it when you look out your window, or turn on your television. You can feel it when you go to work; when you go to church; when you pay your taxes. It is the world that has been pulled over your eyes to blind you from the truth.

NEO: What truth?

MORPHEUS: That you are a *slave*, Neo. Like everyone else you were born into bondage: born into a prison that you cannot smell or taste or touch. A prison…for your mind. Unfortunately no one can be *told* what the Matrix is. You have to see it for yourself… [Morpheus extracts two pills from a silver case.] This is your last chance. After this, there is no turning back. [He opens his left hand and reveals the blue pill.] You take the blue pill. The story ends. You wake up in your bed and believe…whatever you want to believe. [He opens his right hand and reveals the red pill.] You take the red pill. You stay in Wonderland, and I show you how deep the rabbit hole goes… Remember, all I'm offering is the truth, nothing more.[154]

This memorable scene has been parodied and referenced in major media uncountable times, talked about, thought about, and reflected upon for over thirteen years by people in countries all over the world since its release in 1999. As it represents both an innate sense of intrigue and creeping danger in the face of human decision, the audience's continual contemplation of the implied double consequence and high stakes on Neo's shoulders is not surprising. Note, however, that it's not simply *any* decision that could inspire such a stirring within the hearts of the onlookers. There is an intensity about the decision to educate one's self to the secret, dark, dangerous truths around us that nobody can deny. When people observe a canvas of human nature with its strengths, weaknesses, and passions such as is in this example, they can't help but identify with the character in that moment.

Anyone reading the irrefutable evidence within this book that makes a case for the sinister goings-on in the upper rungs of our American ladder finds themselves "knowing something" also. What they know, they may not be able to explain, but they *feel* it. This gut instinct tells them that there is something wrong with the world and, just as in the above case, it needles at them and provokes a constant state of insecurity and a lack of confidence in our government leadership. It affects everything around us and we see validation in our concerns every which way we turn and every day. Not many would be surprised to see that with as much as our government is capable of, there are details that remain hidden beneath the surface of the shiny front, like a deep-sea predator waiting for fresh meat to disturb the top of the calm waters. Yet, how *far* these details actually go might surprise some.

Both sides of the decision of what reality to swallow have their benefits; the "blue pill" benefits of living in ignorant bliss are the more obvious to see initially. But anyone who has ever experienced a more dramatic case of "hindsight syndrome" will attest that the happy, responsibility-free lifestyle that accompanies a dose of the blue pill is only temporary and, unfortunately, negative side effects include being unprepared for the consequences of such ignorance when the storm hits. The red pill (although certainly far safer in the long run for the majority, as it represents taking action to spread the word and be prepared) has a major and immediate side effect that nobody seems to like: responsibility. It's such an ugly word. It inspires action; it questions your current involvement; it requires that you choose your priorities wisely and organize them all to fit into your busy schedule; therefore, it is much easier to ignore.

A few decades back, Bantam Books began releasing the *Choose Your Own Adventure (CYOA)* children's books, and many of us at a young age took part in early, cognitive decision-making development as a result. Although the series has now decreased in popularity, the books remain a fresh and innovative landmark in the history of literature. Unlike many standard, turn-the-page books, a *CYOA* book involved the reader's interactive participation. Each began with a short introduction of the plot and conflict, and from there, presented the reader with a choice of what the character in the book would do next (listing the decisions at the bottom of the page, such as, "If you choose to go down the path to the left, go to page 4. If you choose to ignore the path and open the box straight ahead, go to page 27."). The reader was then directed to another page in the book where the story continued and eventually led to other choices, and finally to the end of the story. However, any fan of the *CYOA* books will tell you that the "end" was never really the end—until you had reread the books enough times to experience every possible outcome.

It's ironic as adults to look back on these books we loved so well and realize that our lives are still similar to these tales. We don't often choose the position we are placed in, but we always have the ability to look at the options we have in each scenario and take the path we see as the best opportunity of ensuring safety and success in our future. Unfortunately, in real life, there will always be only one final choice of which path to take, and in a world with an ever-ticking clock where time is precious and can't be reversed, there is no starting from the first page and trying again for a better outcome.

When the rubber meets the road, whether you choose to swallow the cushy, comfy, but temporary blue pill or the dangerous but educational red pill, your future and the future of your loved ones is coming at you fast, and what role you play will ultimately be up to only you.

Luckily for Keanu Reeves, his role, Neo, was only science fiction.

The Short, Ruddy Sheep Kid vs. the Colossal, Armored Giant

We've all heard the story, but have you really stopped to think about what can be learned by comparing the account of David and Goliath to modern times? The story in (recorded in 1 Samuel 17) is too long to include in this chapter completely, but certain profound parts beg to be broken down to help us see where we stand today as related to the actions of young David when *he* was presented with the red pill/blue pill fork in the road.

To begin, and most obviously, David was just a pale, small, redheaded kid ("for he was but a youth, and ruddy, and of a fair countenance," verse 42). He was not a soldier or warrior. What run-ins he did have requiring battle (against lions and bears) did not bring him any kingdom fame, so it wasn't as if anyone was expecting anything from the little sheepherder when he arrived at the battle site to deliver food to his soldier brothers. As far as anyone else knew, he had spent his days running errands for his father and chilling out in fields watching the sheep graze, and this happens to be how he *did* spend the majority of his time. His weapon of choice was a sling, which, compared to the tempered steel blades of the king's fully armored troops, probably looked like a useless little pea-shooter to someone of his time. As an opposite extreme, Goliath was enormous. Measuring between nine and ten feet tall (according to the Hebrew Bible, "six cubits and a span," verse 4), he had to at least be muscular and commanding enough to be the leader of the Philistine army, and he was carrying the following items: a "helmet of brass" and a "coat of mail" weighing "five thousand shekels of brass" (verse 5); "greaves of brass" and a "target of brass" (verse 6); and a spear weighing "six hundred shekels of iron" (verse 7). (As this is not a chapter devoted to the study of Goliath's armor, we will not go into detail about the various weights and how much brass five thousand shekels would have bought during this time of history, or even suggest that's an exact translation of the verse. Many scholars have already done that for us, and their numbers land between 140–210 pounds that he carried only in his coat of arms and spear; once all of the pieces of armor mentioned here are added up [including the greaves, target, and helmet, which were not assigned a direct weight in the Scriptures], there is evidence that he was bearing hundreds of pounds at the moment he met David. Some scholars on the Internet have made estimates in the 550–650-pound range. If we looked merely at the least weight mentioned [140 pounds] and pretended that the greaves, target, and helmet weren't a part of a larger number we can't calculate, it would still prove that Goliath was a threatening, towering, massive hunk of a man, the likes of which there is no modern-day comparison. In other words, the two, David and Goliath, were on dramatically opposing ends of the spectrum.) And, since David was completely unarmored (verses 38–39), this would be, in canine terms: the world's largest and most ferocious pit bull versus a small, sweet Chihuahua.

But in addition to the most obvious differences in weight or measurement, there is a leap between the political offices of the two. Goliath was the leader of the Philistine army: an army so fierce that the people of God, Himself (the Israelites), cowered in fear from it. The power Goliath held over his own people and the people of God's army was unprecedented. Who was David? Besides being a boy who kept the mildest of creatures to nibble at the grass as his foremost responsibility, to both the Philistines and the Israelites, David was a nobody. David wasn't even as accomplished as the average soldier in the Israelite army. Yet, there had to be something different about him when he bravely approached for the chance to defend God's people, as King Saul allowed the confrontation to commence.

The endless hours of calm shepherding David had spent had been a perfect atmosphere in which to commune with the Holy Spirit. He had sung and danced and worshiped the Lord, developing such a closeness that when he went up against the lion and bear, he did so fearlessly. To David, this behemoth of a man at the frontlines of battle was no more frightening than the wild animals he had already fought and killed to save his sheep:

> And David said to Saul, Let no man's heart fail because of him; thy servant will go and fight with this Philistine. And Saul said to David, Thou art not able to go against this Philistine to fight with him: for thou art but a youth, and he a man of war from his youth. And David said unto Saul, Thy servant kept his father's sheep, and there came a lion, and a bear, and took a lamb out of

the flock: And I went out after him, and smote him, and delivered it out of his mouth: and when he arose against me, I caught him by his beard, and smote him, and slew him. Thy servant slew both the lion and the bear: and this uncircumcised Philistine shall be as one of them, seeing he hath defied the armies of the living God. David said moreover, The LORD that delivered me out of the paw of the lion, and out of the paw of the bear, he will deliver me out of the hand of this Philistine. And Saul said unto David, Go, and the LORD be with thee. (1 Samuel 17:32–37)

Can you imagine this fateful moment in history? When Saul warned David that he was going up against a man who had been a warrior since his youth, and a large one at that, David basically said, "Nah, I've killed a bear and a lion. I can handle this guy, 'cuz God's got me covered." Saul must have seen something in this young boy to allow him to approach Goliath. There must have been a countenance (the power of God, perhaps?) that David presented at a glance. Had it been otherwise, it's not far-fetched to imagine a response such as, "Guards! Get rid of this skinny, teenage rock-flinger before he aggravates somebody and gets us all killed!" Yet, the fearless tenacity within David won him the right to fight, *and* the king's blessing: "Go, and the Lord be with thee."

Notice that David did not stand around considering his options or his situation. When he saw the threat, he recognized it as the evil that it was, and he did so *instantly*. He didn't stop to be objective and/or try to talk things through with the enemy to see if there was another side to things. He approached the battle lines to deliver food to his brothers and, when he observed Goliath as the enemy of the Israelite God, he quickly and efficiently challenged the threat head-on. As the Scriptures above tell, the only hesitation was from the leadership above him (verse 33). Thankfully, David remained steadfast; otherwise, we might have been left with a different ending to one of history's most amazing tales of war.

Where are the Davids?

When Saul had David dressed in his own armor, David took it all off, saying that the armor was not "proven" (verse 39). Besides Saul's armor being too large, David obviously didn't place much faith in man-made material to protect him, anyway. That was man's contribution to safety in battle. David, the small-fry that he was, had so much faith in the protection and assistance of the Lord that he saw no reason to weigh himself down with fancy, man-made metals. The only protection he needed to confront Goliath was the spiritual armor he had tempered in his many hours alone in prayer. Thus, with no armor or shield, no soldiers beside him, and no social or political influence, our little, redheaded David marched forward with nothing but a sling in hand and obliterated the giant in one fatal shot. Goliath fell to the ground and was quickly beheaded, ending the threat of the Philistine army.

To recap:

A battle can be fought and won quickly and efficiently when God decides it can be, despite the size or influence of the warrior.

When instinct hits to protect our families or communities (or sheep), it is an instinct that should be heeded instantly, without hesitation or questioning.

Each time we are delivered from the hands of our enemies or danger, we are further strengthened; future Goliaths seem no more frightening than the bears or lions we have already slain. However, the willingness to act upon our convictions in the early battles helps us gain the experience that will help in more substantial times.

Communing with God must be an important priority for anyone who will make a difference for His kingdom.

When we stand in tenacity against the evil we recognize (and when filled with the power of the living God), we will radiate in a way that ignites an inspiring fire within the Sauls around us who might otherwise discourage our action.

Yeah, But...What Would My Role in This Be?

A popular reason so many people choose to do nothing when the winds of action and change blow toward them is the mindset that they aren't in the position to do anything. Some think that they have nothing to offer; others think they don't have time to address or deal with the issue; still others may believe in their ability and have time, but see themselves as simply too far away from the problem to be useful. Perhaps you're a soccer mom or average Joe. Maybe you believe nobody listens to you, or you are now older and feel that the youth are too quick or busy to still bend their ear toward you. To all of these groups, I have one thing to say: *Everyone has a role.*

> First they came for the communists,
> and I didn't speak out because I wasn't a communist.
> Then they came for the trade unionists,
> and I didn't speak out because I wasn't a trade unionist.
> Then they came for the Jews,
> and I didn't speak out because I wasn't a Jew.
> Then they came for me
> and there was no one left to speak out for me.[155]
> —MARTIN NIEMÖLLER

Don't be discouraged. It's a common battle tactic of the enemy to deter us from accomplishing good by planting distracting thoughts of self-uselessness. The Lord will not give you a role to play that you aren't strong enough to carry through to the final curtain call. If He begins a project in you and sees you fit to accomplish a goal, He will see it through to completion and give you the strength, wisdom, and maturity to do it ("Being confident of this very thing, that he which hath begun a good work in you will perform it until the day of Jesus Christ," Philippians 1:6). But regret may be a very relatable verb in your future if you, like World War II survivor Martin Niemöller, whom the famous quote above is attributed to, find yourself saying or doing nothing while you have the opportunity.

Do not forget that your role may not be as complicated as you may think. Not everyone is a Jonah: given a task so grievously large and unfathomable that he had to spend days in the belly of a whale to finally succumb to what God is asking. Not every task is as intimidating as turning the wicked city of Nineveh heavenward. Not everyone is chosen to be a David to charge against the odds with no armor and nothing but a sling. David wouldn't even have been present at the time of Goliath if his mother (a soccer mom of her time?) hadn't sent him to deliver food to battle. Maybe your role is to plant a seed. Maybe your role is to *raise* the David; to buy your friend Jonah a cup of coffee and share with him your convictions about what is going on in your country before he gets thrown overboard; to stand for what is right in the midst of so much wrong, so that when they come for you, there will be someone beside you to speak out for you... One thing is assured: Without educating yourself to know what evil is afoot, you will not instantly recognize it as David did. Recognition of the evil is the first step in fighting it.

I'm Way Too Busy

We do not see it necessary to spend too much time convincing the reader that time-absorbers and distractions of today are numerous and counter-productive. It's obvious. Every time we go out to lunch with a friend, we spend half of it answering our cell phones. While on a long drive alone with a loved one where a conversation could have accomplished some-thing in our relationship, we fight to be heard above the GPS suctioned to the windshield and end up missing our turn just to get back on track and hear the electronic voice alert us that it's "recalculating." We *would have* heard Pastor So-and-So's sermon last week, but we couldn't resist the urge to text back when our phone vibrated in our pockets. When we get home from work, we can't walk past the computer anymore without catching up with all 275 people on our friends list over Facebook or Twitter. We may have had time to do something about the issues we read in that book that warned us of American government evils, but we just *had* to catch up with the characters in our favorite television show or video game…

In a world as derailing as our present one, with a never-ending barrage of intrusive vibrations, ringings, beepings, social obligations, television shows, video games, etc., who has time to think about the grand-scale problems of our country or government? Who has time for anything anymore? The distracted lifestyles we live now are shocking to the older generations and "normal" to the younger ones. *What one generation allows in moderation, the next allows in excess.* And the more time-consumers materialize (regular phones, desktop computers, etc.), the more time-savers and quick-fix conveniences replace them with promises of less time spent (such as cell phones, or laptops and electronic notebooks, just to name a couple of examples). Ironically, however, the faster-thinking we become in embracing these quick-fix solutions, the less we have the ability to stop for a while and focus on things that simply *take time to focus on* and that should hold a major importance in our daily/future lives. (Thank goodness for fast food, or we'd all starve to death.)

It's easy to become too busy with smaller priorities than the education of current evils. ("And this I speak for your own profit; not that I may cast a snare upon you, but for that which is comely, and that ye may **attend upon the Lord without distraction**" [1 Corinthians 7:35, emphasis added]. "Wherefore we would have come unto you, even I Paul, once and again; **but Satan hindered us**" [1 Thessalonians 2:18, emphasis added].) Any one of the items on the list above, *when used in excess*, can be a distraction from our time spent on something more important, such as educating ourselves to the existing troubles in our society. Would any good have come from a story wherein David *would have* done something about the Philistines just after he beat *The Mario Brothers* on his handheld gaming console in his field of sheep?

There is no doubt about it. Satan loves a good distraction.

Turning Back to a Life of Ignorance

When Lot and his family left the sinful cities of Sodom and Gomorrah, they were told to flee and never look back. When Lot's wife disobeyed this angelic warning and turned back, she was turned into a useless pillar of salt. Note, however, that she didn't accidently stumble and catch a glimpse of the cities during a fall; that's not how the Bible describes it. It is the opinion of the authors of this chapter that it was with yearning for the life of blissful ignorance in her heart that she turned back, and it was that deliberate yearning for the ignorant life that brought upon God's wrath and her useless, salty fate.

If the question were to be asked, *How much do you truly desire ignorance?*, I imagine most would quickly respond with the notion that they do not desire it at all. But is there a deeply buried craving for ignorance within the heart of every man? Is ignorance, alongside distraction, another tool of the enemy to drag down a whole country under the burden of secret, clandestine operations? Is our government playing the classic *Wizard of Oz*, "Pay no attention to the man behind the curtain," card? And if so, are we, as believers and God-fearing people, becoming as useless pillars of salt like Lot's wife, turning away from the educated future and looking back on the life of no responsibility?

Charles Darwin said many things in his life that we strongly disagree with. However, his famous quote about ignorance is worthy of mention: "**Ignorance more frequently begets confidence than does knowledge.**"[156] Profound, isn't it? That a person would have more confidence in a situation as a result of less education or knowledge is ironic.

It is, nonetheless, true. If you find yourself believing confidently that there is nothing going on behind the curtain in our recent government, and that the authors of this book are a bunch of conspiratorial crazies, we challenge you to add the details within this book to your progressive, American history class education, and see how confident you remain.

To *ignore* the writing on the wall is to be *ignorant*; being ignorant leaves you and your loved ones vulnerable. Ignorance is bliss… But is it really?

Choose Your Own Adventure

You, like Neo, have a choice.

Let me tell you why you have purchased this book. It is because you know something. *What* you know, you can't explain, but you *feel* it. The Matrix is all around us. You can see it when you look out your window, turn on the news, go to work, attend church, and pay your taxes. It is the world that our government has pulled over your eyes to blind you from the truth. Like everyone else in this country, you live in bondage or slavery in a prison you can't smell, taste, or touch. It is a transparent prison for your mind and it affects every aspect of your life.

After reading this book, there is no turning back to ignorance. You can never look back, lest you become as useful to your family and fellow man as a pillar of salt. You take the blue pill. The story ends. You wake up in your comfy bed and believe whatever you want to believe. Or, you take the red pill, you stay in the real world, and learn how deep the rabbit hole goes.

Our nation has been asleep at the wheel for far too long. The blue pill is what put us here to begin with, and it is what contributed to establishing the evils that will be addressed in the following pages. Your family, friends, loved ones, and people you meet on the street are all depending on you to arrest the opportunity to not only know what is happening around you, but to care, and to play your part in being proactive and preventative in years to come. Turn off your cell phone, resist the urge to update your Facebook profile, alleviate all distractions, and really think about your decision. The cast has all been chosen. The orchestra pit is silent and the conductor has raised his baton. The curtain is lifting...

What role will you play?

"Remember, all I'm offering is the truth, nothing more."[157]

If you choose to take the red pill, go to page 153.

If you choose to take the blue pill, close this book, return it to the shelf, and go back to bed.

chapter eight

WHEN ONCE WE WERE A NATION OF

Values

By Josh Peck

A merican values are degrading. Most should find it difficult to argue that statement, regardless what end of the spectrum a person is coming from. To conservatives, liberals are degrading American values by allowing our freedoms to be stripped while replacing them with political correctness and over-sensitivity. To liberals, conservatives are degrading American values by pushing legalistic/religious views and becoming increasingly insensitive to the opposing views of others. The more time goes by, it seems, the more of the American way of life is being forgotten and replaced by something far uglier and upsetting. That begs the question, what exactly are these values we are losing?

In 1970, American sociologist Robin Williams Jr. set out to define America's core values.[158] The ten he defined are as follows:

1. Equal Opportunity
2. Achievement and Success
3. Material Comfort
4. Activity and Work
5. Practicality and Efficiency
6. Progress
7. Science and Scientific Thought
8. Democracy and Free Enterprise
9. Freedom
10. Group Superiority

We can examine the original interpretation of these values and see how they are being stripped from our American lives. We once were a nation of values, but today, these values are consistently redefined.

The First Four

The United States was meant to be a society in which everyone has an opportunity to succeed. Of course, due to differing talents and efforts, some are more successful than others. However, everyone is supposed to have the opportunity, if they desire, to become a successful individual. All people should have the opportunity to provide for themselves and their family.

Moreover, our society is supposed to reward personal merit, hard work, and determination. In a sense, we are to have a healthy amount of competition. This competition is to be handled ethically, of course; we should not want to get ahead of others by beating them down unfairly, but by using their successes as personal motivators toward our own goals. In this way, everybody truly wins. Of course, this is not descriptive of the goals and successes of society today. Unfortunately, we live in an age and society where it is far easier to climb over someone rather than alongside him or her.

The idea that money is the root of all evil is an inaccuracy. In fact, the Scripture states, "The *love* of money is the root of all evil" (1 Timothy 6:10, emphasis added). Material comfort was once a strong American value, but this was not meant as a motivation of greed. It is important for us to be able to provide for ourselves and families in the way they, as fellow human beings and Americans, deserve. Material comfort doesn't have to mean having a large mansion with a golf course for a backyard; in fact, it can just mean having a home for your family with the tools you need to succeed. However, with the massive imbalance in financial distribution across the country, this value has become nearly impossible for more than half of American citizens.

Activity and work (the willingness to work for your money and to be fairly compensated), sadly, is not being adequately honored in our modern day. That, along with the previous three values mentioned, has been squelched by the 1 percent of the population that holds more wealth than the other 99 percent. In fact, it was reported that the wealthiest sixty-two people in the world have as much wealth as the 3.6 billion poorest—a scale that is becoming more imbalanced every day.[159]

Specifically, in the United States, roughly one out of two American families earns $60,000 or less a year, lives below 250 percent of the federal poverty level, and yet is still headed by an adult who has attended college.[160] Back in 2010, it was believed that the ideal salary for comfort and overall happiness was $75,000 a year.[161] Now in 2016, at the time of this writing, that number would have to be increased due to inflation.

Unfortunately, we are not a nation of equal-opportunity values. The more time goes on, the more of a gamble financial security becomes. As of now, the average American has about a 50 percent chance of not being in financial misery, and that is even after having attended college. Americans have an even smaller chance of thriving financially. However, despite what the polls and figures say, we do not have to rely on wealth for our happiness. Ecclesiastes 5:10–12 states:

He that loveth silver shall not be satisfied with silver; nor he that loveth abundance with increase: this is also vanity.

When goods increase, they are increased that eat them: and what good is there to the owners thereof, saving the beholding of them with their eyes?

The sleep of a labouring man is sweet, whether he eat little or much: but the abundance of the rich will not suffer him to sleep.

2 Corinthians 12:10 states:

Therefore I take pleasure in infirmities, in reproaches, in necessities, in persecutions, in distresses for Christ's sake: for when I am weak, then am I strong.

Practicality, Efficiency, and Progress

It used to be that the American people would value what people *did* over what they *said.* The fact is, anyone can say anything. It's the actual *doing* that counts. We used to be a nation of people who would show their effectiveness instead of merely talking about it. Every election year, we are bombarded with more and more promises that are likely to never be fulfilled. Yet, every election year, we as a society keep falling for those promises. Even more, we have a nation divided: certain citizens who adhere to the party of the elected president ignorantly defend his broken promises while the opposing party maliciously condemns him. There is no common ground. Needless to say, this is the least effective way to behave if we expect to have a thriving nation.

Practicality, efficiency, and progress all really go hand in hand. The most effective way to progress as a nation is to be practical. Keep things simple and effective. Yet, it seems that this is the exact opposite of what we see. In every area of our government, and even of our culture, complications and difficulties continually arise. We can see this in virtually all areas of life, yet these complications seem to only target certain individuals and groups. For example, it might be more efficient and practical to buy food from the supermarket and trust that it is safe to eat. However, to really know for sure, we would have to farm our own food, free of pesticides, and work hard to raise those crops. In a perfect country, new innovations to make the farming process easier and more efficient would be the norm. However, what is most popular are innovations that make food in supermarkets more cost-effective, regardless of whether it means a decrease in actual food quality and health. This can pose a problem for individual Christians and other religious groups who do not wish to consume unhealthy or dangerous food due to religious beliefs.

Food consumption is just one of many areas where we can see how the value of practicality has been abused. Easier does not always lead to better. Another area where we can see this drastically is in the American value concerning scientific advancements.

Science and Scientific Thought

America has always been a nation of science. The main idea is that, through science, our lives can become easier and more meaningful. The quality of the American life is supposed to increase through scientific innovations and discoveries.

We have seen this in certain areas. After all, it is far easier to take a plane to visit family across the country rather than to visit them by traveling on horseback. Through technologies like cell phones and social media, we have an easier time communicating with one another. In fact, the Internet as a whole seems to have made life easier for the modern family. But, as we looked at in the previous section, does easier lead to better?

Scientific innovations have brought new problems into the family. While pseudo-anonymous online communication has increased in the life of the average American teen, face-to-face communication with family members in the home seems to have dramatically dropped. In fact, recent studies have shown some troubling statistics about the way this current generation of teens is making and keeping friends.[162]

According to the Pew Research Center, 57 percent of all teens have made friends online, yet only 20 percent have ever met an online friend in person. Gone are the days of parents getting to know other parents to decide whether their kids can socialize with a new family. Now, in most American homes, the responsibility or safety is left up to the child's judgment. Also, only 25 percent of teens spend time with their friends in person after school on a daily basis, yet 55 percent will text message friends every day. Sixty percent of teens spend an average of twenty hours per week in front of computer and television screens, while roughly a third of teens spend about forty hours a week in front of a screen.[163]

All of this time our kids are spending in front of computers and engaged in their cell phones should cause us to wonder who is raising our kids? How are a child's social skills going to suffer due to online socialization? Should anything change, or is this just the world now and we need to adapt?

Many in our country have chosen to adapt. After all, convenience is king. It is far easier to allow our kids to spend hours a day on the computer rather than putting in the effort to be an active part of their lives. Of course, not all families behave this way, but the number of those who do is rising.

Part of the issue of accepting new technologies is the ignorance of many parents regarding how these technologies actually work and the possible dangers involved. By and large, children find it easier than their parents to learn and apply new online innovations. However, parents are catching up. One study has shown that 75 percent of parents are using social media for parenting-related information and social support.[164] Ninety-five percent of teens are online and 81 percent use social media.[165]

Outside the typical American home, the country itself is developing new technologies that will drastically change how we live our lives. One such innovation on the horizon is gene-editing technologies. In fact, according to *MIT Technology Review*, the pharmaceutical industry is "doubling down" on CRISPR for novel drug development.[166] The review states there has been a recent $300 million joint venture between Bayer AG and CRISPR Therapeutics. The goal is to develop new drugs, using gene-editing technologies, to treat and even cure such health issues as blood disorders, blindness, and congenital heart disease.

The American value of science and scientific thought is intended to make life easier and more meaningful. A higher quality of life is the goal. However, is this what we see in our country? Are these innovations making life easier for the average American, or only for targeted individuals?

For the average Bible-believing Christian family, in many ways, life is becoming more difficult. The issue is that the phrase "quality of life" means different things to different people. For some, a higher quality of life means not having to deal as much with children by allowing television and strangers online to raise them. For some, a higher quality of life means editing one's own genes to eradicate disease and illness.

For others, however, a quality life is a simple, God-fearing one. A high-quality life means being a part of their children's lives without pressure from the outside world to do the opposite. A high-quality life means not having to worry about higher-ups in the country putting substances in our medicine and food that will drastically alter and degrade the bodies God has given us. Most of all, a high quality life means living by the very Word of God, the gift of the Holy Scriptures, and being free to do so without others forcing us to do differently.

Democracy and Free Enterprise

Democracy plays a huge role in an individual's sense of self-worth. Democracy defines what we as Americans can achieve and our overall freedom of how we reach our goals. Enterprise is included with the freedom of those goals and achievements. Free enterprise defines how we make our economic choices to succeed.

This applies to business owners just as much as it does to employees of corporations or franchises. If we choose to run our own businesses, we plan how to produce, distribute, and market our goods. The way we decide to do this determines our profit. A large part of this endeavor includes choosing the best employees for the job. If we choose to manage a corporation or franchise business, we plan how to run the operations to make our goals possible. If operations succeed, then the business makes a bigger profit. This results in promotions and higher pay. Higher pay usually means more money can be put back into circulation by making bigger purchases. For example, a business might need newer vehicles for transportation or larger homes for growing families of employees. More money in circulation brings forth a better economy.

Sadly, nowadays, the nation's work ethic seems to be declining drastically. Certain Americans feel entitled and believe they shouldn't have to work as hard as others. This is part of what brings down an economy. No work ethic equals no production. No production equals no pay. No pay equals less money put back into circulation. After that, the economy crashes. We need to teach our children and future generations the importance of honest work. If done properly, this will correct the attitude of self-entitlement.

The Bible says a lot about our work and how it pays off. Proverbs 12:11 states:

He that tilleth his land shall be satisfied with bread: but he that followeth vain persons is void of understanding.

Proverbs also talks about the hard worker as compared to the one who is lazy. Proverbs 12:24 states:

The hand of the diligent shall bear rule: but the slothful shall be under tribute.

If we can return to biblical values, we can return to the original definition of American values.

Freedom

Freedom is an important value that really ties together all ten core American values. This includes our freedom of speech, worship, privacy, education, and many more. Instead of America thriving on these values, we are, in a sense, "rewriting" them to appease the self-entitled individual. Freedom seems to be slipping away at a fast rate. There is now higher security at our airports, which sometimes leaves passengers feeling violated before they board an aircraft.

Of course, our rights of religious freedom and speech are being attacked aggressively. Christians are continually being put down for voicing their opinions and exercising certain religious rights. We are being told we are intolerant and judgmental, and we have "no right" to feel the way we do about certain things, such as abortion and immigration issues. It has now reached the point that we can see it in the news and social media on a daily basis.

This might lead us to wonder why it is okay for Americans to harass their own. Sometimes we hear that it is a practice of the freedom of speech, however, it is obvious that harassment is something different entirely. Regarding security issues, we often hear they are put into place because of prior terrorism. We can all understand this to a certain extent, but it is easy to see how certain people of authority have sometimes gone overboard with their searches of airline passengers. In reality, it is plausible to suggest that this puts more fear than comfort in people's minds.

Lastly, instead of encouraging our future generations to work and become educated, they learn from our culture that it is easier to demand an increase of the minimum wage. Of course, the result of this is an escalation of our cost of living, which leads to another demanded increase of minimum wage, and on the cycle continues. Therefore, some have chosen to follow more of a socialistic route. In this view, no matter how hard you work or have worked to get where you are, ultimately it doesn't matter. Financial equality and opportunity rules. Of course, this goes against clear biblical teaching. Not only does the Bible teach us to put our money aside for our children and grandchildren, it also teaches us that the wealth of the sinner is saved for the just. Proverbs 13:22 states:

A good man leaveth an inheritance to his children's children: and the wealth of the sinner is laid up for the just.

The country is heading in a direction that teaches that we can be as lazy as we want—which, of course, is sinful, according to biblical definition—yet earn as much as the just and hardworking.

Obviously, no one should have the right to take someone else's hard-earned money that is saved for themselves and their descendants. Hard work and determination, as the Bible defines it, is the answer, not socialism. It's time to take back our true American freedom.

Group Superiority

We as a nation have come far with this one. Race, gender, and other physical attributes should not play a role in positions of authority. There are supposed to be equal rights given to employees.

Women are treated somewhat better than they had been in the past, yet there is still work to do. Women are given equal rights concerning the education of their choice. For example, women can join the military, pilot aircraft, or be engineers if they want. In the past, women were limited to what trades they could go into based on skills they already possessed. These usually included positions as nurses, waitresses, retail sales clerks, or house wives. This ties right back to equal opportunity.

Now, in the workplace, for the most part, discrimination against women is intolerable. If someone is harassing a woman, that person is typically reprimanded or fired. This is one area that has seen an improvement. However, overall, a woman working in a position is paid a lower salary than a man in that same position. On average, women in America make seventy-nine cents to every dollar a man makes.[167]

This core value is meant to ensure that everyone is treated equally in the workplace. It should be based on the skills and requirements that need to be met specific to the job. This includes education and work ethic. Every human being is created equally by God, and this fact should be reflected in the work place.

Conclusion

Getting back to these core values and treating them as such can turn our country around. We need to treat our fellow men and women with respect, educate ourselves and our children, and keep our American work ethic. If we follow the proper interpretation of these American values, we will work together as a team instead of beating each other down to reach the top. The original intended purposes of these values should ensure that we all can reach the top if we just work together.

However, what we have seen in recent decades runs against this concept. Instead of "us first," we live in a "me first" nation. Instead of living by values that will benefit everyone, we live by values that benefit the individual. While it may seem impossible to change the course of the nation, it isn't. The change doesn't start at the top. We can't expect to suddenly overturn the entire American government just because we don't like what's going on. Unfortunately, that is a "me first" attitude, and it is what has brought the nation to where it is today.

Instead, the change needs to begin at the bottom: the foundation. The change starts within the home. Specifically and biblically, it is the father's responsibility to guide the course of the family. First Timothy 5:8 states:

> But if anyone does not provide for his relatives, and especially for members of his household, he has denied the faith and is worse than an unbeliever.

1 Corinthians 11:3 states:

> But I want you to understand that the head of every man is Christ, the head of a wife is her husband, and the head of Christ is God.

The husband and father of the household needs to provide for the family in all ways. We do this by making sure Jesus Christ is in the center of the family. As fathers, we should talk to our children as we would want our Heavenly Father to talk to us. We should treat our wives as we would expect Jesus to treat the church. We should provide proper guidance and instruction to our family the way we expect God to do for us.

This is how we can truly take our country back. The degradation of American values is not a political problem, it is a spiritual one. This means there will never be a political solution for this spiritual problem. We need a spiritual solution. We need to bring the country back to Christ. We start by bringing Christ back into the family. Our Lord and Savior Jesus Christ is the solution.

chapter nine

———— WHEN ONCE WE WERE A NATION ... ————
Under God, Indivisible

By Joe Ardis

Despite its title, this chapter is not a righteous railing against the secular world to convert lest they perish. Nor is it an attempt to promote a theocratic worldview.

In fact, it's quite the contrary...

What I Wanted to Become

Throughout American history, remarkable activists have ascended out of anonymity in the right appointed place and at the right appointed time to carry their impassioned pleas to a nation starving for political and societal reform. From these leaders and the various organizations they propelled have come beneficial and paramount civil, constitutional, ethical, and social benefits to our culture. Some of these men and women saw vices and wickedness within our government that threatened national morality, and they surrendered everything—at times, including their lives—toward the cause of upright conduct. Others observed concerns within the development of our laws that endangered freedoms, and they threw caution to the wind, led marches and rallies, and united parties to band together in pursuit of maintaining liberty and justice for all. The numbers of those who have risen to such higher causes is abundant.

It is to these champions that we owe our comfort and independence. It is these advocates—who gave everything to ensure a better existence for future generations—that we can never thank enough. It is to these conquerors that America has for so long been the great nation that she is.

Once upon a time, I, Joe Ardis, *wanted* to be one of these heroes. But the Holy Spirit had something else in mind for me, as you will learn.

What I Was Shaped to Become

As a child, I was taught to use my brain more for reasons of conscience—and the personal actions and choices this propelled—than for any other purpose. My mother and father did all they could from my birth forward to shape me into a man of God. Intellect, articulation, oratory demonstration, good grades in school…all of that mattered only *after* I had utilized my mind to determine right from wrong, and the role I had chosen to play toward the goal of morality for me and others around me. It was an age-old, "wisdom over knowledge" upbringing. Getting a golden star on a spelling test or math paper was celebrated, but the eternal implications these endeavors held within my household were moot when compared to the proverbial golden star earned when making the world a better place while serving God first and foremost. My greatest responsibility was to *think with wisdom* and to *play my part* in the cause—whatever cause that might be in each particular case.

From this nurturing came an underlying zeal to be a leader, even when that was not related to Christianity or witnessing. I was never content to just wander and exist. In every arena, if there was something more I could do, some position that needed filling, some responsibility left wanting, I felt it was my duty to take up arms and charge full steam ahead. This has manifested itself in many ways throughout my life up to the time of this writing, and it was *particularly* interesting when I was a kid.

For example, during a stint that lasted the whole school year, I hosted my own live role-play gameshow at the front of the school bus on the ride home, in which the other kids reluctantly participated, pretending to be contestants. I would even use art class to paint cardboard signs displaying words like "lucky winner" and "final round" that I would intermittently stick to the bus windows, swapping them out from time to time to increase the other kids' perception of the constantly escalating intensity of each phase of the game until finally we would reach the day's grand-prize winner, who was usually rewarded with a stick of gum, a new pencil eraser, or anything else I could conjure up during the school day. At times, these impromptu gameshows created quite a bit of laughter and helped the bus driver keep the other kids entertained. Later, when my family brought home our first VHS camcorder, I would pull out my guitar and record "shows" that my exhausted family members were coerced to contribute to, including "Joebo" and "Dr. Joekyll and Mr. Hyde"—parodies of Rambo and Dr. Jekyll/Mr. Hyde, which at the time I thought were clever but now find embarrassing. I had created a long list of fictitious characters, each with its own function and personality, and I absolutely *lived* in-character. There was "the jaw," a boy who spoke animatedly with his jawline jutting outward; "the umpire," whose sole purpose was to call "you're out!" over and over with his hands flailing about in the air; "Grampa Sam," who found anything and everything to vociferously gripe about in his outrageously thick southern accent; "Danny," an incredibly shy teenager who always formed his sentences incoherently and didn't want to eat his vegetables; and many others. I'm sure a modern child psychiatrist would have a heyday hearing all the identities I became throughout each day. From the moment I woke up to the moment I went to bed, I was never just "Joe." I *had* to find some exorbitant way of proclaiming my presence to all around me. One could imagine a young Jim Carrey on steroids for an idea of what being around a young version of me was like. I wasn't an unhappy child trying to escape reality. In my view, I was just a boy having a ton of fun that often manifested in very silly but incredibly obnoxious ways.

Most of the time I was a total clown, and today I wonder why anyone would have paid me any attention, save for the fact that I demanded it from them, whether they liked it or not. Paradoxically, I was often unpopular in grade school (throughout nine different moves to new schools) and spent much of those years applying emotional salve to layers of tough skin in order to survive the pestering from bullies and jocks. One might *think* that getting picked on would silence me, but as puzzling as it is to wrap my brain around now, despite the flack that my tomfoolery earned me socially, I forged on in making my statement, determined to be the presiding mayor over my own world. And, as ludicrous as those decisions may seem now, one thing was always true of those days: As I was busying myself trying on all these identities and turning heads with my annoying stunts (which either brought laughter, indifference, or annoyance), I was learning to be comfortable at the center of attention, whilst not exactly being everyone's favorite guy… circumstances that would groom me for later ventures.

In my teen years, I became less awkward in my approach, and I largely let go of the idea that I had to be the personality to whom all eyes were focused upon. During this time, my off-the-wall, sarcastic, exaggerative sense of humor—polished through the previous years of being the official school bus gameshow host and other nonsensical endeavors—gained me the admiration of kids nearby. For a while, that was my niche. Before long I was assisting in children's church, running puppet shows, acting in skits, and writing Christian songs for all ages. By my late teens and early twenties, after honing my guitar skills further, I was standing in front of significant gatherings to host public outreach events, play concerts, share testimonies, lead worship, or pray…and I was not ashamed of the gospel, or swayed by the opinion of naysayers. The music I wrote then gained momentum, and one song even won an international award from a substantial pro-life organization, receiving recognition from the Billboard Music Awards in the early 2000s for best new original song in the independent categories.

All those years of self-directed "stage training" I had shown from my childhood was paying off. All the signs seemed to be pointing to this notion that the Lord had a great purpose for me, and I was ready to be used!

Or so I *thought*.

What I Turned Myself Into

Even the most elementary Christian teaching tells us that in order to grow spiritually and prepare our hearts and minds to be used by Him for His purposes, we need to read the Word and pray. Interestingly, I was an incredibly analytical person, and evidently this "read and pray" concept was too basic for me to appreciate. It wasn't because of outright arrogance or defiance that I didn't correctly implement this credo in my daily walk (at least never intentionally). I just somehow found myself constantly busy with what was happening at church socially, where I was going on the weekend, the lyrics to a new song, and so on. So at best I would speed-read the Scriptures, memorize the quips and quotes I heard others saying, and thus be "equipped" to "drop a verse" to someone when the moment called for it. This was accompanied by my nearly memorized prayer before bed, going down the list of items that needed to be said in order to complete the assignment, and then I was free to play my guitar and wait for a worship song to reveal itself, or call my non-believing buddies and listen for an opportunity to witness to them about this amazing God I knew. Easy-peasy. Check! Done… I may not have actually, truly, deeply *known* God with the maturity I voiced to my friends, but I didn't know that at the time. I honestly didn't. After all, I was "doing what I needed to do," and whatever feelings I had about Him in those days were as close as I was going to get to having a relationship with Him while I wandered around waiting for signs and wonders that curiously never came.

I wish that I had a noble testimony that follows the description above. I wish now that I could say I had some great epiphany that drove me into a wholehearted fellowship with God, and that I tapped into the fullness of my potential as a strong servant of Christ, putting away childish things in trade for spiritual maturity. That Rock on which I could have been standing would have carried me through the rest of this story more impressively to you as a reader. But, truth is, this half-hearted, checkmark-style devotion life was my norm well into my early years as a husband and father.

In 2000, I married my wife, Katherine. In 2005, we had our first child, Kate.

I had, by this time, started noticing a concerning trend sweeping across the states. It appeared as if people my age and younger were making decisions about political leaders based on very risky ideologies. I knew innately that we, as Christians, were not commissioned primarily to debate politics, but I also knew instinctively that we, as Christians, are commissioned to do what we can to make the world a better place, and as far back as the anointed kings of Israel, due diligence as one nation under God involved a responsibility to position the best chiefs over our temporal territories.

One of the 2004 presidential candidates had declared a stance in favor of God and against abortion. I could see why, then, all of my Christian friends immediately proclaimed, and in no uncertain terms, that he would have their vote. But so many of those who discussed the election in my social circles were basing their passionate support of this candidate entirely on two of his stated positions about religious convictions he claimed publicly to hold, and not on his intelligence, articulation, leadership skills, foreign and domestic policies, plans for the economy, tax and capital gain strategies, positions on educational systems, social security perspectives, medical care plans, or anything else that a governmental captain with an entire country in his hands for the duration of *at least* four years is responsible for. This particular candidate shared stated positions on most of these other matters, and again proclaimed publicly how his plans to deal with them were better than his rival for the White House. But to many of my closest friends, these other topics were largely just background noise and fell way down the checklist of important issues.

This was somewhat understandable, but superficial, I thought, so I dug a little deeper. When I questioned my friends, asking their opinions on other important social and governance matters, a haze fell over their features as they fumbled for words, gave trite responses, and redirected their official stance back to that one agenda that flattered their conscience: The *only area* of politics they were able to engage in discussion was the fact that their choice administrator had said he was *for* God and *against* abortion. I am too, but was he sincere or simply giving conservative voters what they needed to hear to gain their support? The more I spoke to those in the church, the more I received responses that began with, "Yeah, well, my dad talked to our pastor, and *he* says..." or "You know, last Sunday my youth pastor said his neighbor thinks..." or "My friend's boss at work says..."

I was honestly astounded. The young people of my own home country didn't have a clue what a president was supposed to be. Had they educated themselves, stopped quoting short soundbites, and actually conducted some deeper research into the candidates and the issues—and then still maintained their position for this candidate—I may have smiled and silently disagreed with their perspective on my own, but I would have respected that their decision was an *educated* one. Instead, they were flocking to the ballot centers by the scores, voting cards in hand, willing to radically and blindly alter the direction of our children's potential future forever because they "knew a guy who knew a guy" who gave them an abbreviated rundown of only one aspect of this candidate's character.

And now I was a father, myself. It was *my* child who would inherit the land my fellow youth were shaping for her.

Don't misunderstand. My issue was not as much with *whom* the youth of the nation was voting for, but with *why* they were voting how they were. It was as if they listened and researched politics just long enough to hear what they wanted to hear about a candidate, something that flattered their personal agenda but of which did not necessarily flatter the interests of a country's future, and then stopped considering any other consequences.

What were they thinking? Or *were they* thinking? Where was the *wisdom* in this logic? It just ceaselessly got under my skin that people my own age were casting votes as if they were casting lots. At best, it was a gamble.

By 2006, I had long since relented arguing about the 2004 election and reset my sights on work, family, and keeping my eyes open for that doorway into ministry. But that campaign, and the discussion of it in the following year, had left a deeply troubling stamp in the recesses of my mind like an invisible, slow-release poison that would continue to damage my confidence and contentment each time political principles were brought into conversation.

In 2007 and 2008, life continued in the same, checkmark-devotion way. I watched as new questions were being raised regarding political legislation and policies. For many, these were new questions that had posed a lot of sudden, unexpected consequences. For *me*, however, they were questions I had been asking for five or ten years while I had been studying movements within the government and the evolving aspirations of the American public. I continued to shake my head in wonder, realizing that the home I had been brought up in—the home that taught children to study and think beyond the walls of a public school education; the home that edified wisdom, discernment, and deliberation beyond what one's friends and associates decree; the home that advocated the challenging of whether or not something is too good to be true when it seems to be—was more unique than I ever imagined. Onward I trod, determined as of yet not to allow these concerns to take over my life, but a bitterness was swelling...

In 2009, about the time the nation was climbing aboard the train of an Affordable Care Act, I began to reach an all-time low. More and more over time, the Bible was placed on the shelf to collect dust in between check-list style devotions, while I scoured the daily online updates listing the pros and cons of historically unparalleled legislation. Prayer time was quickly becoming a routine shared in equal spurts with incessant grumbling regarding those in the nation who continued to blare their opinions on *select* categories, while refusing to educate themselves on the long-term implications of their desires. All around me, rallies were forming, comprised of people with an entitlement mentality. They shouted for anything that was free. They claimed rights to anything they didn't have to work for. The decisions they were making were feeding their immediate wants, but paving the way for all kinds of devastating costs to liberty and freedom down the road.

I couldn't escape the all-consuming saturation of political agenda. Everyone wanted something. Everyone was making demands. Everyone was jumping up and down claiming he e or she knew the best route to take. One law or policy after another was being passed to satisfy the entitlement generation. And all the while, from the angles available to me at the time, it appeared that not nearly enough people were standing up to challenge the administrations or legislations that threatened the long-term freedoms of "we the people," because the confetti exploding from the party cannons had already obscured the peoples' view of the prospective aftermath. The future of the nation was looking extremely grim.

I couldn't help but repeat the same pessimistic and depressing thoughts regarding my children: Would they believe in free speech, or be driven to silence through gradual oppression? Would they be able to go after their dreams and desires making use of their God-given talents like I had been given, or would their futures be clouded in debt brought on by the unjust laws that my own generation had hastily and impulsively engineered? Would they someday be allowed to choose their own doctors based on the best match for their needs, or would they be forced to receive substandard care from a list of healthcare professionals the government had assigned to them? Would they be *free*…or would they end up imprisoned by the future America my dark thoughts were shaping?

One day, during an effort to temporarily take a mental break from all the negative, exhausting brooding over the calamitous direction the nation seemed to be heading, I was playing a video game while my daughter was away from the house. Distracted from my virtual world by the real one, I paid little attention to the duties of my avatar as I ran my computer character around on-screen, aimlessly defeating bad guys as my thoughts raced with anxiousness.

A scene played out in my mind. In a daydream, my daughter had walked in, gazing over my shoulder at the computer.

"Whatcha doin', Daddy?" four-year-old Kate said in my imagination.

I watched my response to her play out like a movie.

"Just relaxin', hon. Go along and play now. Daddy's just relaxin'."

"How come, Daddy?" she asked, as if my taking a break in the middle of the day was confusing to her.

I considered the free will I was exercising in that moment I was resting at my computer. I thought about the current liberty I was enjoying, the cost of which had been paid by yesteryear's hard-working, great American heroes.

"I'm squandering your freedom," I said to the little girl in my mind's eye. "I'm sitting on my backside playing video games while your rights are disappearing. Now, Daddy's tired, honey. Run along."

I was shocked by the transparency of my own words to her. Yes, it was just a daydream, and no, I would never say anything like that in reality. However, it had strangely rung out as truth. And then it was her words—the comeback my psyche assigned to her lips in that moment—that shook me to my core.

"Daddy, why aren't you fighting for me? Why aren't you fighting for my future while there's still time?"

And there it was. I was sure of it.

My sign.

My wonder.

My *calling*.

The great U.S. of A. was doomed unless people—people like *myself*—put down the video game controllers and stepped up to the plate of activism as others had done before me. I could no longer wait for my peers to fight the good fight or organize demonstrations or march at the head of rallies. It was *my* responsibility to get off my backside, think with wisdom, and play my part in making my daughter's world a better place.

I had been in training my entire life. I was the "character." I was the leader of the bus. I was "Joebo" and "Dr. Joekyll"—the personality that persons of all ages listened to even when they didn't agree. I was the winner of international songwriting awards. I wasn't afraid of opposition or doing whatever it took to pull peoples' attention toward the things that mattered most. But now the despair and confusion that had been consuming me over the appearance of losing our nation had so depleted my energy and focus that it stifled my ability to see an effective way forward in terms of using my gifts for justice, to efficiently use my abilities to help rescue a politically deteriorating nation. I suddenly realized I was *supposed* to be a groundbreaker. I was *supposed* to rise up and act. I was *supposed* to be the defender of the little princess who depended on me.

And I had failed.

I had always been a sincere appreciator of those who had given themselves over to establishing a country "of the people, by the people, and for the people," but in that instant, right then, right there, in the modest computer room of my home, I was a born-again patriot. Tears welled up in my eyes and spilled over my cheeks for the first time since I was a boy. I couldn't even remember the last time I had cried with such helpless and hopeless fury. So incensed was I when it truly hit home how my sweet daughter was being robbed that my own eyes and heart were blinded to any other pursuit than the enlightenment *of*—and by extension *for* and *by*—we the people.

I knew I had to do something, so I considered my musical talents and got to work immediately. From the depths of my disquieted soul, following the daydream incident in my computer room, and through the growing concern I was now developing over the political administration of that year, the song "Freedom" was born. Through the words my lyrically gifted older sister had helped me write, I told a few select chiefs of our land exactly how I felt:

I swear, I swear before God above,
  When I look into my daughter's eyes, and I think about your lies,
  I won't be pushed aside. I'm not about to hide.
  Drop your political disguise. Don't expect me to stand idly by,
  While you take away her world, not my little girl.
  You better step aside....
  You take for granted the red, white, and blue.
  Your position you abuse. It's the little ones who lose.
  It's not for you to choose.

Freedom isn't yours to give away.
Liberty's been bought for us in blood.
We won't give it up, so help us God.
We won't be pushed aside. We're not about to hide.
(endnote includes a link to the video)

   Immediately after the song had been recorded in my studio, I got together with the other of my two sisters and filmed the music video. In it, my daughter, Kate, was a central character. There were scenes of me twirling her around in the park, followed by scenes with a politician in a pig mask luring her over to trade her piggy bank for a collection of balloons that said "tax," "debt," and "socialism." The pig mask was shown being stomped on the asphalt later in the song. Other scenes included a forlorn military wife, now widowed, walking through the cemetery with the American flag in her hands—and another wife with a baby in her arms hugging her husband goodbye as he descended the steps of his front porch in his camouflage with a bunker backpack slung over his shoulder, headed out for duty. The latter two scenes involving the military wives were not in any way supposed to suggest that the sacrifices men and women make for our country should be viewed with a victim mentality, but that their sacrifices should be *appreciated* by our country's leaders, not misused or taken for granted, as I believed they were becoming. Not only was the imagery strong, bold, and forthright in its unabashed symbolism, but even the passion on my face and in my body language revealed that I was already clenching my fists in preparation for a personal war against Washington.

   About this time, the Tea Party was escalating across the states. Patriots from all faiths and backgrounds, all angry about the same things that had riled me, were forming into activist groups and launching awareness events all over the country. I made contact with the highest ranks of the Tea Party movement, including Lloyd Marcus, who was touring with the Tea Party Express at that time. They listened to my song, watched the music video that I had created for it, and responded emphatically, inviting me to the "Tea Are the World" recording project the following fall, where choice patriots across the states were hand-selected to participate in the development of a two-disk compilation set. Raiders News Update (now known as SkyWatch TV) also latched on to my song, believing that even though politics was not the news company's focus, the message behind my latest passion was one that many Americans—Christians or otherwise—could relate to. Through these two channels, World Net Daily caught word and published an article called "Patriot Rocker Fights for Little Girl's 'Freedom,'" which resulted in tens of thousands of views on my YouTube upload the same day. By the time I attended the Tea Are the World recording event—which occasioned significant connections for me, such as American Mighty Warriors' founder Debbie Lee and the band Foghat's former guitarist John Rainey, as well as many other politically active networking moguls—my music, as well as my story and motives, were popping up in news all over the nation. Independent pro-freedom radio shows were booking me to voice my pleas over nationally syndicated airwaves. I launched the instantaneously successful organization Artist's Expressway, providing a conduit for other frustrated patriots—from painters to musicians to comedians to photographers and many others—to express their political grievances, and they did so with fervor.

Opportunity was knocking. I had a voice, and people were listening. I was doing my part!

And yet, something was missing.

This train was moving fast, and I was the man feeding the coal to the engine as fast as I could load it, but the more momentum I gained, the farther away I felt from contentment. Not to mention the onslaught of feedback that attacked my decision to use my daughter to make a political statement. The "how dare you" emails I found in my inbox for several months straight confounded me. Somehow, these people had seen my "Freedom" music video, and of all things the trolls could get worked up over, my casting my little girl in the footage was the issue. Not politics.

My initial thought had been that if I just applied myself toward the cause as hard as I could, I would go to sleep at night in the comforts of accomplishment. But the opposite was happening. I was only growing more and more depressed and anxious every single day. I wasn't just immersed in the cause, I was drowning in it.

For months, I continued onward. Even the apostle Paul had an irremovable thorn in his side that caused him intense discomfort while he stood unshakable in the position in which God had placed him, using the talents he had been given behind the prison walls in Rome, so that no man could tear asunder the message he had been sent to deliver. Even David had uncountable times fled to the wilderness and dark caves to escape his oppressor, writing Psalms that encapsulated the very things I was feeling, while he vigilantly maintained his footing on the path toward reformation for God's people. Both of these men (and *so many others* from Scripture) had faced grievous opposition and heartbreaking turmoil on the journey. If *they* could do it, then I *must!*

My response to the spirit-crushing feelings that were spreading inside me like a plague was to ramp it up. I wasn't fulfilled, because I wasn't doing enough. I wasn't happy doing this work because this work wasn't producing adequate results. I had to fight harder, be stronger, yell louder, and go against this thing with every ounce of my energy like the heroes of America's past. I had to make my mark on the world and back it up with a bounding voice no man or woman could ever forget, lest our children be left with a country that paled in comparison to the glorious one that had been built for me.

I decided to take a different approach. Maybe humor, sarcasm, and parody would be more effective. Maybe the inner gameshow host at the front of the bus needed to take the wheel for a while, using wit as my new medium.

"The Devil Went Down to Washington"—a parody of the 1979

"The Devil Went Down to Georgia" by the Charlie Daniels Band—was the result. I spent hours in my studio laying down some hot guitar chops, vocals, and mixing over and over again until I felt the song was ready to meet the world. Then, just as before, I got together with the younger of my two sisters and filmed the video. Lyrically, many statements were made regarding what I viewed to be extremely concerning recent legislation trends propelled by the then-current administration, including healthcare issues (that had already left my grandmother in financial ruin the year prior). The imagery included a man in a Barack Obama mask challenging me to a guitar duel near some old train tracks outside an abandoned building, saying, "I bet the nation's soul whose throne I stole I'm a better player than you." In another scene, the Obama character was playing cards with a man in a devil mask on a stop-sign table; the masked Obama pulled an ace out of his sleeve and snickered as if he'd really gotten away with something. In another scene "a band of politicians joined in" Obama's guitar duel—two pecking chickens in suits banging a bunch of nonsense on Stratocaster guitars. In the end, I won the duel, my challenger was seen fleeing the town, and I faded away while walking down the train tracks.

Many, *many* responded to the music video positively, understanding the message behind the humor. I was still making my statement, and yet, now people were laughing instead of shaking their heads in miserable demoralization. It was for these individuals the song had been written, so that they may be given a moment of levity amidst a sea of worry, and it was through these individuals that my parody was skyrocketing overnight into viewership ratings that instantly put my former song to shame. Hundreds of thousands of views, shares on Facebook, Twitter feeds, LinkedIn posts…the song was just everywhere all at once, including on large screens at Tea Party rallies around the nation.

This was really happening. I was all over the country.

I knew before I had ever created it that the song would be controversial, and I believed I was egging on a battle of debate that I would have to face in the coming months about my concepts of healthcare and other laws, which I had readied myself to tackle. But the flood of hatred I initiated against myself from Internet trolls was more incredible than anything I had prepared myself to handle, and it stemmed from the most pretensive and asinine reasons.

From the onset of the video's appearance on YouTube (video viewable from this endnote link), comments abounded (mostly from younger people) that this Joe Ardis guitarist was a *racist*! (It should be stated on the record that I have *never* been a racist, and some of my closest friends as early as my childhood have been African-American, Hispanic, and other ethnicities whose upbringing and lifestyles dramatically differ from my own. However, in our country at that time, especially since President Obama was the first non-white president, a popular insult dropped by Obama supporters was that anyone standing against him or his administration was a "racist." There was *not one racial implication* in the lyrics, or imagery, of my video, and yet that was the most popular backlash claim.) I had become a "hater," a "pig," a "bigot." Maybe this was, again, a symptom of our youth's tendency to fight politics based on non-political convictions, but challenges against my *political* statements regarding alarming legislation were few and far between. Those who were irate over the video were mad that I was a *white* man defeating a "black president" (their words) in a guitar duel.

I couldn't understand it. For what felt like the billionth time in my life, I was observing my own generation supporting, or attacking, ideologies based on things that have nothing to do with the responsibility of our government. My musical parody had nothing to do with race, but for scores of people, an attack against skin color was all I had set out to do. Never mind legislation. Never mind policy. Never mind economic, social security, or educational strategies. It was never clearer to me than it was in that instant: Today's generation couldn't possibly understand or appreciate the lives that had been lived on this soil before us, and what concepts of "freedom" or "liberty" had cost to implement. For far too long, our nation had been asleep at the wheel, merely enjoying these gifts, and from that, the entitlement age was born. Unless I came to flatter the immediate wants or needs *of* the people of this generation, *by* the people of this generation, and *for* the people of this generation, my message would always be buried under the *railings* of this generation, who didn't appear to comprehend what they were even arguing about. At least that's how it felt.

People were arguing just to hear themselves argue. People were hating just to jump on the bandwagon of activism. People were shouting about politics just to ensure that their social circles were aware of their fearlessness. Everyone was *radical!* But few within my purview were truly *educated.*

And now here I was, absolutely right in the very middle of all of this conflict, my reputation amongst the people I was trying my hardest to reach was now the "rocker racist," instead of the young man whose unique perspective on politics might otherwise benefit national policies.

I couldn't check my email without the daily deluge of animosity. Threats against my safety were pouring in every minute. I wasn't afraid of them, but I was stirred by how far off the mark these people seemed to be. How easy it was for them to see straight *past* the point I was trying to make and render my work mute in the roar of petty squabbling.

Rage and emptiness was teeming inside. Nothing I did or said seemed to persuade the very people I was trying to reach the most, the very ones I viewed as confused, and in need of a better understanding of how to take steps to create a better tomorrow for everyone in the nation and especially the future generations that would inherit what we leave behind. Though I was receiving tens of thousands of positive comments, shares, likes, thumbs-ups, twitters, etc., I felt that the number of stone-throwers seemed significant as opposed to those who heard my message with an open mind. When I had been speaking quietly, it felt like nobody listened. When I ramped it up, so did they, and in the worst of ways. None of this was making sense. I had hundreds of thousands of supporters on my side, but only those whose political opinions had always *been* on my side. I was preaching to the choir. My intention had been to reach those outside my circle, and within *that* field of effort, I was failing. I felt like the wedge between my ideology and theirs was only increasing. I was not motivated to "do more" by the praise of my fellow, like-minded patriot pals, nor was I deterred in the slightest by those who expressed opposing world views from my own, but I certainly began to wonder if, for all my energy spent fighting for my country, battling in politics, using the methods I had so emerged myself into was effectively helping my cause, or just furthering vitriol and fueling anger to those I was trying to help the most.

It started consuming all areas of my life and effecting my health. From the ceaseless panic and dread, I developed ulcers and diverticulitis. Then I was diagnosed with a lethargic liver and adrenal fatigue. Two different doctors wanted to put me on antidepressants, which I refused because I didn't see medication as the answer. I didn't need medication to alter my personality, or to make me generally care less about everything troubling me. I was stronger than that; I had to forge ahead.

In the meantime, the only father my child knew had become a harbinger of doom, the man who patted her head with weariness before letting out yet another deep sigh. The only husband my wife knew was a zombie, lifelessly reporting for duty at my computer to write my latest political opinion, read the latest discouraging headlines, and moan day in and day out about all the American foundational shattering perceived within my worldview. What an exhausting life I had created, and my family were victims of it. Such strain. Such constant, *constant* strain. Tension was my bread, worry my wine. I took communion every day at the table of woe in remembrance of the country that I believed had been lost. All too replaced was the gospel in my heart and mind as I continued to only give Scriptures and prayer time the leftovers of my energy, while I continued the checkmark approach to skimming through them. After all, I was exhausted. At times it felt like my heart was vaguely in to reading the Word. How could it have been more so? I hardly had time to think about that. Those freedom-march songs and presidential parodies wouldn't write themselves…

But the emptiness inside was well fed as I trod this path daily.

Was this, or was this not, what I was supposed to be doing with my life?!

The answer to that question eventually arrived, and it forever changed me…

What God Had to Say about Who I Had Become

One afternoon, I sluggishly but obediently dragged myself to the computer with a deep breath to once again take in the condemning protestations of those pusillanimous pollywogs who opposed me. One email stood above the others. This man made his intentions perfectly clear.

He hated me.

He thought my decision to use my daughter in my first video was detestable.

He believed my second video was racist.

And his email detailed a series of "things he would love to do to me" and my little girl.

The anger inside me began to swell in my chest so quickly that my eyes darted away from the words contained in the email, and I had zero intentions of continuing to read whatever sick, sadistic hateful items this troll may have included just beyond the introduction I had started to read. In the past, I had received several emails or witnessed comments online to the effect that someone wanted me dead, or "wished I would die of cancer" or "would love to find me to (fill in the blank)" and other hatred. The threats I had received prior to this sounded empty and contrived as if they had been written by people who didn't really plan to carry out their hollow terrorizations, but who wanted to shower me with the worst verbiage they could come up with to rattle me away from the messages I was sending the nation. This email, however, felt different. Whether this man had truly been capable of doing the horrible things he fantasized about doing to me and my daughter like he said he wanted to or not, the vitriolic intentions bled off the computer screen like a target forming above my home.

I wasn't *afraid* of him; I was *infuriated!* I fumed with an unrecognizable revulsion against this man, feelings in my gut I never thought I was capable of harboring. Who—*who in the world*—did he think he was?! He didn't like a political role I was playing for my country, so he was daydreaming about committing horrible atrocities against me and my child? Like some grandeur and visionary John Wilkes Booth? Like some copycat Lee Harvey Oswald who believed my end would bring about the country he wanted to live in? How insane! How absolutely and totally irrational!

I do believe I would have reacted differently if his crosshairs had only been centered upon me, but my sweet, loving, and innocent little girl?

Rage.

Pure, unadulterated rage.

From somewhere I can't explain, a bubbling, putrid ball of contempt arose within me. Thoughts flew around in my mind with a chaotic hum, as if the epicenter of my brain was filled with wasps, stingers protruding, sending out the small shockwaves that were about to initiate an earthquake of hatred that, once loosed, would create a new Joe completely unrecognizable as the man I had been. My jaw clenched, and my fingers curled into fists, white at the knuckles. I started to shake with indignation.

Then, my lips parted, and I started to whisper under my breath the things I would do to this man if our paths crossed.

It was then that I heard from the Lord.

It was my sign.

My wonder.

I hadn't even completed my sentence of revenge when a still, small voice from the Holy Spirit interrupted me, saying, "Joe, *this* is why you're empty inside."

It was only one second, but in that moment, hundreds of layers of truth dawned upon me. It was like I had spent the last ten years downloading this Holy Spirit file, and when it was finally opened in my mind, multiple pop-up windows mounted all at once, flooding my consciousness with convicting and bombarding tiers of reproach, each one a larger blast of clarity than the previous. I immediately shut down my loathing and listened, so that this voice might be allowed full entrance and domination over my own finite, human thoughts.

"This is why you're empty inside. This is why you're still living in great fear over the political climate of your temporary home. This is why you're so angry. You've become distracted from your true purpose, which is to *preach the Gospel.* When you annunciate the Word of God, it heals the hearts of those that by your own admission are a part of the problem. Unless change happens in the heart of men, they will continue to usher in their own destruction. Politics are man's earthly game. The gospel is My eternal truth, and its power trumps even the greatest governmental policy. Jesus Christ is My eternal truth, and His death on the cross trumps even the greatest presidential candidates."

I can't really explain what happened that day. I was permanently and positively changed. I calmed my nerves, closed my eyes, and allowed what became a life-changing revelation from the inside out—not the politically charged outside-in—to begin a work in me that literally saved me from myself!

How had I traveled so far away from my real, legitimate calling? Paving the way for our children to inherit a wonderful country with liberty and freedom and justice for all had been a worthy endeavor, but balance had so long been missing from my "doing my part" and "playing my role" that I was completely consumed to the point of substituting the gospel for politics. Putting on political boxing gloves and beating people over the heads is only going to further drive in the wedge between their perceptions of what Christianity is and their being open to hearing the gospel, and I had done a fair amount of radio/media in which I talked openly about "what's wrong with all these folks who couldn't see the obvious problems in the world spelled out in front of their very eyes!" than I had talked about the gospel that may have potentially changed their hearts and worldview. People are *never* going to talk about what truly matters, when all they see are angry mobs out there waving flags, making demands, and waging wars against Washington. Legislation had my attention, while God had the back seat. Policies and tax concerns had caught my eye, while God remained on the sidelines. Freedoms within this lifetime and in my home country had filled my heart with concern, while the eternal liberties promised by God had been left for others to share with the lost world.

And then it occurred to me...

I had *decided* to immerse myself in politics. God didn't tell me to go that direction. I had never been close enough to Him to hear what He was calling me to do. I suddenly couldn't remember a single time that He had ever given me clear, concise direction that I was on the right track during those rough few years of activism. The Holy Spirit voice that was speaking to me now was not the same Joe-Ardis-conceived voice that spoke to me just after I had daydreamed about my daughter. That had stemmed from human reasoning. Now, this voice was clear, concise, and Divine...and it was telling me to *stop*!

"You have *replaced* your calling to spread the gospel in exchange for championing a political agenda," the still, small voice went on to say. "You've traded the gospel for standing on your own soap box, and now you're warring in a political arena of *men*, which is doomed to be infiltrated by sin and selfishness. You're at war with institutions for your children, when My plan all along was to use you as a soldier in the war against the principalities of darkness so that more might come unto Me."

187

I thought about all those times I had heard people cleverly refer to treating symptoms instead of the source of the problem. The *symptoms* of this country's fall from grace—and by extension its own political mess—traces back to the root, which is the concept that we are no longer "one nation, under *God.*" We can stand on soap boxes all day and enlighten our listeners with the radiation therapy that might temporarily fire them up to take complaints to the White House, but the cancer is our nation's godlessness, and the cure for this cancer is at the foot of the cross.

I have never seen a people so divided...so *divisible.* If suddenly our country were to return to a focus upon God, most areas of disagreement and radical arguing would take care of themselves, and we might once again shine as "one nation, under God, *indivisible.*"

If I had met that man who sent me the email threat under different circumstances, we might have been friends. He may have laughed at all my moronic jokes; he might have liked the same kinds of movies I liked; he may have had a personality that refreshingly complimented mine; he may have had a daughter of his own who could have played dolls with my little girl; he and I might have hit it off magnificently and become the best of friends; he might have really enjoyed my music, my *Christian* music, and been open to hearing what I had to say about Christ. Instead, he became an enemy of me and everything I stood for; instead, I showed him that a Christian man was willing to set God aside and preach the gospel of politics, feed from the trough of dispute, clobber those who disagreed with my righteous views while on radio, and rail against governments; instead, I obliterated any chance I ever had to lead him to the cross; instead, he and I were divided against one another, *divisible.*

Not only was I treating the symptoms of those whom I saw to be part of the problem, but I, myself, had become part of the problem. In my passion to better the finite proving grounds of men, I had stirred the pot of dissension and had drawn lines in the sand between myself and the potentially lost, and I had been a *terrible* example of Christ's character.

How grateful I am that the Holy Spirit spoke to me when and how He did.

What We Should All Strive to Become

Some of my closest friends today, including a list of names I connected with during my stretch of radical patriotism, believe that without our liberties, constitutions, etc., we will eventually lose our freedom of speech and therefore lose our ability to preach the gospel or openly live as men and women of faith. This expands into the ideology that you can't separate politics from religion. To a degree, that's true. We need stable and balanced politics to keep us liberated under man's law, and we need a relationship with God to keep us free from sin. But we cannot mandate morality or force men to be righteous, charitable, good natured, or loving because we've voted for the things that enforce that lifestyle any more than the government can tax a man's pocketbook a hundred dollars per month to support the needy and expect his gift to mean more than mere begrudging compliance to an earthly mandate.

So what is the answer? How can we become a nation that is truly "under God"?

We should *educate* ourselves and our children. We should be willing to think beyond our immediate needs and consider long-term implications each time we vote. We should know exactly who or what we are voting for and then proceed to do our duty, pull the lever, and vote at each and every opportunity. We should be a *thinking* people instead of an *impulsive* people, and not fall prey to the convincing—but potentially false—promises political campaigns plaster within our line of sight. And when something or someone appears too good to be true, it is our most patriotic duty to stop dead in our tracks and reconsider what we are about to stand for before we check that box on the card.

But, more than anything, we should love our fellow man. We should

189

not turn our pulpits into picket signs, create division between ourselves and others, and give in to the temptation to debate politics when a door may be opening to talk about the cross. Our most important war is not here on earth. We absolutely *must* turn our attention toward the cure for the cancer, and not toward the symptoms.

For when *hearts* are changed, legislation will follow.

So what should we strive to become?

Fishers of men *first*, American patriots *second*.

I believe that when you look at the current political atmosphere, especially in America, it is an incredible opportunity to reach people with the gospel. Our nation is heavily divided spiritually, morally, and ideologically. Today's generation is longing for answers, and they will never find the peace, joy, and stability they are looking for in a political figure, no matter how pure that person's intentions may be. People are looking for a Savior, so much so that a large percentage of our nation's population seems to be tuning out the specific plans, ideals, and social engineering that should define a good, moral leader, in the quest for someone who will simply make the promises that appeal to their sense of wants and desires. Perhaps a nation ripe and ready to receive an Antichrist? It is our job as believers to broadcast the wonderful news of Jesus Christ to everyone we have the opportunity to share His love with. Ephesians 6:12 says, "For we wrestle not against flesh and blood, but against principalities, against powers, against the rulers of the darkness of this world, against spiritual wickedness in high places." While I do hold out hope for a reconstituted representative government in the United States, Psalm 146:3 says, "Put not your trust in princes, nor in the son of man, in whom there is no help." People who hold positions of leadership and responsibility *should* be held accountable to the highest moral and ethical standards, yet each of these people live in a fallen state with a natural leaning toward selfishness and sin. When we place hope and faith in human beings, we set ourselves up for disappointment, fear, and anxiety. However, the Bible also promises, "If my people, which are called by my name, shall humble themselves, and pray, and seek my face, and turn from their wicked ways; then will I hear from heaven, and will forgive their sin, and will heal their land" (2 Chronicles 7:14).

With that, we may still have hope for a nation "under God, and indivisible."

chapter ten

<hr>

——————— WHEN ONCE WE WERE A NATION OF ———————
Creationists

By Sharon K. Gilbert

<hr>

We hold these truths to be self-evident, that all men are created equal, that they are endowed by their Creator with certain
unalienable Rights, that among these are Life, Liberty and the
pursuit of Happiness.
—UNITED STATES DECLARATION OF INDEPENDENCE

If today you can take a thing like evolution and make it a crime
to teach it in the public school, tomorrow you can make it a
crime to teach it in the private schools, and the next year you
can make it a crime to teach it to the hustings or in the church.
—CLARENCE DARROW, Day 2 of the Scopes Trial

T he world changed in 1776, when a small group of British rebels
proclaimed the "self-evident" truth of a Creator who endowed
all His creation with "unalienable" rights. Since the very name of this
book implies that the United States has radically shifted from its foundation, one presumed to be based on a divine Creator and not the descent
of man from lower species, it is important to first determine just how

firm—or infirm—our country's foundation actually was with regard to this essential belief.

As a born-again believer in Jesus Christ, and one who grew up in a conservative, Bible-based small town in Indiana, it was a shock to learn that the founders wrote from a philosophical and scientific framework radically skewed from my own. Philosophers in the eighteenth century embraced what they considered to be "enlightened" thought, which was in truth a twisted philosophical tree grown from a diabolical root. The Enlightenment—a quest to explain God's truths through science—produced men and women whose names echo throughout political and scientific history, but this insatiable thirst for "knowledge" commenced long before 1776.

Ancient Greek philosophers, including Aristotle, taught "essentialism," a philosophical and "scientific" belief that each and every part of creation is composed of essential elements unique to that type of plant or animal. This essential set of substances or elements, again unique to each particular species, is what defines it. Essentialism forms the bedrock for taxonomy, the science of categorizing every biological entity on earth—known in ancient times as "the great chain of being" or *the scala naturae* (Latin for "ladder of nature"), which presumes a Creator, but does not necessarily follow all biblical traditions. Essentialism does, however, by definition, prohibit evolution, since each species is considered to be discrete, and each reproduces "after its own kind," with offspring containing the same set of "essential elements" as the parent.

However, in 1735, a Swedish scientist named Carl Linnaeus reshaped and redefined the *scala naturae* into the *systema naturae* (system of nature), consisting of animal, mineral, and plant kingdoms. By shifting away from discrete entities (that is, a collection of unique and individual animals and plants that reproduce according to their essential elements), the Linnaeus hierarchy provides the basis for progressive alteration. It also removed humans from their position of superiority. Mankind was to now be included within the animal kingdom under mammalia and within that under the classification primates, which is nearly identical to today's taxonomical hierarchy, listing *Homo sapiens* as nothing more than a type of advanced primate.

Linnaeus' scientific publications and philosophies form a primary foundation stone in the Enlightenment pyramid of thought. Linnaeus influenced Jean-Jacques Rousseau, who denied original sin (despite being a Catholic) in favor of a philosophy of education and social structure that celebrates mankind's innate goodness (the noble savage). The ancient Greek notion of a *tabula rasa* (Latin for "blank slate") found revival in the Enlightenment period, when Rousseau published a study called *Emile* (banned in Paris and burned, which probably succeeded in making it more popular with social scientists), in which he proclaimed that all children began life with no knowledge or inherited inclination, and that each should be raised in nature and essentially allowed to choose their own subjects once commencing a formal education (in their early teens) with a tutor (Rousseau was not a fan of institutional education). In fact, Rousseau believed that society is what corrupts natural man, not original sin. I imagine he'd find the current day expression, "it's all good," a satisfying one when it comes to his theoretical pupils.

Linnaeus's taxonomy and scientific works had a major influence upon a man who may be unfamiliar to you, one Erasmus Darwin, the grandfather of Charles Darwin and Sir Frances Galton (Galton is considered to be the Father of Eugenics). If you've not heard of the elder Darwin before, then let me unpack his contributions to our modern eugenics and evolutionary thought dogma for you.

Erasmus Darwin, physician and philosopher, was a member of the Darwin-Wedgewood family in England. Josiah Wedgewood created the pottery dynasty (yes, it's *that* Wedgewood), but when his original partner died in 1780, Josiah asked his good friend Erasmus Darwin to help him run the business. The two families grew close and sealed the bond through marriage (Josiah's daughter Susanna to Erasmus' son Robert), and the fruit of this marriage was Charles Darwin.

Sir Francis Galton, Charles Darwin's cousin, also derived his existence on this earth from the friendship and eventual marital union of these two enlightened men. Sir Francis would have taken Rousseau to task on the subject of *tabula rasa,* for Galton believed each person was born with a fixed tendency toward behaviors, strengths, and weaknesses, depending on his blood heritage. His theories helped to inaugurate the English and American eugenics movements, and he even served as honorary president of the Eugenics Education Society.[168]

Ironically, the Wedgewood-Darwin family's descendants continued to intermarry with cousins in a process called consanguinity, which may have led to less fit generations. Even Charles Darwin suspected that his children's ailments might have been attributed to close interbreeding amongst the cousins. A recent study indicates that at least one mitochondrial defect may have lingered within the Wedgewood-Darwin family tree as a consequence.[169]

The close relationship between Erasmus and Josiah produced not only offspring of the human sort, but also a curious organization called "The Lunar Society" (sometimes called the "Lunarticks"), whose original founding five members included both men. Benjamin Franklin is said to have attended Lunar Society meetings.[170] The society's name derives from the time of the month when the club met, the first Monday that lay closest to the night of a full moon (hence the "Lunarticks" nickname). This is claimed to be their chosen night because they preferred to have a bright night on which to walk home (no street lights, I presume). Other notable members included James Watt (steam power inventor and the man for whom the electric "watt" is named), Joseph Priestly (discoverer of "fizzy water," so all those who love carbonated beverages owe much to him), Swiss inventor Argand (who pioneered the development of the balloon and the gas lamp—but whose work apparently couldn't help the members get home without a full moon), and even Thomas Jefferson and Benjamin Franklin, as mentioned above.

Based on Erasmus Darwin's writings, it's clear that this philosopher physician held deist beliefs, typical for those within the Enlightenment period:

> For instance, the ideas of the transfer of inherited characteristics and of a struggle for existence are already lively depicted in The Temple of Nature[171] [a reference to a work Darwin had previously published—a curious title, is it not?]. Darwin's evolutionary account of the origin of man did not cause him to doubt the existence of God as the **"Great Architect"** of the universe. In *Zoonomia* (vol. 1, sect. 1), he explained that God was the **"Great First Cause"** who infused spirit and life into the primal filament, thereby giving it the potential to evolve.[172] (emphasis and endnote for "Temple of Nature" added)

This idea of an architect or a "first cause" reveals a singular deist concept akin to the Divine Watchmaker notion. The Lunar Society's influence over Enlightenment thinking and the eventual cataclysmic shift from a belief in the Genesis creation account as rock-bed truth for Christians to one which pays little attention if any to a creative Genesis event or the concept of original sin is profound. And even when Erasmus Darwin's influence and interest faded, the Lunar Society's celestial influence did not wane, but rather the next leader kicked it up a notch:

The nature of the group was to change significantly with the move to Birmingham in 1765 of the Scottish physician William Small, who had been professor of Natural Philosophy at the College of William & Mary in Williamsburg, Virginia. **There he had taught and been a major influence over Thomas Jefferson,** and had formed the focus of a local group of intellectuals. **His arrival with a letter of introduction to Matthew Boulton from Benjamin Franklin** was to have a galvanizing effect on the existing circle, which began to explicitly identify itself as a group and actively started to attract new members.[173]

It's important to understand the philosophical bent of the deist with regard to America. It is true that our country's earliest settlers established colonies here as places of refuge from religious persecution, and most if not all believed in the inerrancy of the Bible in the original languages, but the long procession from Jamestown and Plymouth Rock to the signing of the Declaration of Independence and the construction of the U.S. Constitution, where "We the People" (not God Almighty) are first and foremost is certainly a harbinger of things to come, if not a radical paradigm shift. That being said, it is my personal belief that, despite what our governmental authorities and scientists might claim, the *citizenry* of our nation during the seventeenth, eighteenth, and nineteenth centuries were still primarily and fundamentally Christian in philosophy, and these dear souls would have balked at being called anything other than followers of Jesus Christ. Like Christians living today—and you who now read this book—these ancestral believers rested upon a Solid Rock, not shifting scientific sands. The deists who peppered the aristocratic leadership found this immoveable and intractable position to be disconcerting and intrusive. Deists, you see, believe in a God who doesn't really care much, so it is up to the individual to shape himself, and by derivation to shape God in their own image. It's a self-directed climb toward heaven. An autodidactic sacred scribbling on their own *tabulae rasae.*

In essence, a deist can do *whatever is right in his own eyes.*

Many now argue that the founders of our country, those who penned our "sacred texts" (the Declaration of Independence and the Constitution), actually espoused deist if not anti-theist philosophies (Franklin and Jefferson certainly hobnobbed with them in the Lunar Society). Reference to a Creator in the well-known opening to the Declaration (quoted in the opening to this chapter) is proof that these founders believed in some kind of designer, but that does not necessarily mean that their idea of a Creator God tracks with those of most Christians. Deists believe in a Creator, but he is an absent and disinterested "watchmaker" who started the world turning, who gave it a set of clockwork cosmic rules, and then skipped off to start again elsewhere. Deists were passionate about belief in such a God, but they also insisted upon a sort of libertarian brand of faith, one where each man gets to choose just how he wishes to define God.

In fact, one such revolutionist, Thomas Paine, known for his deist philosophies, said the following in 1787:

> It has been the error of schools to teach astronomy, and all the other sciences and subjects of natural philosophy, as accomplishments only; whereas **they should be taught theologically, or with reference to the Being who is the Author of them**: for all the principles of science **are of divine origin**. Man cannot make, or invent, or contrive principles; he can only discover them, and he ought to look through the discovery to the Author.... **Instead of looking through the works of creation to the Creator Himself, they stop short and employ the knowledge they acquire to create doubts of His existence.** They labor with studied ingenuity to ascribe everything they behold to innate properties of matter and jump over all the rest by saying that matter is eternal. And when we speak of looking through nature up to nature's God, we speak philosophically the same rational language as when we speak of looking through human laws up to the power that ordained them. **God is the power of first cause, nature is the law, and matter is the subject acted upon. But infidelity, by ascribing every phenomenon to properties of matter, conceives a system for which it cannot account and yet it pretends to demonstrate.**[174]

I've found references to this speech as a defense of Paine as a traditional Christian, but look again at the language. He insists only that God created the universe and (to Paine's mind) the clockwork of this world includes all the rules instilled within it by the Creator. Paine would have us look to an Intelligent Designer but no further. To the deist, mankind is now in charge of the earth as discoverer and arbiter of the laws imprinted upon it. In fact, deism taken to the extreme might even be defined as a brand of early Mormonism or even transhumanism, since this philosophy argues that each man achieves apotheosis through his own works (transhumanism or self-directed evolution) and then that "new god" moves on to create his own new world (and become its "god"). At the very least, it smacks of Russian cosmism, which grew up in that curious, transitional breeding ground between the nineteenth and twentieth centuries.

Here's what is curious about Paine's proclamation regarding the teaching and propagation of a Creator God in our society. In his pamphlet, *The Age of Reason*, Paine appears to say that no person can require another to follow a deity according to a set of rules:

> No one will deny or dispute the power of the Almighty to make such a communication, if he pleases. But admitting, for the sake of a case, that something has been revealed to a certain person, and not revealed to any other person, it is revelation to that person only. When he tells it to a second person, a second to a third, a third to a fourth, and so on, it ceases to be a revelation to all those persons. **It is revelation to the first person only, and hearsay to every other, and consequently they are not obliged to believe it.**[175] (emphasis added)

In that same publication, Paine also stated:

> Soon after I had published the pamphlet Common Sense, in America, I saw the exceeding probability that a revolution in the system of government would be followed by a revolution in the system of religion. **The adulterous connection of church and state, wherever it had taken place**, whether Jewish, Chris-

tian, or Turkish, had so effectually prohibited by pains and penalties, every discussion upon established creeds, and upon first principles of religion, that until the system of government should be changed, those subjects could not be brought fairly and openly before the world; but that **whenever this should be done, a revolution in the system of religion would follow. Human inventions and priestcraft would be detected;** and man would return to the pure, unmixed and unadulterated belief of one God, and no more. (emphasis added)

It's clear from this excerpt that Paine considered preaching the gospel to be an infringement of the listener's rights to make his choices regarding the practice of religion. Christians are called to preach and teach the gospel message to all. Priestcraft is akin to "human invention," Paine and most, if not all, true deists would tell us that Creationism is not a firm requirement for faith, and my insistence that all faith rests upon a literal interpretation of Genesis is little more than "human invention" and "hearsay."

Deism is a belief that a Creator did indeed precipitate all the known material universe through a divine cosmological event; however, this is the very basis upon which so-called Intelligent Design, which has become so popular today, rests. This is sometimes referred to as the Watchmaker theory, which presumes a nebulous "Creator" fashioned all the worlds at some point in the past (many believe this to have occurred billions of years ago), and then this Watchmaker, seeing His work as complete with sets of rules and a happy clockwork to keep it running, departs for greener pastures. This ambiguous tenet provides a massive launch pad for the current belief that humanity was either directly created by aliens or arose through a space seed accident sometimes called "panspermia." To paraphrase the famous "turtle" story—though the actual source of the phrase is up for debate (some say Bertrand Russell, others Joseph Berg)—the idea of a creator who had a creator who had a creator leads ultimately to "creators all the way down."

WHEN ONCE WE WERE A NATION

This erroneous interpretation of Genesis provides the loophole that evolutionists have used since the Enlightenment took root in antiquity (Genesis 3: "ye shall be as gods"), which then sprouted in the sixteenth-century world of "I think, therefore I am" (*Cogito ergo sum* in Latin), a summation of mankind's hubris given to us by Rene Descartes; flowered in the eighteenth century when Rousseau denied original sin and advocated the natural method to child-rearing, allowing the child to essentially raise himself and select his own way to go (rather than being reared *in the way he should go* by a parent or guardian); leading to the formation of the Lunar Society philosophies and Darwin-Wedgewood blood lines from which sprang Charles Darwin and Sir Francis Galton, whoin the nineteenth century, cultivated the Age of Reason into full maturity when it sowed the demonic seeds of modern eugenics and transhumanist thought.

However, lest you still think that Charles Darwin alone birthed the idea of a descent of man, allow me to include this excerpt from an 1801 Daniel Webster speech to Dartmouth College, called "On the Goodness of God as Manifested in His Work," which says this:

Even the infidel writer, of modern times, however, in the pride of argument they may have asserted it but believed or not, for they could not help perceiving that **if mankind with their inherently intellectual powers, and natural capacities for improvement, had inhabited this Earth for millions of years, the present inhabitants would not only be vastly more intelligent than we now find them, but there would be vestiges of the former races,** to be found in every inhabitable part of the Globe. Floods and Earthquakes notwithstanding; **Unless we adopt Lord Monboddo's** [a Scottish judge, philosopher, and deist] **supposition that Mankind were originally Monkeys,** it is impossible to admit the idea that they could have existed millions of years without making more discoveries & improvements than the early histories of nations warrant us to believe they had done.[176] (emphasis added)

Go, Daniel! The erroneous assumption that mankind evolved from a progression of lesser species was known to this eminent gentleman, and he clearly found its patently flawed philosophy to be anathema.

The latter part of the nineteenth century saw radical scientific changes in all western nations, particularly in the United States and England. The combustion engine replaced the horse. Electricity replaced gas and candle power. Telegraphy, radio, wireless communication, and telephony provided instantaneous communications for governments, militaries, and financiers. Revolution and work riots toppled governments and led to the First World War, and among these mighty shifts arose a singular new science called biology, the study of life.

My degree is in biology, and I chose to pursue this discipline because of my intense curiosity about and respect for God's intricate and beautiful creation. The science of biology is a relatively recent one, but the study of genetics (which formed the four-year core curriculum of my molecular biology concentration) is quite new. It began with the discovery of "colored bodies" in the human cell ("chromosome" means "colored body") as a means to explain inherited characteristics. This nascent science took further shape when Hugo de Vries and Carl Correns co-discovered Mendelian Inheritance patterns, or perhaps one might say re-discovered it, because the unearthing of Gregor Mendel's research in the early twentieth century proved *he* had actually been the first, so the eponymous monk is now credited with being the Father of Mendelian Genetics.

This simplistic theory of dominance and recession, helped along by the odd mutation, prompted eugenicists like Sir Francis Galton and David Starr Jordan to believe they might succeed in breeding a new and improved race of humans. This ignited a firestorm of scientific study, based partly on Charles Darwin and partly on Mendel, where men of science partnered with politicians to eliminate poverty, drunkenness, promiscuity, and feeble-mindedness from society via a program of positive eugenics (breeding—meaning they tell you who to marry) and negative eugenics (sterilization—bad luck, you don't get to breed, but rejoice since we're letting you live).

Genetics also provided a scientific means by which evolution might be forced into curricula. If colleges included eugenics (self-directed evolution), then secondary and primary schools would automatically follow suit, since educators in the sciences would certainly be swayed and influenced by their professors' opinions and in turn seek to influence their own pupils.

Following the publication of *The Descent of Man* in 1870, many theologians, preachers, and teachers, began to write and preach about what Christians perceived as the promulgation of a heresy into mainstream thought. However, the idea of any public school teaching evolution as an alternative to creation more than worried the American people (who as a whole still subscribed to the belief in a Creator, Adam and Eve, and original sin) and eventually led to the famous Tennessee law prohibiting the teaching of evolution in their schools and from there to the seminal test case that forever unhitched the U.S. public school system from Creation.

Known as the Scopes Monkey Trial, this legal battle began when the American Civil Liberties Union convinced a substitute teacher named John Scopes to "teach evolution" in defiance of the new law in Tennessee prohibiting it.

On March 13, 1925, the Tennessee House passed this law:

AN ACT prohibiting the teaching of the Evolution Theory in all the Universities, Normals and all other public schools of Tennessee, which are supported in whole or in part by the public school funds of the State, and to provide penalties for the violations thereof.

Section 1. *Be it enacted by the General Assembly of the State of Tennessee,* that **it shall be unlawful for any teacher in any of the Universities, Normals and all other public schools of the State which are supported in whole or in part by the public school funds of the State, to teach any theory that denies the story** of the Divine Creation of man as taught in the Bible, and to teach instead that man has descended from a lower order of animals.

Section 2. *Be it further enacted,* that any teacher found guilty of the violation of this Act, shall be guilty of a misdemeanor and upon conviction, shall be fined not less than One Hundred $ (100.00) Dollars nor more than Five Hundred $ (500.00) Dollars for each offense.

Section 3. *Be it further enacted,* That this Act take effect from and after its passage, the public welfare requiring it.[177] (emphasis added)

Almost immediately, the ACLU stepped in to test this new law, and the trial of the century (eclipsed later on by the O. J. Simpson trial, of course) commenced on July 20, 1925, in the sweltering heat of a Tennessee summer.

The 1920s were a wild time in the United States. Many older Americans had grown up in the Victorian age and watched with a mixture of awe and horror as the industrial revolution, Russian Revolution, World War I, and the Spanish Flu epidemic brought the entire world to the brink of ruin. Younger people reveled in the atmosphere of modernity and loose morals. Social debates over slavery, alcohol prohibition, women's rights, and science tore families apart, and the Scopes Trial further ruptured those families.

According to the University of Missouri at Kansas City website on the Scopes Trial, the entire dog-and-pony show (or one might better describe it as a "man-and-monkey show") was a setup:

The Scopes Trial had its origins in a conspiracy at Fred Robinson's drugstore in Dayton. George Rappalyea, a 31-year-old transplanted New Yorker and local coal company manager, arrived at the drugstore with a copy of a paper containing an

American Civil Liberties Union announcement that it was willing to offer its services to anyone challenging the new Tennessee anti-evolution statute. Rappalyea, a modernist Methodist with contempt for the new law, argued to other town leaders that a trial would be a way of putting Dayton on the map. **Listening to Rappalyea, the others—including School Superintendent Walter White—became convinced that publicity generated by a controversial trial might help their town**, whose population had fallen from 3,000 in the 1890s to 1,800 in 1925.

The conspirators summoned John Scopes, a twenty-four-year old general science teacher and part-time football coach, to the drugstore. As Scopes later described the meeting, Rappalyea said, "John, we've been arguing and I said nobody could teach biology without teaching evolution." Scopes agreed. "That's right," he said, pulling a copy of *Hunter's Civic Biology*—the state-approved textbook—from one of the shelves of the drugstore (the store also sold school textbooks). "You've been teaching 'em this book?" Rappalyea asked. Scopes replied that while filling in for the regular biology teacher during an illness, he had assigned readings on evolution from the book for review purposes. "Then you've been violating the law," Rappalyea concluded. **"Would you be willing to stand for a test case?"** he asked. **Scopes agreed. He later explained his decision: "the best time to scotch the snake is when it starts to wiggle."** Herbert and Sue Hicks, two local attorneys and friends of Scopes, agreed to prosecute.[178] (emphasis added)

Dayton, Tennessee, was a small town, but the entire nation—if not the entire world—watched the events that unfolded during that sleepy summer, thanks to the daily reports by "the Sage of Boston," reporter and satirist H. L. Mencken. Mencken, a German-American who opposed America's entry into World War I, sympathized with those who espoused eugenics and social Darwinism. In fact, according to an article at the *Los Angeles Times* in 1989, Mencken actually supported the Nazis during World War II:

> The previously secret diary of writer and social critic H. L. Mencken **discloses virulent anti-Semitism, racism and pro-Nazi leanings,** shocking even the sympathetic Mencken scholar who edited it.
>
> On Mencken's instructions, the diary, typewritten on 2,100 pages from 1930 to 1948, remained sealed for 25 years after his death in 1956. The *Baltimore Evening Sun*, where Mencken once worked, published excerpts Monday. The diary has been available to scholars since 1981, but quoting either directly or indirectly from the 2,100-page document was prohibited.
>
> On the subject of Jews, Mencken wrote in December, 1943, that the Maryland Club had **decided against admitting any more Jewish members after the only one on its rolls died. "There is no other Jew in Baltimore who seems suitable,"** he said.[179] (emphasis added)

This philosophical leaning toward race fitness and privilege may explain Mencken's keen interest in the Scopes case.

The players in this "trial of the century" included William Jennings Bryan, a three-time Democratic candidate for president (yes, he was an old-style Democrat in the days before these donkeys switched to elephant duds and became neo-conservatives), who led the charge to uphold the Tennessee law as the trial's prosecution attorney, but more to the point he wanted to defend the right of families to determine what their children learned in schools funded by public monies. Bryan had been spearheading a fundamentalist agenda across the nation to include anti-evolution laws, so now he led the defense on behalf of his outraged Christian constituency. Mencken referred to

Bryan as a "sort of fundamentalist Pope" (an odd choice of phrase that reveals the journalist's shallow understanding of fundamentalist Christian doctrine).

On the opposite side, Clarence Darrow chose to defend Scopes against the state, and claimed he could win. Darrow was coming into the trial fresh from Chicago's trial of the century (there seem to be a lot of these "trials of the century") in which teenage genius thriller killers Leopold and Loeb had been tried in 1924 for the kidnapping and murder of fourteen-year-old Bobby Franks.

If you're not familiar with this case, it is a tragic story of two young men with little to do but seek ways to heighten the thrill of life amidst their dull and privileged existence, even if it meant murder. Alfred Hitchcock's groundbreaking film *Rope* is based on this crime. Darrow had achieved notoriety and even infamy for agreeing to defend the two teenagers, and he saw the Scopes trial as another rung on the celebrity ladder, but more so as a means to further establish his own philosophical viewpoint in American schools:

> The Scopes case was a dream come true for Clarence Darrow. In his autobiography, *The Story of My Life*, [he] admits that as soon as heard William Jennings Bryan had joined the prosecution team, "at once I wanted to go." (SOL, 249) On a speaking tour in Richmond at the time, a confidant Darrow confided to a friend, "I believe I could bring him down." (Stone, 432) **The trial, as he saw it, provided the opportunity "to focus the attention of the country on the program of Mr. Bryan and the other fundamentalists in America." (SOL, 249) Religious "fanaticism," as he called it, threatened public education and the spirit of inquiry and skepticism that sustained civilization.** Darrow described the upcoming trial apocalyptically in remarks shortly after his arrival in Dayton: **"Scopes isn't on trial; civilization is on trial."**[180] (emphasis added)

Darrow himself made his position clear during the trial. He postured for the press and presented himself as the advocate for the people. His legal arguments echo and reverberate even today on issues far beyond human evolution and Creationism. The idea of a "slippery slope" is here presented by Darrow from Day 2 of the trial:

> If today you can take a thing like evolution and make it a crime to teach it in the public school, tomorrow you can make it a crime to teach it in the private schools, and the next year you can make it a crime to teach it to the hustings [author's note: "hustings" is an older term for political speechmaking or platforms from which such speeches are made] or in the church. At the next session you may ban books and the newspapers. Soon you may set Catholic against Protestant and Protestant against Protestant, and try to foist your own religion upon the minds of men. If you can do one you can do the other. Ignorance and fanaticism is ever busy and needs feeding. Always it is feeding and gloating for more. Today it is the public school teachers, tomorrow the private. The next day the preachers and the lectures, the magazines, the books, the newspapers. After while, your honor, it is the setting of man against man and creed against creed until with flying banners and beating drums we are marching backward to the glorious ages of the sixteenth century when bigots lighted fagots to burn the men who dared to bring any intelligence and enlightenment and culture to the human mind.
> —CLARENCE DARROW, Day 2, State of Tennessee vs John Scopes[181]

I suspect that Thomas Paine and other deists such as Erasmus Darwin and Francis Galton would heartily agree with much of Darrow's argumentative reasoning in that the esteemed attorney believed it completely wrong for one person to foist his opinion upon another. *However, by allowing evolution to be taught in schools as fact, isn't that precisely what educators are asked to do?* Once upon a time, America was indeed a nation of people who believed in Creationism. Our country, however, is not an island; it reflects societal shifts in other Anglophone countries, particularly in England. Eugenics and the new scientific imperative toward improving mankind through self-directed evolution could never have succeeded without a national decision on evolution in schools. Darrow was right in a way, restriction in one arena leads to restriction in all. We Christians have watched in horror as our rights have been stripped away to a bare-bones set of permissions.

The Scopes trial was the final nail in the coffin of Creationist thought and in many ways personal freedom in this nation. The wily Clarence Darrow chose to waive his right to make a final summation to the court (I suspect, he did this to prevent Bryan from having that privilege, for Tennessee law prohibited the prosecution from presenting a summation if the defense chose not to present one). However, William Jennings Bryan distributed copies of his summation to reporters, and so we have it for posterity. I can think of no better words to close out this chapter.

Mr. Bryan, would you care to offer your final remarks for this case?

Science is a magnificent force, but it is not a teacher of morals. It can perfect machinery, but it adds no moral restraints to protect society from the misuse of the machine. It can also build gigantic intellectual ships, but it constructs no moral rudders for the control of storm tossed human vessel. **It not only fails to supply the spiritual element needed, but some of its unproven hypotheses rob the ship of its compass and thus endangers its cargo.** In war, science has proven itself an evil genius; it has made war more terrible than it ever was before. Man used to be content to slaughter his fellow men on a single plane—the earth's surface. Science has taught him to go down into the water and shoot up from below and to go up into the clouds and shoot down from above, thus making the battlefield three times a bloody as it was before; but science does not teach brotherly love. Science has made war so hellish that civilization was about to commit suicide; and now we are told that newly discovered instruments of destruction will make the cruelties of the late war seem trivial in comparison with the cruelties of wars that may come in the future. **If civilization is to be saved from the wreckage threatened by intelligence not consecrated by love, it must be saved by the moral code of the meek and lowly Nazarene. His teachings, and His teachings, alone, can solve the problems that vex heart and perplex the world....**

It is for the jury to determine whether this attack upon the Christian religion shall be permitted in the public schools of Tennessee by teachers employed by the state and paid out of the public treasury. **This case is no longer local, the defendant ceases to play an important part. The case has assumed the proportions of a battle-royal between unbelief that attempts to speak through so-called science and the defenders of the Christian faith, speaking through the legislators of Tennessee. It is again a choice between God and Baal; it is also a renewal of the issue in Pilate's court....**

Again force and love meet face to face, and the question, "What shall I do with Jesus?" must be answered. A bloody, brutal doctrine—Evolution—**demands, as the rabble did nineteen hundred years ago, that He be crucified.** That cannot be the answer of this jury representing a Christian state and sworn to uphold the laws of Tennessee. Your answer will be heard throughout the world; it is eagerly awaited by a praying multitude. **If the law is nullified, there will be rejoice wherever God is repudiated, the savior scoffed at and the Bible ridiculed. Every unbeliever of every kind and degree will be happy.** If, on the other hand, the law is upheld and the religion of the school children protected, millions of Christians will call you blessed and, with hearts full of gratitude to God, will sing again that grand old song of triumph: "Faith of our fathers, living still, in spite of dungeon, fire and sword; O how our hearts beat high with joy Whene'er we hear that glorious word— Faith of our fathers—Holy faith; We will be true to thee till death!"

—WILLIAM JENNINGS BRYAN'S closing speech (never made), *State of Tennessee vs John Scopes*[182]

Thank you, Mr. Bryan. Those prescient remarks regarding the role of science and warfare have been proven all too true. Evolution has claimed victim after victim as human value has dropped precipitously, leading to abortion, self-loathing, and abandoned and abused children; and now propels us toward a dystopian future where those who can afford an upgrade will compete with those who cannot. Animals are elevated to a position equal or superior to humans, while human children lose their rights as they are proclaimed "not self-aware."

Once we were a nation—a people—who believed in Creation. It is to our shame that we have left the God of the Bible in legal limbo. Or worse, relegated Him to the back of the line.

Even so, Lord Jesus, come!

chapter eleven

—————WHEN ONCE WE WERE A NATION OF ———
Civil Liberties
By Sheila Zilinsky

The American way of life is in a war to the death. Not a war against nation, but a culture war. It is every bit as deadly as if we were outright attacked by a nation. America is being radically transformed at break neck speed as our most fundamental rights, to life, liberty and the pursuit of happiness, are under all-out assault. America was not the last bastion of freedom; it is the first and the only one. For that, it is under attack as it represents everything the Founding Fathers envisioned, a nation of free people under God. The steady derivation and stealthy erosion of civil liberties and rights across our nation over the past twenty years is the result of willful neglect and calculated design. Patrick Henry said, "We are not weak if we make a proper use of those means which God has placed in our power."

Today, incidents that would have caused our grandparents to be fighting in the streets barely cause us to bat an eye. Events that have already transpired and those on the horizon have deep significance for our personal lives and profound implications for our nation. Two hundred and forty years ago our forefathers, tired of royal oppression of their God-given rights, revolted against the British crown in 1776 and created the greatest country in the world, the United States of America. In 1776, there were many in the Continental Congress and throughout the colonies who were still not all that keen on breaking away completely from Britain. It wasn't until English seaman and schoolmaster, Thomas Paine, arrived in the colonies that, with the help of Benjamin Franklin, he a little pamphlet in which he set forth his views on the need for American independence from England. He called it *Common Sense.* In simple terms, it said the king was a brute, with no reasonable mandate to rule in England, let alone America; that England was a leech feeding off the back of American enterprise; and that it was time for the colonies to stand up and become a beacon of freedom for the world. The pamphlet electrified the country, selling a staggering five hundred thousand copies that were read by soldiers and politicians alike.

On June 7, 1776, Congress began to deal with the issue in earnest. Virginian Richard Henry Lee prepared a resolution that the colonies "are, and of a right ought to be, free and independent states." In the days to follow, the representatives appointed a committee of five to draft a formal declaration backing Lee's resolution. The group consisted of Benjamin Franklin, John Adams, a Connecticut lawyer named Roger Sherman, a New York iron mine owner named Robert Livingston, and a thirty-three-year-old red-haired lawyer from Virginia named Thomas Jefferson. Jefferson produced a document that has come to be regarded as one of the most eloquent political statements in human history declaring that "all men are created equal." On July 4, 1776, Congress formally adopted and signed the Declaration of Independence. The Declaration's most famous sentence reads: "We hold these truths to be self-evident, that all men are created equal, that they are endowed by their Creator with certain unalienable rights; that among these are life, liberty, and the pursuit of happiness." Even today, this inspirational language expresses a profound commitment to secure these rights, defining the system of limited government set forth by the Founders to protect the rights and freedoms with which all people are endowed by their Creator. These lines suggest that the whole purpose of government is to secure the people's rights, and that government gets its power from "the Consent of the Governed." If that consent is betrayed, then "it is the right of the people to alter or abolish" their government. When the Declaration was written, that was a radical statement; the premise that people could reject a monarchy and replace it with a republican government based on the consent of the people. The signers of the Declaration articulated principles that are still vital markers of American ideas and the commitment to protect civil liberty.

Americans are more rights-conscious and liberty oriented than the citizens of any other nation, past or present. It is what defines Americans as a free and open society in which diversity and difference are not only tolerated but actually encouraged. The Declaration of Independence heralded the birth of a nation on the sole basis that it was needed to secure the inalienable rights of the people to protect the individual from arbitrary governmental action and overreach.

Throughout history, there have been instances of trade-offs. America's commitment to civil liberties has been put to the test many times past. To name a few: the Alien and Sedition Acts of 1798 and 1918; the denial of habeas corpus relief during the Civil War; the massive relocation and internment of Japanese-Americans during World War II; the guilt by accusation of the McCarthy era; and the government's campaign of surveillance targeting opponents of the Vietnam War. These were driven by a perceived need to protect the United States against foreign adversaries or internal subversion. These ominous chapters of American history, especially those involving crackdowns against dissent, have almost always occurred during times of war or the "threat" of war. The protection of civil liberties rests upon the commitment of the American people to their fundamental law. To preserve liberty by trampling upon it is senseless. Taking away the civil liberties of some to protect us all seems like a reasonable trade-off to many, but the threat is much greater as it impinges upon the rights of far more persons than those under specific governmental scrutiny. Ben Franklin said, "Those who give up essential liberty to obtain a little temporary safety deserve neither liberty nor safety."

The USA Patriot Act

Consider the ubiquitous post-9/11 measures. Take the USA Patriot Act, short for this Orwellian mouthful: Uniting and Strengthening America by Providing Appropriate Tools Required to Intercept and Obstruct Terrorism Act of 2001. More than three hundred pages long, the law sailed through Congress with scant dissent only a short six weeks after the attacks. It was signed into law by President George W. Bush on October 26, 2001, and quickly became the quintessential salvo for government abuse and overreach. The Patriot Act undeniably expanded the government's surveillance and spying powers and the scope of criminal laws, and it marks the point at which preventive detention and limitations on subversive speech became commonplace. The Patriot Act amended many existing statutes, including immigration laws, banking laws, anti-money-laundering laws, and the 1978 Foreign Intelligence Surveillance Act (FISA), which set the groundwork for surveillance, collection, and analysis of intelligence gathered from foreign powers and agents of foreign powers, up to and including any individual residing within the United States who was suspected of involvement in potential terrorist activity. Under this sweeping legislation, the government can obtain intelligence surveillance orders that identify neither the person nor the facility to be tapped, conduct secret intelligence surveillance of U.S. and non-U.S. persons who are not affiliated with a foreign organization, engage in dragnet surveillance of emails sent in the United States, search your home without your permission, demand your information from telephone, Internet, and credit card companies without your knowledge, label you a "terrorist," monitor what Internet sites you visit, and take away your property without a hearing. And here's the kicker: The government can put you in jail indefinitely. Yes, indefinitely.

Warrantless Wiretapping

Soon after the September 11, 2001, terrorist attacks, President George W. Bush issued an executive order that authorized the infamous National Security Agency (NSA) warrantless wiretapping program. This secret eavesdropping program allowed the surveillance of certain telephone calls placed between a party in the United States and a party in a foreign country without obtaining a warrant through the Foreign Intelligence Surveillance Court. In December 2005, the *New York Times* reported that the National Security Agency was eavesdropping on telephone calls between people in the United States and associates in foreign nations. Under an ongoing program, the NSA was monitoring calls even without obtaining a FISA warrant either in advance or retroactively. Bush had secretly authorized the program, claiming that the Constitution afforded him broad, inherent powers that superseded legislation like FISA. Bush repeatedly cited new post 9/11 legal assertions he claimed authorized him to use force in combating terrorism. Despite the president's sweeping assertions, a U.S. District Court judge found the NSA wiretapping program to be illegal and unconstitutional under the First and Fourth amendments, and ordered warrants to be obtained for all wiretaps, including warrantless wiretaps of American citizens. However, despite the judge's ruling, there continue to be countless cases of U.S. corporations that have cooperated with the NSA by providing it with data, including e-mail and telephone communications between persons in the United States, as well as between abroad.

The TSA

If you think it's bad enough that the government eavesdrops on your phone calls and reads your emails, consider now your family members being abhorrently groped before boarding a plane. Before 9/11, airport security in the United States was a private enterprise. It was handled by companies under contract with government, and security proced- ures were largely standardized, with metal detectors and other measures common to all major airports and carriers. Passengers were required to submit to searches of their persons and property as a condition of buying their tickets and boarding their flights. In 2001, Bush signed the Aviation and Transportation Security Act, which authorized the Transportation Department to federalize airport security. The depart- ment created the Transportation Security Administration (TSA), which oversees security for highways, railways, mass transit, ports, and domes- tic airports. In 2003, the TSA was placed under the new Homeland Security Department. The TSA, which today employs more than fifty thousand screeners, has been criticized by air travelers and civil liber- ties groups alike. Many of the complaints have developed into lawsuits concerning privacy issues, but they have been largely unsuccessful. The Fourth Amendment generally protects Americans from searches of their persons or property without warrants; however, the courts have granted wider and wider latitude to government agents under the guise of ter- rorism and other crime prevention. Random searches are allowed under certain circumstances, and law enforcement officials are given the bene- fit of the doubt in identifying probable cause for any specific search in light of their specialized training. Passengers are also now subject to random additional searches if deemed necessary. A no-fly list of suspected terrorists had been in use prior to 9/11, but was greatly expanded post 9/11. While the list had fewer than twenty names prior to September 11, 2001, CBS' *60 Minutes* claimed that a March 2006 copy had forty-four thousand names and hundreds of false identifications in which individuals are delayed or prevented from flying because their names are similar to those on the list. Following a lawsuit brought by the ACLU in 2004, the government agreed to release details of how the list was compiled and used, and it was discovered the Patriot Act was severely limiting the constitutional rights of US citizens and Immigrants alike. The Act permitted both citizens and non-citizens to be jailed based on mere suspicion without charges and detained indefinitely. It broadened the definition of activities considered "deportable offenses," including defining soliciting funds for an organization that the government labels as "engaging in terrorist activity." The Patriot Act additionally expanded the ability of law enforcement to conduct secret searches and engage in phone and Internet surveillance, and gave law enforcement access to personal medical and financial records, etc.

The National Defense Authorization Act

It wasn't just George W. who was a disaster to American Civil Liberties, issuing 291 executive orders over eight years. Obama has also issued 184 orders so far in his presidency. The damage done under Obama's tenure will be felt for decades to come. Consider the National Defense Authorization Act (NDAA), signed into United States law on December 31, 2011, by Barack Obama. This pernicious law poses one of the greatest threats to civil liberties in all of United States history. Under Section 1021 of the NDAA, foreign nationals who are alleged to have committed or who are merely "suspected" of sympathizing with or providing any level of support to groups the U.S. designates as terrorist organizations or an

WHEN ONCE WE WERE A NATION

affiliate or associated force may be imprisoned without charge or trial "until the end of hostilities." It has no parameters or timetable, and can be used by authorities to detain (forever) anyone the government considers a threat to national security and stability—potentially even demonstrators and protesters exercising their First Amendment rights. The astonishing part is that the NDAA's draconian detention provisions, which include American citizens, are an affront to everything our nation's founders fought for. It is indeed a threat to the inalienable due-process rights afforded to every American citizen under the Constitution.

Spying, Surveillance, and Data Mining

Government secrecy and privacy infringement are the order of the day. The top-secret world the government created in response to the perceived War on error has become so large, so unwieldy, and so secretive that it is truly astonishing in every sense of the word. It is cleverly hidden under the guise of "sensitive" and "classified." Perhaps the greatest assault on the privacy of the ordinary American is the rapid expansion of data collection, storage, tracking, and data mining. Privacy is supposed to be an essential right, yet no one bats an eye while our right to privacy is being trampled and expunged. Americans who claim they'd defend this right to the death apathetically shrug their shoulders while the powers that be hack, track, and attack us. Intrusive government surveillance powers have grown more powerful and more secretive. Often the surveillance takes place with no or little oversight by the courts or by the public. Government agencies—including the FBI and the Department of Defense—have conducted their own spying on innocent and law-abiding Americans. The sweeping legislation includes tracking cell phone service, Internet records, and email. Data retention legislation has dangerously expanded the government's ability to monitor its citizens, damage privacy, and chill freedom of expression.

The CEOs of Facebook and Google have both said essentially the same thing: The age of privacy has ended. Get over it. Internet companies sell personal data for profit, often by using cookies on our computers to track activity. Facebook sold users' video rental records. Google pulled Americans' personal information via WiFi when it created Street View. Apple iPhones were tracking and storing their owners' movements. The government is already using corporate data, many times without subpoenas. Corporations have voluntarily allowed the government to use their technology to spy on citizens. With smart devices and smart grid, we are being data mined into oblivion. Store smart-saver cards are used to collect data about the items we buy. Smart TVs, smart phones and computers watch us.

Today, the government is spying on Americans in ways the founders of our country never could have imagined. George Orwell's *1984* is playing out more like a newspaper than a dystopic novel from the 1940s. The FBI, federal intelligence agencies, the military, state and local police, and private companies are gathering incredible amounts of personal information about ordinary Americans that can be used to construct vast dossiers that can be widely shared with a simple mouse click. The fear of terrorism has led to a new era of overzealous police intelligence activity against political activists and religious minorities.

This surveillance activity is not directed solely at suspected terrorists and criminals. It's directed at all of us. Increasingly, the government is engaged in suspicion-less surveillance that tracks sensitive information about innocent people. The U.S. Department of Homeland Security claims that its agents have the right to look though the contents of a traveler's electronic devices, laptops, cameras, and cell phones, and to keep the devices or copy the contents in order to continue searching them once the traveler has been allowed to enter the U.S., regardless of whether the traveler is suspected of any wrongdoing. Reports indicate that as many as one million travelers, nearly half of whom are American citizens, were subjected to electronic device searches at the border between 2008 and 2014. The Federal Bureau of Investigation can now dig through and search our trash and even examine our databases at will. The government can also monitor and record prescription drug use by all citizens via "Prescription Drug Monitoring Programs." A plethora of other intrusive surveillance programs allow the U.S. government to store vast amounts of data about our private activities—everything from domestic telephone calls to travel activities.

The 2005 Real ID Act rammed through Congress enacted the 9/11 Commission's recommendation that the federal government "set standards for the issuance of sources of identification, such as driver's licenses." The Act establishes minimum security standards for state-issued driver's licenses and identification cards and prohibits federal agencies from accepting for official purposes licenses and identification cards from states that do not meet these standards. States have considerably pushed the Real ID agenda. Under the law, states are required to standardize their driver's licenses and link to databases to be shared with every federal, state, and local government official in every other state. Real ID requires people to verify legal residence in the U.S. in order to get a driver's license, permits secret deportation hearings and trials, reduces judicial review of deportation orders, and makes non-citizens, including long-time permanent residents.

The use of Biometric ID national identity cards, RFID chips, and the collection of biometric identification continues to grow around the world. Various endeavors in many countries are seeking to promote RFID technology and biometric identification. According to a report in 2014 by Acuity Market Intelligence, it was estimated that in five years, roughly half of the world population will be registered with national biometric identification cards. The program has already been well underway in many countries for years now, and it continues to grow. The surveillance state not only grows inexorably, but so does the secrecy and unaccountability behind which it functions.

The results of this mindset are as clear as they are disturbing. A

three-part *Washington Post* series entitled "Top Secret America" provided a clear picture of what is now crystal clear: We live under a
surveillance system so vast and secretive that nobody—not even those
within the system—knows what it does or how it functions. Among
the series' more illustrative revelations: "Every day, collection systems
at the National Security Agency intercept and store 1.7 billion e-mails,
phone calls and other types of communications." To call that an out-of-
control, privacy-destroying surveillance state is to understate the case.
What makes this Big Brother mammoth particularly odious is that it
does not even supply the very security it claims to invoke. It actually
does just the opposite. As many surveillance experts have repeatedly
argued, the more secret surveillance powers we give the government,
the more unsafe we become.

Perhaps the most disturbing aspect of our leviathan surveillance
state is that the bulk of its actions are carried out not just by shad-
owy government agencies, but by large private corporations that are
beyond the reach of democratic accountability. It is accurate to view
the U.S. government and these huge industry interests as one gigantic,
amalgamated, inseparable entity. In every way that matters, the separation between government and corporations is nonexistent. As the
NSA scandal revealed, private telecom giants and other corporations
now occupy the central role in carrying out the government's domestic surveillance and intelligence activities—almost always in the dark,
beyond the reach of oversight or the law. The Surveillance State thus
provides its own fuel and own rationale to ensure its endless expansion,
all while resisting any efforts to impose transparency or accountability
on it. We've gotten so used to the security trade-off that it's worth
reminding ourselves that surrendering privacy does not make us more
secure. Systems of surveillance can themselves be a major source of
insecurity. Benjamin Franklin once said: "Those who would give up
essential Liberty, to purchase a little temporary Safety, deserve neither
Liberty nor Safety."

Freedom of Religion and Expression.

The First Amendment to the United States Constitution prohibits the making of any law respecting an establishment of religion, impeding the free exercise of religion, abridging the freedom of speech, infringing on the freedom of the press, interfering with the right to peaceably assemble, or prohibiting the petitioning for a governmental redress of grievances. It was adopted on December 15, 1791, as one of the ten amendments that constitute the Bill of Rights. There are primary reasons why freedom of expression, which encompasses speech, the press, assembly, and petition, is essential to a free society, namely that freedom of expression is the foundation of self-fulfillment. Self-expression is vital to the attainment and advancement of knowledge. The right of individuals to express their thoughts, desires, and aspirations, and to communicate freely with others affirms the dignity and worth of every member of society. The First Amendment is under attack in America like never before, and it is being destroyed by death from a thousand cuts.

On the one hand, the disciples of "political correctness" want to make all forms of speech that are "offensive" to anyone against the law. On the other hand are those obsessed with "national security" who want to ban all speech that is critical of the U.S. government. These twin forces are constantly seeking to push the First Amendment into a smaller and smaller box. If you say the wrong thing in America today, your website might be shut down, you could be fired, suspended from school, or even arrested and shipped off without a trial. Conservative Christians and pro-Second Amendment groups are being ubiquitously targeted for their speech. Instead of seeing the value in allowing everyone to say what he or she thinks, we are being taught in America today that there is speech that is "acceptable" and speech that is "unacceptable." Obama's unconstitutional reign of lawlessness plans to continue to rack up notches in its belt for every way it can manage to silence dissent, aka "free speech."

A recent CNN article quoted government officials saying that "domestic terror groups" are a greater threat to America than ISIS or al Qaeda. By "terror groups," of course, they aren't referring to the over twenty-two confirmed terrorist jihad camps in the United States belonging to a Pakistan Muslim Brotherhood and Al Qaeda-related branch. No, they are referring to anyone who criticizes the government or its agenda. There is an entire manual dedicated to dealing with "Right-Wing Extremists" that has been around for some time. As Geoffrey R. Stone, a professor of law at the University of Chicago and chairman of the American Constitution Society, wrote in the *New York Times* on January 2011: "The so-called Shield bill, now introduced in both houses of Congress in response to the WikiLeaks disclosures, would amend the Espionage Act of 1917 to make it a crime for any person knowingly and willfully to disseminate, 'in any manner prejudicial to the safety or interest of the United States,' any classified information 'concerning the human intelligence activities of the United States.'" In addition, the government is curbing free speech by prohibiting an expansive right of others to disseminate information to the public. The Stop Online Piracy Act and the Protect Intellectual Property Act would give the U.S. government the ability to shut down literally millions of websites. The U.S. Department of Justice has authority that would require Internet companies to retain data and records of user activity online posing a grave threat to free speech and the freedom of the Internet. Hillary Clinton recently said that certain "political, cultural, and religious beliefs" are obstacles to promoting alternative lifestyles around the world and therefore must not be tolerated. Loretta Lynch, the U.S. attorney, told attendees at a Muslim Advocates Dinner in December 2105 that the Justice Department will take action against "anti-Muslim rhetoric" and "violent talk." She went on to say, "Now obviously this is a country that is based on free speech, but when it edges towards violence, when we see the potential for someone lifting that mantle of anti-Muslim rhetoric or, as we saw after 9/11, violence against individuals...when we see that, we will take action." These are only a few examples of how free speech is being "not tolerated."

Freedom of religion is just as vehemently under attack. Take the case in Colorado, where a baker was ordered to make wedding cakes for same-sex couples, trumping his religious objections to the practice. Surprisingly, in our once-Christian nation, courts have now ruled that it is unconstitutional to use the name of "Jesus Christ" during certain official government meetings. In Texas, the Department of Veteran Affairs tried to ban prayers that include the words "God" or "Jesus" during funeral services for veterans. The government is also using laws to crush dissent. We have seen case after case of law enforcement authorities brutally dragging female protesters to the ground by their hair. Over and over we see authorities using brutality and force against citizens and using pepper spray, tear gas, rubber bullets, and flash-bang stun grenades against protesters. Whenever government gains the power to decide who can speak and what can be said, the First Amendment rights of all of us are in danger of being violated. But when all people are allowed to express their views and ideas, the principles of democracy and liberty are enhanced. As Ron Paul says, "We don't have freedom of speech so we can talk about the weather. We have the First Amendment so we say controversial things." Without the uninhibited exchange of ideas, even those that give offense, all other freedoms are of little value. Somewhere along the way we have compromised this essential and inalienable right for the illusion of faux societal harmony.

The Right to Keep and Bear Arms

A well-regulated militia, being necessary to the security of a free state, the right of the people to keep and bear arms, shall not be infringed.

—THE SECOND AMENDMENT TO THE UNITED STATES CONSTITUTION

At the point of the triangle-shaped Lexington Green battlefield can be found one of the most celebrated American symbols: sculptor Henry Hudson Kitson's statue of Captain John Parker, who commanded the Minutemen Militia on April 19, 1775. On that day and at that place, the opening salvo was fired in the American war for independence. The Minuteman statue captures the essence of an armed, free citizenry. It also symbolizes the inescapable connection between the right of Americans to bear arms and our national independence. The iconic symbol is therefore an affront to the sensibilities of those who believe that "peace" and "security" are best preserved through disarmament not only of Americans but civilians worldwide. The clash of arms at Lexington Green and Concord's North Bridge was triggered by the world's mightiest power attempting to seize weapons and bring their weapons under the government's control. Captain John Parker's Minutemen and Lieutenant Colonel Francis Smith's Redcoats fought a battle over the issue of disarmament. It was the intention of the British imperial power to disarm the Americans that provided the impetus for America's war for independence. The logic of gun prohibition dictates that the best way to fight crimes committed with firearms is to focus on the weapon rather than the criminal. This in turn leads to restriction on the liberties of the law-abiding which supposedly will help prevent crimes committed by the lawless. Many Americans are wearily familiar with these policies that play such a prominent role in our domestic debate over what is misleadingly called "gun control." These fallacies are being enforced by the United Nations' global gun grab with this ominous twist: Americans are being told that the right to keep and bear arms must be abolished in order to prevent crimes committed by foreign regimes' terrorist and crime syndicates. Those who see government as a benevolent parent looking out for our best interests are sadly duped. To those who see the government as inherently corrupt, the Second Amendment is a means of ensuring that the populace will always have a defense against threats to their freedoms. The U.S. government has adopted a "do what I say, not what I do" mindset when it comes to Americans' rights overall. Nowhere is this double standard more evident than in the government's attempts to arm itself to the teeth, all the while viewing as suspect anyone who dares to legally own a gun, let alone use one. A provision in a Washington State bill authorizes police to search and inspect gun owners' homes yearly. Connecticut has adopted a law banning the sale of large-capacity magazines and assault weapons. And a New Jersey legislature would reduce the number of bullets an ammunition magazine could hold from fifteen to ten. These are just a few examples in addition to the vilification of anyone seeking mental health treatment—no matter how benign—and finding themselves entered into the FBI's criminal background check system, joining the ranks of some 175,000 veterans who have been barred from possessing firearms based solely on the fact that they received psychiatric treatment through the Department of Veterans Affairs. Concurrent to this is an all-out draconian police state. The government's efforts to militarize and weaponize its agencies and employees is reaching epic proportions, with federal agencies such as the Department of Homeland Security and the Social Security Administration placing orders for hundreds of millions of rounds of hollow-point bullets. Moreover, under the auspices of a military "recycling" program involving the acquisition of military-grade weaponry and equipment, more than $8 billion worth of equipment has been transferred from the Defense Department to domestic police agencies since 1990. Included in the government's arsenal are tank-like, twenty-ton Mine Resistant Ambush Protected (MRAP) vehicles, tactical gear, and assault rifles. Also included in its arsenal are armed surveillance Reaper drones capable of reading a license plate from over two miles away, assault weapons that can shoot five 12-gauge shells per second and can fire up to nine thousand rounds without being cleaned or jamming, ADAPTIV invisibility cloaks that can make a tank disappear, PHASR rifles capable of blinding and disorienting anyone caught in its sights; Taser shockwave weaponry that can electrocute a crowd of people at the touch of a button, enhanced sniper rifles with built-in sound and flash suppressors that can hit a man-sized target nine out of ten times from over a third of a mile away; and grenade launchers that can be programmed to accurately shoot grenades at a target up to five hundred meters away. These are just a few items in the government's arsenal of weapons, which makes the average American's handgun look like a Tinkertoy©. We have overlooked the most important and most consistent theme throughout the Constitution that was intended to be a clear shackle on the government's powers. The Second Amendment reads as a clear rebuke against any attempt to restrict the citizenry's gun ownership. The Constitution is not neutral. It was designed to take the government off the backs of people. In other words, it thwarts government overreach. The freedoms enshrined in the Bill of Rights in their entirety stand as a bulwark against a police state. To our detriment, these rights have been steadily weakened, eroded, and undermined in the past two decades. Without the Second Amendment right to own and bear arms, we are that much more vulnerable to the vagaries of out-of-control police state, malevolent dictators, genuflecting politicians, and overly ambitious bureaucrats. Gun control and gun rights advocates obviously have very different views about whether guns are a force for violence or for good. It is hard to read the Second Amendment and not honestly conclude that the framers of the Constitution intended gun ownership to be an individual right. It is true that the amendment begins with a reference to militia: "A well-regulated militia, being necessary to the security of a free state, the right of the people to keep and bear arms, shall not be infringed." Accordingly, it is argued, this amendment protects the right of the militia, not the individual, to bear arms. More important, the mere reference to a purpose of the Second Amendment does not alter the fact that an individual right is created. The right of the people to keep and bear arms is stated in the same way as the right to free speech or free press. The statement of a purpose was intended to reaffirm the power of the states and the people against the central government. At the time, many feared the federal government and its national army.

Gun ownership was viewed as a deterrent against abuse by the government, which would be less likely to mess with a well-armed populace. As twentieth-century libertarian Edmund A. Opitz observed in 1964, "No one can read our Constitution without concluding that the people who wrote it wanted their government severely limited; the words 'no' and 'not' employed in restraint of government power occur 24 times in the first seven articles of the Constitution and 22 more times in the Bill of Rights." The Second Amendment's statement of the right to bear arms serves as a check on the political power of the ruling authorities. It represents an implicit warning against governmental encroachments on one's freedoms, the warning shot over the bow to discourage any unlawful violations of our persons or property. As such, it reinforces that necessary balance in the citizen-state relationship. As George Orwell noted, "That rifle hanging on the wall of the working-class flat or labourer's cottage is the symbol of democracy. It is our job to see that it stays there."

Conclusion

The loss of rights happens gradually. The steady decline of our liberties over the last twenty years has, sadly, been a case of the frog in the boiling water. We are slowly acclimated to giving up one right at a time, one freedom at a time. Today, we shrug off things our nation's founders would have never tolerated. Little by little, one right at a time slips away and, once established, tomorrow, that same authority becomes a basis for ignoring the entire Bill of Rights. One step at a time, with each step being justified by the noblest rhetoric, our freedom is lost forever. The war on perceived or real terrorism poses an indefinite threat to civil liberties. There never will be a formal end to it, so the loss of liberties it entails will seemingly continue forever. In his book, *All the Laws But One—Civil Liberties in Wartime*, author William Rehnquist advanced the thesis that civil liberties are restricted in wartime, but then restored after the completion of the wars. The widespread assumption since September 11, 2001, has been that this pattern would be followed once again, that the loss of liberties would be temporary, yet not one repressive action has been backed off of. Our Founding Fathers endowed with us a heck of a trust fund—not in gold, but in protection for our God-given rights. The Bill of Rights and the Constitution are not granters of our liberty; rather they are guardians of it. They knew when writing these documents the effects of big government. They knew the importance of having the right to defend one's self, the right to free speech, the right to own property, and the right to trial by one's peers. They didn't know this because they had them, but because at one time they *didn't* have them. They understood the effect a tyrannical dictator or ruthless king can have on a life. America has become the country it is today not because of a massive government, but because of its denial of massive government. America still is the greatest country in the world, but it is losing what made it great. Religious liberty and fiscal freedoms are slipping away from us faster than at any other time in history, and the silence is deafening. Paine's impassioned plea in 1776 didn't just foreshadow much of the substance of the Declaration of Independence, but it ignited a spark in the hearts of people. His urging of a new beginning in the struggle for freedom was distinguished not only by his ideas, but more importantly by his passion—a fervent passion that heartened Washington's despondent army and countless others. The father of modern conservatism, Edmund Burke, once said, "The only thing necessary for the triumph of evil is for good men to do nothing." Consider the words of John Hancock, one of the signers of the Declaration of Independence, urging, "I conjure you, by all that is dear, by all that is honorable, by all that is sacred, not only that ye pray but that ye act." One is left with the question: Why haven't we acted? Freedom comes at a price. We choose freedom or slavery. When signing the Declaration, America's founders pledged to each other their lives, fortunes, and sacred honor. Hundreds of thousands more have made the supreme sacrifice to protect our liberties and freedoms with their passion, blood, sweat, and tears—and even their very lives. If we do not do the same, our once-great nation, our liberties, and our prosperity will be perhaps lost forever. To God and to our children we are each accountable.

chapter twelve

————————— WHEN ONCE WE WERE A NATION OF —————————
Industry
By Cris Putnam

I turned fifty this year. That is half a century and nearly one-fourth as old the United States. I recall when the American Freedom Train exhibit visited my hometown in 1976, our nation's Bicentennial. I got to see George Washington's copy of the U.S. Constitution, the original Louisiana Purchase, and even the dress Judy Garland wore in my favorite movie *The Wizard of Oz*. Back then, I was a patriotic Cub Scout and the enemy in my assortment of G.I. Joe toys was a German Nazi Stormtrooper. Hogan's Heroes, a lampoon of the bumbling Nazis, was one of the best shows to watch on the three (sometimes four with the new attachable circle antenna adjusted just right)-channel television with a big dial and no remote. I watched the first Apollo missions and the Vietnam War on an electron cannon called a cathode ray tube designed to fire electrons through a phosphorescent screen. It was the first time a war was covered with live video feeds, and I remember Walter Cronkite, cigarette in hand, warning parents to make small children leave the room. The first time my dad didn't make me leave the room, I saw a man get cut down by machine gun fire and many wounded, confused-looking young men. Back then, they were all lauded as heroes to us boys. I remember wondering if I would be drafted when I turned eighteen.

But our nation is not what it was then. In the year I was born, 1965, manufacturing accounted for 53 percent of the American economy. The words "Made in America" meant something about the quality of the products they described because American workers famously took pride in their work. However, now, very few consumer goods are made domestically. I'm afraid my G.I. Joe wouldn't like what goes on in Washington today, but, unfortunately, the Nazi action figure might approve. Not that long ago, it became widely known that some of the Army's standard-issue black berets were being made in China. Swiftly engaging in the damage-control mode, Deputy Defense Secretary Paul Wolfowitz recalled the Asian-made berets and ordered them destroyed.[183] Heaven forbid! If we faced a threat from the nuclear-armed remnant of Soviet-era communism, China, American soldiers might have to defend us deprived of proper headwear. Though I write that somewhat musingly, the potential loss of the manufacturing sector of our economy has more ominous implications than expressed by the media-savvy sound bites offered by politicians. In terms of economic ramifications, the existential threat to the middle class is very serious.

The sharp decline in manufacturing is not just an economic trend; it touches many of us personally. For example, members of my extended family in rural western North Carolina lost their jobs in textile mills and furniture plants, which meant the bills weren't always paid on time and vacations were canceled. Even so, the cheaply produced goods were purchased by the freighter load by major retailers because they are highly profitable. As more jobs moved to the Far East, small local retailers like Stamey's in Fallston, North Carolina, were replaced by Walmart Supercenters. Around that time, my Dad, an engineering executive for a large American firm, used to say things like, "If we were as smart as the Founding Fathers, we would throw our own tea party by pushing Toyotas into the ocean." But I doubt anyone ever will. Although there is a consensus that outsourcing hurts the overall economy, who doesn't want to save money? After all, economic theory seems arcane to many folks and, more disturbingly, many young people probably don't understand why the archenemy of my G.I. Joe was a German Stormtrooper.

According to data published by the Bureau of Labor Statistics, the number of manufacturing jobs peaked in 1979 with 19,676 citizens employed (not adjusted for seasonal workers). At that time, those hard-working Americans made up over half of the U.S. economy. During the seventies, the number of jobs was relatively the same, but the workforce grew enough to decline slowly. By the time I was in college, manufacturing had shrunk to 39 percent of the workforce, but the changeover to the second millennium was devastating. From 2000 to 2001, America lost more than 1.2 million manufacturing jobs, making it one of the single worst years for unemployment in the past two decades. By 2004, it accounted for a mere 9 percent.[184] According to *The Economist*, "For the first time since the Industrial Revolution, fewer than 10 percent of American workers are now employed in manufacturing."[185] In fact, 42,400 factories have closed down since 2001.[186] When the Big Three automakers—Ford, Chrysler, and General Motors—admitted they were in danger of collapse and the Great Recession of 2008 set in, it seemingly marked the demise of the once proudly displayed slogan, "Made in America." Today, the G.I. Joe American kids want for Christmas is made by Hasbro's plant in Taiwan.[187]

Arguably, the Cold War or *arms race* against the USSR was won by America's more productive industrial output. In a very real sense, it was a manufacturing contest that cost the Soviets when their economy imploded under the economic pressure to keep pace. The term "cold" denotes that there was no direct combat between the two sides, although there were proxy wars—meaning "indirect," like when the U.S. fought the Soviet-supplied Viet Cong in Vietnam or when the USSR battled the Taliban, equipped by America, in Afghanistan. But during the Cold War (1947–1991), we still made most of our own weapons as well as supplied our enemy's enemies and, for ethical reasons, even the most miserly supply officer wouldn't contemplate outsourcing officially sanctioned apparel to China and Sri Lanka, Romania, Canada, and South Africa.[188] G.I. Joes and Army berets aside, the Big Three make a more pertinent example. Their car plants were turned into the most massive war machine the world had ever known, producing almost two-thirds of the Allied military equipment: 297,000 aircraft, 193,000 artillery pieces, 86,000 tanks, and 2 million army trucks.

Ford Motor Company's vast Willow Run plant in Ypsilanti, Michigan, ran twenty-four hours a day, assembling 1,550,000 parts every sixty-three minutes into a B-24 Liberator long-range bomber designed by Consolidated Aircraft in California to have longer ranges.[189] General Motors made airplane engines, tanks, guns, and trucks, Chrysler made airplane fuselages. After the war, the American auto industry soared, eventually building cool muscle cars like the Ford Shelby Cobra, Chrysler Super Bee, and Chevrolet Corvette. In 1970, GM, consisting of Cadillac, Buick, Pontiac, Oldsmobile, and Chevrolet—was the largest U.S. corporation and world's largest automaker. Almost all of the blue-collar employees labored until they retired with a full pension, including medical insurance, prescription drug coverage, and dental care. Today, well-paying blue-collar jobs are extremely rare, and even highly educated applicants are fortunate to receive such benefits. When the United States was at its manufacturing peak in 1979, GM employed more than six hundred thousand people. In sharp contrast, sixteen years later, they employed less than one-sixth of that number, only eighty-six thousand workers.[190] In 2008, GM was surpassed by Toyota Motor Corporation as the world's largest automaker. Less than a year later, GM admitted it was $173 billion in debt and filed for Chapter 11 bankruptcy protection.[191] It seemed hopeless. Even so, the GM story isn't over yet and, perhaps, offers a faint glimmer of hope.

Since the Second World War, our country's superior technology, coupled with the means to manufacture it, has been the underlying force behind America's military prowess. Manufacturing empowered America to defeat the Nazis and Japan in World War II. Shortly after the Japanese bombed Pearl Harbor, President Franklin D. Roosevelt challenged the Congress and U.S. citizens with these words:

> We cannot outfight our enemies unless, at the same time, we outproduce our enemies. It is not enough to turn out just a few more planes, a few more tanks, a few more guns, a few more ships, than can be turned out by our enemies. We must outproduce them overwhelmingly, so that there can be no question of our ability to provide a crushing superiority of equipment in any theater of the world war.[192]

The president presented seemingly impossible manufacturing demands to Congress, but the American people stepped up to the challenge. He asked for sixty thousand aircraft to be manufactured in 1942 and more than doubled the goal for 1943, up to 125,000.[193] Roosevelt's critics were quick to denounce his production goals as arbitrary and impossible.

Over the course of the Second World War, American industrial production, already the world's largest, doubled in size. Of course, the new war's demands created jobs. African Americans and Latinos found previously inaccessible opportunities and, controversial at that time, eight million *women* went to work in factories. Daniel Inouye, the former U.S. senator for the state of Hawaii, not only fought in World War II as part of the 442nd Infantry Regiment, he lost his right arm due to an enemy grenade and received several military decorations. Senator Inouye recalled those years in the PBS documentary series *The War*:

> I believe that war was the only war in which Americans involved themselves as a nation. In the Revolutionary War, one-third were for it, one-third were against it, one-third didn't care. But in this war, children went around collecting pennies or spare tires. We had victory gardens where they planted lettuce and carrots and cabbages. Women took the part of their husbands or boyfriends and got on the assembly line. It was a war that, I think the whole nation, took part in and did so magnificently. *We would not have won the war if it weren't for that.*[194] (emphasis added)

The American ethos of the early twentieth century contributed significantly to defeating the totalitarian juggernaut led by Adolf Hitler. But I wonder if that ethos still exists. For all intents and purposes, probably not. What would happen if we faced a similar threat today? If the trucks stopped delivering groceries to stores and the power grid went down, eliminating refrigeration, I feel confident there would be chaos and a massive death toll due to starvation in many urban areas. Personally, I'm heading for the hills. Much less, are young Americans today familiar enough with recent history to recognize the biblically foretold, emergent world leader (often compared to Hitler)—the one foretold as the "man of sin" or "man of lawlessness" (2 Thessalonians 2:3) who would "make war with the saints, and to overcome them"? Why believe globalism and global connectivity heralds his arrival? In the New Testament, God clearly assigns him global dominion: "Power was given him over all kindreds, and tongues, and nations" (Revelation 13:7). Although some of young folk surely are well informed, I was troubled by Ray Comfort's anti-abortion video entitled, *180*.

The majority of the thirty-three-minute-long documentary *180* features Comfort walking around Venice Beach, California, interviewing and evangelizing various interesting people. He draws a clever analogy

OF INDUSTRY

by comparing the Nazis' Holocaust of the Jews to abortion in the United States by asking questions like these that everyone ought to consider:

- Finish this sentence: "It's okay to kill a baby in the womb when..."
- What if a construction worker was about to blow up a building, but wasn't sure if there was a person in there or not? If we're not sure, we should always err on the side of life, right?
- What if someone had aborted you?

Not many youths have ever been challenged on the issue of abortion, and, through this line of reasoning, Comfort led eight to make a 180-degree turn by deciding that abortion is immoral. Considering the culture's embrace of moral relativism, nonsense like, "That's just *your* truth, not everyone's," C. S. Lewis points out that a person who claims there is no objective morality will complain if you break a promise or cut in line.[195] I'm rather fond of Greg Koukl's advice. I was encouraged that the Holocaust comparison was still persuasive to at least eight of today's youth concerning abortion, but, overall, I was profoundly disappointed by the ignorance of relatively recent history displayed.

The film begins with Comfort asking a young lady, "Have you heard of Adolf Hitler?" She answers, "No." He asks her again for clarity, "You don't know who he is?" The woman reiterates the seemingly preposterous response, "No."[196] Marching music swells as the video flashes to authentic, black-and-white film of a Nazi military procession. Comfort commences the presentation, "I am Ray Comfort. I am Jewish and I am deeply concerned that a generation is forgetting one of the greatest tragedies in the history of the human race. Adolf Hitler sanctioned the murder of eleven million people, including six million Jews."[197] This caught me off guard. What? Is he *really* concerned that an *entire generation* is ignorant of the Nazi-perpetrated Holocaust? Indeed, his demeanor indicates he *really is* deeply concerned, and he goes on to present truly disturbing evidence for his claim.

For a while, I mentally fumbled in search of a reasonable explanation

239

for such historical obliviousness. I thought, "Maybe it's just California," or "Perhaps it's the failure of public education." I wondered if it was possibly a consequence of our ever-shortening attention spans due to television. While all of those possibilities have some truth to them, I finally settled on the following rationale: "The Second World War seems like ancient history, which seems irrelevant to many of our youth." While that seems to be the most likely explanation, it's not really true. Knowledge of the past is essential for improvement in the future. In other words, you cannot learn from forgotten mistakes. Philosopher George Santayana famously wrote, "Progress, far from consisting in change, depends on retentiveness. When change is absolute there remains no being to improve and no direction is set for possible improvement: and when experience is not retained, as among savages, infancy is perpetual. *Those who cannot remember the past are condemned to repeat it*" (emphasis added).[198] Considering Hitler's many atrocities, such ignorance is an ominous portent.

If a significant number of American youth don't even recognize Hitler's name, then even fewer are aware that the term "Nazi" is short for the German word *Nationalsozialismus,* meaning "national socialism." While Hitler's rule over Germany is now, more accurately, deemed fascism, it is also important to remember that Hitler was *elected* by the German people because he offered a solution to their dismal economic situation. Writing under the pseudonym "Adam Smith" borrowed from one of capitalism's founding theorists, George W. Goodman, a financial planner, wrote:

Before World War I Germany was a prosperous country, with a gold-backed currency, expanding industry, and world leadership in optics, chemicals, and machinery. The German Mark, the British shilling, the French franc, and the Italian lira all had about equal value, and all were exchanged four or five to the dollar. That was in 1914. In 1923, at the most fevered moment of the German hyperinflation, the exchange rate between the dollar and the Mark was one trillion Marks to one dollar, and a wheelbarrow full of money would not even buy a newspaper.[199]

A famous photograph shows a man leaving a German bank with a wheelbarrow full of cash, allegedly to buy a loaf of bread. It's not an urban legend, and Germany is hardly the worst example. Inflation may be defined as "a general rise in prices" and occurs naturally when demand outpaces supply. Hyperinflation is imprecisely defined as "monetary inflation occurring at a very high rate," and, thus, begs the question, "What is considered high?" Economists seem to generally agree that a rate of 50 percent *per month* constitutes hyperinflation. Put in simple terms for illustration, that means an item costing $1 would cost about $194 one year from now and close to $17,000 in only two years. So over a year, 50 percent monthly inflation looks like the following:

Hyperinflation at 50 percent per month can be algebraically expressed as the function:

$$S = C * (1 + R)^t$$

Whereas:

C = the value today

R = the monthly inflation rate

S = the inflated value t months from now

t = the number of months

If we use $1 to make it simple, it looks like this:

S = $1 multiplied (1 + 50%) to the power of twelve

$$S = 1 * (1 + .50)^{12}$$

$$S = 1 * (1.50)^{12}$$

$$S = 194.62$$

But after two years, t = 24 months, it starts to get ridiculous at nearly $5 million ($4,914,394.83)

Now imagine if the value of R was 89.7 sextillion percent—that's roughly 9 followed by 22 zeroes! But hyperinflation like that only happens in places like Africa...right?

Actually, during the twentieth century, economists estimate that *over fifty* countries experienced hyperinflation. Examples include Argentina, Brazil, Chile, China, Germany, Hungary, Poland, Russia, and Zimbabwe. In the latter nation, inflation continued to the point that Zimbabwe (Southern Africa) dollars *literally* became a problem for public restrooms because it was often used as toilet paper.[200] The monthly inflation rate reached the 50 percent mark in February of 1999, but since April of 2006, the monthly rate in Zimbabwe has been above 1000 percent, reaching the absurd rate of 2200.2 percent in March 2007 and the upward trend only worsened leading some economists to estimate the monthly percentage in the *billions,*[201] and another writes that it peaked at 89.7 sextillion percent per month. In such a situation, the price of a restaurant meal might become unaffordable before one could finish eating it. At the nadir of the Great Depression, July 1933, the monthly inflation was only slightly above 3 percent.[202] Hyperinflation makes what we've labeled "great" seem picayune. Try to imagine using $100 bills as tissue paper.

But that could never happen here...right?

In America, the subject of economics is so intertwined with political ideology, conservative and liberal, that it is hard to find analytical objectivity. The Swiss economist Marc Faber graduated *magna cum laude* with a PhD in economics from the University of Zurich at the age of twenty-four. He accurately predicted the October 1987 stock market crash and advised his clients to get their money out of the markets and into more stable commodities.[203] In January of 2007, Faber was quoted by Bloomberg as saying, "In the next few months, we could get a severe correction in all asset markets.... In a selling panic you should buy, but in the buying mania that we have now the wisest course of action is to liquidate."[204] A short time later, he was proven correct. Faber not only seems to have an uncanny ability to spot economic trouble on the horizon, but in the same article he recommended both oil and gold instead of stocks, both of which steadily climbed and peaked around 2011. Having a proven track record, Faber's views ought to be carefully considered. The bad news is that two years ago, in 2014, Faber predicted, "hyperinflation in the U.S. is a certainty within the next ten years."[205] So to answer the previous hypothetical, not only could it happen here, but competent experts believe it to be certain.

Much like the pre-war Germans, Americans are increasingly looking to the government for their well-being. While socialists are fond of the canard that President Roosevelt's New Deal pulled us out of the Great Depression, it more likely was the manufacturing and technological demands associated with the Second World War, coupled with the work-ethic of the average citizen, that generated the jobs and prosperity. Burton Folsom, an American historian and author who holds a chair in history and management at Hillsdale College, argues that New Deal enlarged the powers of the federal government, built labor unions, slowed long-term growth, and weakened the business community. Folsom banters by asking rhetorically, "Was the better U.S. strategy for recovery a 79 percent top income tax rate, a doubled national debt, unbalanced budgets, the only undistributed profits tax in the world, and only slow tariff reform—all of which Rooselvelt delivered—or tax cuts, balanced budgets, and immediate tariff reduction, all of which Roosevelt promised?"[206]

Turning back to GM, one could argue that America adopted a socialist ideology—the redistribution of wealth by government intervention—when investment banks like Bear Sterns teetered on the verge of collapse. As the recession of 2008, the Big Three automakers were in danger of collapse. In response, President George W. Bush implemented the Troubled Assets Relief Program (TARP), a $700 billion "bail-out" of those deemed "too big to fail" following their ill-advised venturing resulting in a subprime mortgages crisis and near collapse of the banking system.

Liberal columnist Randy Shaw points out the incoherence of the Bush plan with the free-market tenet that government should not be in the business of "picking winners and losers."[207] *Lemon socialism* is a pejorative term meaning the government only aids faltering businesses, labeled as "lemons,"—that is, enterprises that, theoretically, a free-market should replace with more viable companies in response to demand.[208] While Shaw accurately points out that such intervention was so labeled by free-market advocates, the title of his essay, "The Return of Lemon Socialism," is naive at best. In truth, Marxist ideas never really "left" in order to "return,"— that is, ever since Roosevelt's New Deal expanded government's role in the economy. Shaw also invokes a conspiracy by adding, "Corporate America knows it can espouse free market ideology when it suits its interests and then switch course when it comes time for a government bailout."[209] Whom, exactly, does he mean by "corporate America?" So we're supposed to believe that American businesses like GM and Levi Strauss and Harley-Davidson were conspiring with investment bankers to buy subprime mortgage dividends? Really? What evidence leads to such a radical charge? Moreover, who decides how wealthy an American needs to be in order to qualify as a conspirator? Of course, I doubt Shaw ever bothered to think it through that far. Worse yet, just prior to painting a conspiracy with such broad brushstrokes, he argued that only a "select few" like Bear Stearns were bailed out by Bush's plan, which turned out to be false. The banks took the lion's share, but American bulwarks like GM, Harley-Davidson, and Levi Strauss were also loaned money—most of which has been paid back with interest. Although Shaw correctly pointed out TARP's incoherence with free-market ideology (having his cake), his own essay became logically incoherent when he criticized Bush for intervening, a policy he ostensibly agrees with (he wants to eat it, too).

The American Recovery and Reinvestment Act of 2009 (ARRA, commonly referred to as the Stimulus or the Recovery Act), signed into law on February 17, 2009, by President Barack Obama, funds government as a means of creating jobs. The ARRA's purpose was to quickly end the 2008 recession by spurring consumer spending and saving between 900,000 to 2.3 million jobs. It appears to have accomplished the first goal but, as of October 30, 2009 (when the recovery board stopped tracking data), it had preserved merely 640,329 jobs, widely missing the goal by an entire order of magnitude. While the principle benefit for the middle class amounts to not much more than, "You get to keep *some* of what you already had" (i.e., your job or pension), in that it was not so much a growth stimulus, it was a life preserver. Profiteering has always been condemned; the Bible has been about a *global* catastrophe for thousands of years.

Behold, the Lord maketh the earth empty, and maketh it waste, And turneth it upside down, and scattereth abroad the inhabitants thereof. And it shall be, as with the people, so with the priest; As with the servant, so with his master; As with the maid, so with her mistress; As with the buyer, so with the seller; As with the lender, so with the borrower; As with the taker of usury, so with the giver of usury to him. (Isaiah 24:1–2)

And I heard a voice in the midst of the four beasts say, A measure of wheat for a penny, and three measures of barley for a penny; and see thou hurt not the oil and the wine. (Revelation 6:6)

I believe one's analysis ought to include preposterous notions seldom countenanced by academics, ideas entailing *the potential that current events mark the fulfillment of biblical prophecy.* In our fourth co-written investigation, Tom Horn and I analyzed the Islamic State using what we deemed "a more long-play perspective."[210] In adopting that outlook, one analyzes current events through an immortal's perspective rather than a human one. That entails looking for trends that forecast the culmination of biblical prophecy. For instance, Koinonia Minsitries founder Chuck Missler pointed out that not until the last two decades or so was it even possible for the Antichrist to implement a system entailing that described in the following verse: "And that no man might buy or sell, save he that had the mark, or the name of the beast, or the number of his name" (Revelation 13:17). In addition to his biblical prophecy expertise, as a former branch chief of the Department of Guided Missiles at Lowry Air Force Base, who later went into the private sector as an executive holding a master's in computer science from the University of California at Los Angeles, Missler is uniquely qualified to offer his interpretation of that passage as a technological prediction of a global cashless financial system. "The Coming World Leader—through electronic funds transfer, credit cards, RFID chips, and related technologies of the 'cashless society'—will establish himself by his widespread control of the global economy" (Revelation 3; 17).[211] Where the King James Version reads "no man," the Greek text is *me tis. Tis* is an *indefinite* pronoun, which explains why it is usually translated as "no one" by scholars.

If one takes the "mark of the beast" prophecy seriously enough to do the math, a global communication network with the capability to reach even the undeveloped world seems to be required. When, inspired by the Holy Spirit, John composed the book of Revelation, the technology to implement such a cashless control system was nearly two thousand years away. But it is right on our heels today. Several companies including LightSquared, SpaceX, and OneWeb have been working on solving the technical problems that plagued past designs promising global Internet access via satellite networks.[212] Complications like interference in the spectrum assigned to the Global Positioning Satellites (GPS; see the FCC response to LightSquared[213]) and latency due to the traditional satellites' extreme distance. Amongst the three doing research and development, LightSquared has already filed bankruptcy due to FCC regulation. SpaceX designs, manufactures, and launches advanced rockets and spacecraft for numerous applications, so they certainly have more viability and resources than the others. They plan to deploy a large constellation of small satellites for low-latency, worldwide, high-capacity

Internet service, but have not set a target date I am aware of.[214] SpaceX received a billion-dollar investment from Google and Fidelity in early 2015, but it's not clear how much of that is earmarked for the Internet satellite network project.[215] I believe their competitor, OneWeb, has a more feasible means of implementing global connectivity.

The company's founder, Greg Wyler, states his goal sincerely and concisely: "Enable affordable Internet access for everyone."[216] The means to that end is especially pertinent to the topic at hand. OneWeb's viability and investment value (it already attracted $500 million[217]) is based on innovating a novel means of mass producing cheaper space satellites "in the same way high quality medical and avionics equipment are." Wyler's solution will deploy more than six hundred satellites with a new satellite manufacturing technology capable of mass producing enough satellites at a lower cost as well as inexpensive, easy to set up, more accessible receiving terminals, capable of providing access to literally *anywhere* on earth: corporate leader calls itself "OneWeb: OneWorld."[218 219] One-Web's solution depends on what it calls a constellation of a previously impractical 648 satellites circling the earth that will enable global access. The "ace in the hole" that could propel OneWeb to beat SpaceX is that OneWeb Satellites is a joint venture between OneWeb, a satellite-based Internet provider, and Airbus Defence and Space, the world's second-largest space company.

We see nothing particularly sinister about Wyler or his company, OneWeb Satellites. Wyler really seems well intended, but that can't stop a future despot from commandeering control. Accordingly, the principle of the "long-play perspective" we took in *The Last Roman Emperor* is that one should hold closely to Paul's admonition to the church in Ephesus: "For we wrestle *not* against flesh and blood (humans), but against principalities, against powers, against the rulers of the sin of this world, against spiritual wickedness in high places" (Ephesians 6:12). We are certainly *not* saying that OneWeb is in cahoots with the Antichrist; rather, we are suggesting that the coming world leader will exploit global connectivity in order to implement the "mark of the beast" prophecy. Thus, the otherworldly strategic maneuvers deployed by immortal beings have played out over many human lifetimes and escape journalistic and academic scrutiny due to the widespread scholarly embrace of philosophical naturalism. We believe the fallen immortals' earthly designs will culminate with the war in heaven described in the final book of the Bible (Revelation 12:7–8).

Notes

1. Jennifer Latson, "The Worst Stock Tip in History," *TIME*, September 3, 2014, last accessed April 19, 2016, http://time.com/3207128/stock-market-high-1929/.
2. "Herbert Hoover," *The White House*, last accessed April 19, 2016, https://www.whitehouse.gov/1600/presidents/herberthoover.
3. "Hoovervilles," *History*, last accessed April 20, http://www.history.com/topics/hoovervilles.
4. http://classroom.synonym.com/differences-between-marxism-socialism-communism-17064.html.
5. *World War II Companion*, edited by David M. Kennedy, The Library of Congress, (New York: Simon & Schuster, 2007), pp. XIII–XIV.
6. Ibid, XIX.
7. January 10, 1920: League of Nations Instituted, history.com, http://www.history.com/this-day-in-history/league-of-nations-instituted.
8. *World War II Companion*, p. 5.
9. The League of Nations, 1920, Office of the Historian, U.S. Department of State, https://history.state.gov/milestones/1914-1920/league.

10. *World War II Companion*, p. XVII.
11. *World War II and the American Home Front, A National Historic Landmarks Theme Study*, The National Historic Landmarks Program, National Park Service, U.S. Department of the Interior, Washington, D.C., October 2007, p. 20.
12. *World War II Companion*, p. 163.
13. *World War II and the American Home Front*, p. 3.
14. *World War II Companion*, p. 170.
15. https://en.wikipedia.org/wiki/Alaska_Highway.
16. *World War II and the American Home Front*, p. 19.
17. Ibid, 15.
18. "America Goes to War," National World War II Museum, http://www.nationalww2museum.org/learn/education/for-students/ww2-history/america-goes-to-war.html.
19. "American Women in World War II," History.com, http://www.history.com/topics/world-war-ii/rosie-the-riveter.
20. World War II andthe American Home Front, p. 25.
21. Ibid.
22. Franklin Roosevelt, "Broadcast to the Nation on Rubber," http://www.jewishvirtuallibrary.org/jsource/ww2/rubber.html.
23. World War II and the American Home Front, p. 31.
24. "America Goes to War," National World War II Museum, http://www.nationalww2museum.org/learn/education/for-students/ww2-history/america-goes-to-war.html.
25. World War II and the American Home Front, p. 3.
26. Ibid, 16–17.
27. Ibid.
28. Ibid.
29. Frank Newport, "Almost All Americans Consider World War Just War," Gallup.com, June 3, 2004, http://www.gallup.com/poll/11881/almost-all-americans-consider-world-war-just-war.aspx.

30. Franklin D. Roosevelt's "Quarantine" speech,October 5, 1937, http://www.vlib.us/amdocs/texts/fdrquarn.html.
31. Laurence M. Vance, "The War That Justified Other Wars," The Future of Freedom Foundation, August 1, 2015, http://fff.org/explore-freedom/article/the-war-that-justified-other-wars/.
32. Ibid.
33. Red Mariott, "How the Allied Multinationals Supplied Nazi Germany Throughout World War II," libcom.org, December 13, 2006, https://libcom.org/library/allied-multinationals-supply-nazi-germany-world-war-2.
34. Ibid.
35. Ibid.
36. J. F. C. Fuller, *A Military History of the Western World*, vol. 3 (New York: DaCapo, 1987), p. 631.
37. Mark Weber, "The 'Good War' Myth of World War Two," Institute for Historical Review, http://www.ihr.org/news/weber_ww2_may08.html.
38. Mark McSherry-Forbes, "Week Ahead: Let's Hope Churchill Was Wrong about Americans," National Churchill Museum, October 7, 2013, https://www.nationalchurchillmuseum.org/10-07-13-lets-hope-churchill-was-wrong-about-americans.html.
39. Lend-Lease Act, History.com, http://www.history.com/topics/world-war-ii/lend-lease-act.
40. Victor Hanson, "The Forgotten Realities of World War II," *Washington Times*, May 13, 2015, http://www.washingtontimes.com/news/2015/may/13/victor-davis-hanson-us-contribution-to-world-war-i/?page=all.
41. Ibid.
42. "Anglo-American Chain of Command in Western Europe," June 1944 World War II, Encyclopedia Britannica, http://www.britannica.com/topic/Anglo-American-Chain-of-Command-in-Western-Europe-June-1944-1673115#ref830374.

43. Edgar L. Jones, "One War is Enough," *The Atlantic*, February 1946, http://www.theatlantic.com/past/docs/unbound/bookauth/battle/jones.htm.
44. Ibid.
45. Ibid.
46. Ibid.
47. Ibid.
48. Ibid.
49. Ibid.
50. Ibid.
51. Franklin D. Roosevelt: "Appeal to Russia and Finland to Stop Bombing Civilians," December 1, 1939. Online by Gerhard Peters and John T. Woolley, The American Presidency Project, http://www.presidency.ucsb.edu/ws/?pid=15845.
52. Sahr Conway-Lanz, "America's 'Ethics' of Bombing Civilians after World War II: Massive Casualties and the Targeting of Civilians in the Korean War," GlobalResearch, September 15, 2014, http://www.globalresearch.ca/americas-ethics-of-bombing-civilians-after-world-war-ii-massive-casualties-and-the-targeting-civilians-in-the-korean-war/5402007.
53. Sahr Conway-Lanz, "The Ethics of Bombing Civilians After World War II: The Persistence of Norms Against Targeting Civilians in the Korean War, *The Asia-Pacific Journal*, Vol. 12, Issue 37, No. 1, September 15, 2014, http://apjjf.org/2014/12/37/Sahr-Conway-Lanz/4180/article.html.
54. Kenneth Rose, *Myth and the Greatest Generation: A Social History of Americans in World War II*, p. 218.
55. Conway-Lanz, America's "Ethics" of Bombing Civilians After World War II: Massive Casualties and the Targeting of Civilians in the Korean War.
56. Ibid.
57. Brian Wansink and Craig Wansink, "Are there Atheists in the

Foxholes?," *Journal of Religion and Health*, 52(3), 768079, http://www.ncbi.nlm.nih.gov/pubmed/23760855.

58. Ibid.
59. Michael Snape, *God and Uncle Sam: Religion and America's Armed Forces in World War II*, (The Boydell Press, 2015), p. 322.
60. Ibid., 323.
61. Ibid., 328.
62. Ibid., 317.
63. Ibid., 318.
64. Ibid.
65. Ibid., 319.
66. Ibid., 320.
67. Ibid., 321.
68. Ibid., 336.
69. Ibid., 339.
70. Ibid., 341.
71. Ibid., 342.
72. Ibid., 343.
73. Louis Zamperini, bio.com, http://www.biography.com/people/louis-zamperini.
74. Patrick Christy, "The Lesson from U.S. Aid after World War II," *U.S. News & World Report*, June 6, 2014, http://www.usnews.com/opinion/blogs/world-report/2014/06/06/the-lessons-from-us-aid-after-world-war-ii.
75. Earl F. Ziemke, "The U.S. Army in the Occupation of Germany," Army Historical Series, U.S. Army Center for Military History, June 30, 1974.
76. George C. Marshall, The Marshall Plan Speech, The George C. Marshall Foundation, http://marshallfoundation.org/marshall/the-marshall-plan/marshall-plan-speech/.
77. Christy, "The Lesson from U.S. Aid."
78. "Occupation and Reconstruction of Japan: 1945–52," Office of

the Historian, U.S. Department of State, https://history.state.gov/ milestones/1945-1952/japan-reconstruction.

79. Emperor Hirohito, Accepting the Potsdam Declaration, Radio Broadcast, Transmitted by Domei and Recorded by the Federal Communications Commission, 14 August 1945, ttps://www. mtholyoke.edu/acad/intrel/hirohito.htm.

80. Ibid.

81. "Nuremberg Trials," History.com, http://www.history.com/topics/ world-war-ii/nuremberg-trials.

82. Ibid.

83. Earl F. Ziemke, "The U.S. Army in the Occupation of Germany," Army Historical Series, U.S. Army Center for Military History, June 30, 1974, p.391.

84. Ibid.

85. The Nuremberg Trial and the Tokyo War Crimes Trials (1945–1948), Office of the Historian, U.S. Department of State, https:// history.state.gov/milestones/1945-1952/nuremberg.

86. "Health Expenditure, Total (% of GDP)," *World Bank Data*, retrieved April 14, 2016, http://data.worldbank.org/indicator/ SH.XPD.TOTL.ZS.

87. Drew Desilver, "For Most Workers, Real Wages Have Barely Budged for Decades," *FactTank*, October 9, 2014, http://www.pewresearch.org/fact-tank/2014/10/09/ for-most-workers-real-wages-have-barely-budged-for-decades/.

88. Katie Johnson, "Efforts to Regulate CEO Pay Gain Traction," *Boston Globe*, October 26, 2014, https://www.bostonglobe. com/business/2014/10/25/growing-effort-limit-ceo-pay/1VKKZCuZMkXJvaQRmUb4RN/story.html.

89. For example, it defies logic that the official unemployment rate in the U.S. has dropped from 10 percent in October 2009 to 4.9 percent by January 2016, while during the same period the participation rate in the labor force by adults sixteen and over

declined from 65 percent to below 63 percent—the first time it
has been that low in forty years.

90. Robert B. Reich, "The Limping Middle Class," *The New York Times*, September 3, 2011, http://www.nytimes.com/2011/09/04/opinion/sunday/jobs-will-follow-a-strengthening-of-the-middle-class.html.

91. Alan S. Blinder, "The Mystery of Declining Productivity Growth," *The Wall Street Journal*, May 14, 2015, http://www.wsj.com/articles/the-mystery-of-declining-productivity-growth-1431645038.

92. FRED® Economic Data, Federal Reserve Bank of Saint Louis, https://research.stlouisfed.org/fred2/series/W270RE1A156NBEA), retrieved 3/26/16.

93. Ibid., https://research.stlouisfed.org/fred2/series/MEHOINUSA672N, retrieved 3/26/16.

94. "Historical Statistics of the United States: Colonial Times to 1970, Part 1," U.S. Department of Commerce, Bureau of the Census, https://www.census.gov/history/pdf/colonialpops.pdf, retrieved 4/3/16.

95. Copyright © 1964 (Renewed), 1968, 1969 by Sherman Edwards.

96. Gene Dattell, "When Cotton Was King," *The New York Times*, March 26, 2011, http://opinionator.blogs.nytimes.com/2011/03/26/when-cotton-was-king/.

97. Howard Dodson, "How Slavery Helped Build a World Economy," *National Geographic*, February 3, 2003, http://news.nationalgeographic.com/news/2003/01/0131_030203_jubilee2_2.html.

98. StevenDeyle, *Carry Me Back: The Domestic Slave Trade in American Life*. (New York: Oxford UP, 2005) Print.

99. "Did Slavery Make Economic Sense?", *The Economist*, September 27, 2013, http://www.economist.com/blogs/freeexchange/2013/09/economic-history-2.

100. Ian Fletcher, "America Aping Britain's Decline Through Free Trade," *Economy in Crisis*, December 29, 2010, http://economyincrisis.org/content/america-aping-britains-decline-through-free-trade.
101. Robert F. Bruner, Sean D. Carr, *The Panic of 1907: Lessons Learned from the Market's Perfect Storm* (Hoboken: John Wiley & Sons, 2007), p. 149.
102. This is called Fractional Reserve Banking. It is done to free up capital and expand the economy, and most countries operate under this type of system.
103. Timothy Curry and Lynn Shibut, "The Cost of the Savings and Loan Crisis: Truth and Consequences," *FDIC Banking Review*, December 2000, p. 31.
104. Anne Seith, "Short Selling American Lives: Deutsche Bank Life Insurance Fund in Hot Water," *Spiegel Online International*, November 20, 2009, http://www.spiegel.de/international/business/short-selling-american-lives-deutsche-bank-life-insurance-fund-in-hot-water-a-662447.html.
105. "Banks Don't Do Much Banking Anymore—and That's a Serious Problem," *Pacific Standard*, February 3, 2014, https://psmag.com/banks-don-t-do-much-banking-anymore-and-that-s-a-serious-problem-d9c1fe47d0a8#.8w99xii00.
106. The discount window was opened to investment banks during the height of the bank crisis in 2008. Fed chairman Ben Bernanke and his advisers agreed that because the banking system was too interconnected to allow it to fail, lending cheap money to companies like Goldman Sachs and Morgan Stanley was worth the risk that it might encourage.
107. "Semiannual OTC Derivatives tatistics," Bank for International Settlements, updated March 6, 2016, http://www.bis.org/statistics/derstats.htm.
108. Ben Protess, "Big Banks Get Break in Rules to Limit Risks,"

The New York Times, May 15, 2013, http://dealbook.nytimes.
com/2013/05/15/compromise-seen-on-derivatives-rule/?_r=0.

109. Mike Collins, "The Big Bank Bailout," *Forbes*, July 14, 2015,
http://www.forbes.com/sites/mikecollins/2015/07/14/the-big-
bank-bailout/#11d6965c3723. Collins cites a report from the
special inspector general for the Toxic Asset Repurchase Program
(TARP), which was "only" supposed to cost $700 billion.

110. Tyler Durden, "Obama Reveals What He Will
Discuss with Janet Yellen," *Zero Hedge*, April 11,
2016, http://www.zerohedge.com/news/2016-04-11/
obama-reveals-what-he-will-discuss-janet-yellen.

111. And the fact that the bankers got their bailout plus a lot more the
American public was never told about is why Goldman Sachs is
often referred to as "Government Sachs."

112. Tyler Durden, "The Beginning of the End for Obamacare:
Largest US Health Insurer Exits Georgia, Arkansas," *Zero Hedge*,
April 8, 2016 (http://www.zerohedge.com/news/2016-04-08/
beginning-end-obamacare-largest-us-health-insurer-exits-georgia-
arkanasas).

113. Tyler Durden, "Healthcare Is About to Surpass Housing As
the Biggest Source of American 'Growth'," *Zero Hedge*, March
26, 2016, http://www.zerohedge.com/news/2016-03-26/
healthcare-about-surpass-housing-biggest-source-american-growth.

114. The Trans-Pacific Partnership, for example, would not only
further erode America's manufacturing base, it would also
sublimate American sovereignty. Unelected tribunals would
rule on trade disputes, and the rulings of TPP tribunals would
supersede U.S. law.

115. This is a gentle way of saying that white settlers had guns and
were thus able to more or less take what they wanted—not
without cost, of course, but it was an unfair contest.

116. Matthew 26:11, Mark 14:7, John 12:8. Also see Deuteronomy
15:11.

117. 2 Thessalonians 3:10.
118. http://faithofourfathers.net/.
119. Article 1 Section 7, Constitution of the United States.
120. For more information, visit http://www.archives. gov/ and http://www.internationalcopsforchrist.com/ proof-that-america-was-founded-as-a-christian-nation/.
121. Refer to our first Amendment about Congress making no law respect the establishment of religion.
122. http://hollowverse.com/john-adams/.
123. Ibid.
124. http://news.discovery.com/history/religion/president-abraham-lincoln-religion-god-1104151.htm.
125. Ibid.
126. http://www.greatamericanhistory.net/lincolnsfaith.htm.
127. Michael A. Shea, "In God We Trust: George Washington and the Spiritual Destiny of the United States of America," p.447.
128. http://www.wnd.com/2012/08/ yes-they-can-do-that-in-public-school/.
129. Ibid.
130. All quoted rules can be found at https://www.aclu.org/ joint-statement-current-law-religion-public-schools.
131. http://www.mountvernon.org/digital-encyclopedia/article/ george-washington-and-religion.
132. http://www.ushistory.org/valleyforge/washington/vision.html.
133. http://divorce.lovetoknow.com/ Historical_Divorce_Rate_Statistics.
134. http://www.childtrends.org/?indicators=family-structure.
135. http://peacemaker.net/project/the-effects-of-divorce-on-america/
136. http://www.telegraph.co.uk/news/politics/3235650/ Children-in-single-parent-families-more-likely-to-suffer-emotional-problems-report-finds.html.
137. http://www.factsforlifeglobal.org/03/.

138. http://www.babymed.com/blogs/jaclyun-stewart/
can-child-without-mother-be-raised-normally.

139. http://www.huffingtonpost.com/dr-gail-gross/the-important-role-
of-dad_b_5489093.html.

140. Ibid., emphasis added.

141. http://www.fathers.com/statistics-and-research/
the-consequences-of-fatherlessness.

142. http://people.missouristate.edu/michaelcarlie/what_i_learned_
about/gangs/recruitment_techniques.htm.

143. http://www.fathermag.com/news/2776-USB.shtml.

144. http://www.goodreads.com/quotes/349175-what-one-generation-
tolerates-the-next-generation-will-embrace.

145. http://www.britannica.com/topic/etiquette.

146. https://www.psychologytoday.com/
blog/your-online-secrets/201409/
internet-trolls-are-narcissists-psychopaths-and-sadists.

147. ScienceDirect, Volume 67, September 2014, Pages 97–102.

148. C. Claiborne Ray, "Science Q & A: Dancing Angels," *New York
Times* (11/11/97). Now at http://www.improbable.com/airchives/
paperair/volume7/v7i3/angels-7-3.htm.

149. "Spanish Exorcist Addresses Claims of Satanic Influence in
Vatican," Catholic News Agency, http://www.catholicnewsagency.
com/news/spanish_exorcist_addresses_claims_of_satanic_
influence_in_vatican/ .

150. David Wilkerson, "Witchcraft in the Church," Believers Web,
http://www.believersweb.org/view.cfm?ID=735.

151. Rebecca Evans, "The Internet Unlocked Something Dark in
Humanity," March 24, 2013, http://www.dailymail.co.uk/news/
article-2298600/The-internet-unlocked-dark-humanity-Top-
author-Anthony-Horowitz-uses-speech-make-claims.html.

152. Ibid.

153. Chip Ingram, The Invisible War (Grand Rapids, MI: Baker,
2006) p. 133.

154. Laurence Fishburne and Keanu Reeves, *The Matrix*, DVD, *Warner Brothers Pictures*. Written and directed by Larry and Andy Wachowski, 1999.
155. "First they came…" *Wikipedia*, last modified May 14, 2012, http://en.wikipedia.org/wiki/First_they_came....
156. "Charles Darwin," *Wikipedia*, last modified May 20, 2012, http://en.wikiquote.org/wiki/Charles_Darwin.
157. Laurence Fishburne, *The Matrix*, 1999.
158. John J.Macionis, 2005, Sociology, 10th ed. (Upper Saddle River, New Jersey: Pearson Prentice Hall). p. 66.
159. http://www.cnbc.com/2016/01/17/62-people-have-as-much-wealth-as-worlds-36b-poorest-oxfam-finds-ahead-of-davos.html.
160. http://www.brookings.edu/research/reports/2013/12/12-facts-lower-middle-class.
161. http://blogs.wsj.com/wealth/2010/09/07/the-perfect-salary-for-happiness-75000-a-year/.
162. http://www.pewinternet.org/2015/08/06/teens-technology-and-friendships/.
163. https://www.sciencedaily.com/releases/2008/03/080312172614.htm.
164. http://www.pewinternet.org/2015/07/16/parents-and-social-media/#fn-13802-1.
165. http://www.pewinternet.org/fact-sheets/teens-fact-sheet/.
166. https://www.technologyreview.com/s/545366/big-pharma-doubles-down-on-crispr-for-new-drugs/ .
167. Carmen DeNavas-Walt and Bernadette D. Proctor, "Income and Poverty in the United States: 2014" (US Census Bureau: September 2015), p.41.
168. Nicholas Wright Gillham (2001), *A Life of Sir Francis Galton: From African Exploration to the Birth of Eugenics*, (Oxford University Press) ISBN 0-19-514365-5. (citation found in Wikipedia, available online via https://en.wikipedia.org/wiki/Francis_Galton#cite_note-Gilham-21 (accessed April 30, 2016).

169. Tim M. Berra; Gonzalo Alvarez; Francisco Ceballos, "Was the Darwin /Wedgewood Dynasty Adversely Affected by Consanguinity?" Oxford Journals: Bioscience, Volume 60, Issue No .5, p. 376–383, published online via http://bioscience. oxfordjournals.org/content/60/5/376.full (accessed April 30, 2016).

170. Robert E. Schofield (December 1957), "The Industrial Orientation of Science in the Lunar Society of Birmingham," *Isis* (The University of Chicago Press on behalf of *The History of Science Society*) 48 (4): 408–415, *doi:10.1086/348607, ISSN 0021-1753, JSTOR 227513.*

171. Erasmus Darwin, "The Temple of Nature" is referenced here; this book is available online via http://www.rc.umd.edu/editions/ darwin_temple/ (accessed April 30, 2016).

172. Entry on Erasmus Darwin at Enlightenment-Revolution website. Available online via http://enlightenment-revolution.org/index. php/Darwin%2C_Erasmus (accessed April 30, 2016).

173. Albert Edward Musson, Eric Robinson (1969), p. 177, *Science and Technology in the Industrial Revolution*; footnote from Wikipedia entry on The Lunar Society, found online via https:// en.wikipedia.org/wiki/Lunar_Society_of_Birmingham#CITERE FSchofield1957. (accessed April 30, 2016), emphasis added.

174. Thomas Paine, *Life and Writings of Thomas Paine*, Daniel Edwin Wheeler, editor (New York: Printed by Vincent Parke and Company, 1908), Vol. 7, pp. 2–8, "The Existence of God," A Discourse at the Society of Theophilanthropists, Paris. Found online via http://www.wallbuilders.com/libissuesarticles. asp?id=7846#FN17 (accessed April 30, 2016).

175. Thomas Paine, "The Age of Reason" pamphlet, published in available as pdf online via http://www.deism.com/images/ theageofreason1794.pdf (accessed April 30, 2016).

176. Daniel Webster's senior oration at Dartmouth, translated from the

Latin by John Andrew Murray, available online via http://www.dartmouth.edu/~dwebster/speeches/goodness.html (accessed April 30, 2016).

177. Text of the State of Tennessee, House Bill No. 185, content found online via http://law2.umkc.edu/faculty/projects/ftrials/scopes/tennstat.htm (accessed April 30, 2016).

178. Douglas O. Linder, "State vs. John Scopes (The Monkey Trial)," published online via http://law2.umkc.edu/faculty/projects/ftrials/scopes/evolut.htm (accessed April 30, 2016).

179. Associated Press, *LA Times,* December 5, 1989, "Mencken Was Pro-Nazi, His Diary Shows." published online via http://articles.latimes.com/1989-12-05/news/mn-198_1_h-l-mencken (accessed April 30, 2016).

180. Douglas O. Linder, 2004, "Clarence Darrow," published at the University of Missouri-Kansas City website via http://law2.umkc.edu/faculty/projects/ftrials/scopes/darrowcl.htm (accessed April 30, 2016).

181. http://law2.umkc.edu/faculty/projects/ftrials/scopes/day2.htm (accessed April 30, 2016).

182. http://law2.umkc.edu/faculty/projects/ftrials/scopes/bs.htm (accessed April 30, 2016).

183. "Army Drops Plan to Buy Berets Made in China," *The Washington Post,* May 2, 2001, https://www.washingtonpost.com/archive/politics/2001/05/02/army-drops-plan-to-buy-berets-made-in-china/c55483af-3539-4d78-a9a0-002e3f0e298a/, accessed April 20, 2016.

184. Bureau of Labor Statistics, http://data.bls.gov/pdq/SurveyOutputServlet, see figure Manufacturing Jobs 1965–2016.

185. "Industrial Metamorphosis," *The Economist,* October 1, 2005, http://www.economist.com/node/4462685 accessed April 28, 2016.

186. Richard McCormack, "The Plight of American Manufacturing,"

Prospect, December 21, 2009, http://prospect.org/article/plight-american-manufacturing, accessed April 30, 2016.

187. "China" YoJoe, http://www.yojoe.com/international/china/ accessed April 30, 2016.

188. "Army Recalling China-Made Black Berets," *New York Times*, May 2, 2001, http://www.nytimes.com/2001/05/02/world/army-recalling-china-made-black-berets.html accessed April 25, 2016.

189. Graham M. Simons (2012), *Consolidated B-24 Liberator*. Church Street, Barnsley, Sth Yorks S70 2AS: Pen & Sword. pp. 40–42.

190. Danny Hakim, "G.M. Will Reduce Hourly Workers in U.S. by 25,000," *The New York Times*, June 8, 2005, http://www.nytimes.com/2005/06/08/business/gm-will-reduce-hourly-workers-in-us-by-25000.html?_r=1 accessed April 30, 2016.

191 "General Motors Corporation," in *Encyclopedia Britannica*, http://www.britannica.com/topic/General-Motors-Corporation, accessed April 20, 2016.

192. Franklin D. Roosevelt, "Annual Budget Message, January 5, 1942," http://www.presidency.ucsb.edu/ws/?pid=16231, accessed April 22, 2016.

193. *United States Army in World War 2, Buying Aircraft: Material Procurement for Army Air Forces* (Washington DC: Government Printing Office), 238, https://books.google.com/books?id=L WEeXQzYUgEC&lpg=PA238&ots=agAjwhnDjL&dq=60 %2C000%20aircraft%20in%201942&pg=PA238#v=onepage& q&f=false.

194. "Daniel Inouye: War Production," Interview transcribed from PBS Documentary, "The War," https://www.pbs.org/thewar/detail_5253.htm accessed April 25, 2016.

195. C. S. Lewis, *Mere Christianity* (New York: Touchstone, 1996) p.19.

196. "180" time: 0:0–0:19.

197. Ibid., 0:48–0:52.

198. George Santayana, *Reason in Common Sense, volume I in The Life of Reason*, 1905, Project Gutenberg, http://www.gutenberg.org/files/15000/15000-h/vol1.html accessed April 25, 2016.

199. Adam Smith (George W. Smith), *Paper Money* (London: Futura, 1982), 57.

200. "FREAK Shots: When Money Goes Down the Toilet" Freakonomics, http://freakonomics.com/2008/12/18/freak-shots-when-money-goes-down-the-toilet/ accessed May 5. 2016.

201. "The Runaway Zeros: Zimbabwe's Hyperinflation," http://www.mtholyoke.edu/~moyan20t/classweb/worldpolitics1/hyperinflation.html, accessed April 27, 2014. 2012, April 30, 2016.

202. Tim McMahon, "Monthly US Inflation Rate 1913 to Present," http://inflationdata.com/inflation/inflation_rate/monthly_inflation.aspxS.

203. Ian Sayson and Pimm Fox, "Global Markets Face 'Severe Correction,' Faber Says," Bloomberg, January 8. 2007, https://web.archive.org/web/20140905031713/http://www.bloomberg.com/apps/news?pid=newsarchive&sid=afYGFBA.L8PQ&refer=home, accessed April 30, 2016.

204. Ibid.

205. Mike Patton, "Is U.S. Hyperinflation Imminent?," *Forbes*, April 28, 2014, http://www.forbes.com/sites/mikepatton/2014/04/28/is-u-s-hyperinflation-imminent/#6c8e22f9673e accessed April 30.

206. Burton W. Folsom, *New Deal or Raw Deal?: How FDR's Economic Legacy Has Damaged America* (New York, Simon and Schuster: 2009), 244.

207. Randy Shaw, "The Return of 'Lemon' Socialism," BeyondChron.com, September 8, 2008, http://www.beyondchron.org/the-return-of-lemon-socialism/, accessed April 26, 2016.

208. Jonathon Green, *Newspeak: A Dictionary of Jargon* (Londpolion: Routledge & Kegan Paul, 1984), 142.

209. Shaw, "The Return of Lemon Socialism."
210. Cris Putnam and Tom Horn, *The Final Roman Emperor, the Islamic Antichrist, and the Vatican's Last Crusade* (Crane, Missouri: Defender Publishing, 2016), 57.
211. Chuck Missler, "Technology and the Bible, Part 2: Technology Statements," KHouse.org, originally published in "Personal Update" April 2008, http://www.khouse.org/articles/2008/773/ accessed April 30, 2016.
212. See http://www.spacex.com.
213. "Statement from FCC Spokesperson Tammy Sun on Letter from NTIA Addressing Harmful Interference Testing Conclusions Pertaining to Lightsquared A and Global Positioning Systems," Federal Communications Commission, February 4. 2012, https://apps.fcc.gov/edocs_public/attachmatch/DOC-312479A1.pdf, accessed April 30, 2016.
214. SpaceX, "Question 7: Purpose of the Experiment," FCC Application, https://apps.fcc.gov/els/GetAtt.html?id=162991&x, accessed April 30. 2016.
215. Alex Knapp, "SpaceX Raises $1 Billion in a Financing Round with Google and Fidelity," *Forbes,* January 20, 2015, http://www.forbes.com/sites/alexknapp/2015/01/20/spacex-raises-1-billion-in-a-financing-round-with-google-and-fidelity/#2ad015c62e49, accessed April 30, 2016.
216. Greg Wyler, video: "See How We Are Making Global Internet a Reality," OneWeb.world, http://oneweb.world accessed April 30, 2016.
217. Alex Knapp, "Branson-Backed OneWeb Raises $500 Million to Build Satellite Internet," Forbes, June 25, 2015, http://www.forbes.com/sites/alexknapp/2015/06/25/branson-backed-oneweb-raises-500-million-to-build-satellite-internet/#9dd72ae55297, accessed April 30, 2016.
218. "Solution" at http://oneweb.world accessed April 30, 2016.
219. See http://oneweb.world/#technology.